Epistemology and the Predicates of Education

Exploring the predicates of education from theoretical, practical and historical perspectives, this book revalorizes the central role of the humanities in the ethical and aesthetic formation of the individual.

This book considers timely questions of process and epistemology in today's academy. It examines the subject of learning as it arises in the individual, is defined by educators and is conceived by society at large. In attempting to formulate a lingua franca for contemporary pedagogy, the book highlights the concrete activities of educators and students and the qualities that emerge in the educational process. By synthesizing the writings of educational theorists working in different fields – philosophy, psychology, anthropology and more – *Epistemology and the Predicates of Education* highlights the transformational nature of knowledge and its capacity to invigorate the student through the practice of self-inquiry.

The analytical and focused research offered in *Epistemology and the Predicates of Education* will be of interest to researchers, academics and postgraduate students in the fields of philosophy of education and higher education.

Thomas E. Peterson is a professor of Italian in the Department of Romance Languages, University of Georgia, USA.

Routledge International Studies in the Philosophy of Education

For more information about this series, please visit: https://www.routledge.com/Routledge-International-Studies-in-the-Philosophy-of-Education/book-series/SE0237

Epistemology and the Predicates of Education

Building Upon a Process Theory of Learning

Thomas E. Peterson

Routledge
Taylor & Francis Group

NEW YORK AND LONDON

First published 2020
by Routledge
52 Vanderbilt Avenue, New York, NY 10017

and by Routledge
2 Park Square, Milton Park, Abingdon, Oxon, OX14 4RN

Routledge is an imprint of the Taylor & Francis Group, an informa business

Library of Congress Cataloging-in-Publication Data
A catalog record for this title has been requested

ISBN: 978-0-367-24392-0 (hbk)
ISBN: 978-0-429-28222-5 (ebk)

Typeset in Sabon
by codeMantra

Contents

List of Figures

List of Tables

Acknowledgements

I am grateful to the University of Georgia for its consistent support of my research and to my colleagues in the Department of Romance Languages for their warmth and commitment to creative and passionate teaching.

The following articles are reprinted (with minor changes) by permission of the publisher (Taylor & Francis, Ltd, http://www.tandfonline.com):

Peterson, T. E. (1999). Whitehead, Bateson and Readings and the Predicates of Education. *Educational Philosophy and Theory*, 31, 1, pp. 27–41.

Peterson, T. E. (2008) The Art of Language Teaching as Interdisciplinary Paradigm. *Educational Philosophy and Theory* 40, 7, pp. 900–918.

Peterson, T. E. (2012). Constructivist Pedagogy and Symbolism: Vico, Cassirer, Piaget, Bateson. *Educational Philosophy and Theory* 44, 8, pp. 878–891.

The following article is reprinted (with minor changes) by permission of the publisher (De Gruyter, http://www.degruyter.com):

Peterson, T. E. (2016). Contemporary Approaches to a Pedagogy of Process. *Semiotica* 212 (A. Stables and I. Semetsky, Eds.), pp. 7–26.

Introduction

This book explores questions of process and epistemology in today's academy. It examines the subject of learning as it arises in the individual, is defined by educators and is conceived by the larger society. While the book's immediate context is the Western and specifically American academy, its theoretical reach extends far beyond that to consider the nature of education as such, as the means by which the person is formed, ethically, emotionally and intellectually. With this broad purpose in mind the book addresses a range of specific critical issues that educational philosophers and practitioners have confronted historically and which continue to be pertinent today. By assembling the views of a wide variety of thinkers over diverse eras, the goal is to arrive at a *lingua franca* of the educational sciences, a language of relations derived from competing terminologies, codes and logics, and to use that language to elucidate the perennial importance of humanism and the Socratic method in the academy. By doing so I hope to provide a tool that is practical, efficacious and useful for educators in the future.

To speak of the predicates of education is to presuppose the centrality of speech and dialogue in the educational process. It is to focus on the languages of teaching and remember a time when the humanities retained a central role in the ethical and aesthetic formation of the individual. On the most basic level, the predicates of education are the actions and qualities that activate the student in the learning process. While such predicates depend on the ability of educators to instruct students in a specific subject matter, they only come alive when students learn how the process of learning itself is adaptable and expandable to other life contexts, including the prospect of self-knowledge and self-realization. "Doctor, heal thyself": in the case of today's educator, the biblical admonition rings true. It is widely recognized that a crisis exists in our institutions of higher learning and that the responsibility for addressing it rests with the educators. The crisis has been analyzed as an economic and structural matter in a number of studies.[1] For example, Slaughter and Rhoades' *Academic Capitalism and the New Economy* demonstrates that research universities today view themselves as marketers of a product, that they are "integrating with the new economy, shifting from a public good knowledge/learning regime to an academic capitalist knowledge/learning regime" (Slaughter and Rhoades, 2004, p. 7). One can point to the downsizing of faculties, the outsourcing of teaching jobs and the erosion of the tenure system. Other studies have addressed the changes in the university as a sign of the decline of contemporary culture, or as revelatory of a workplace centered on factors of prestige and status, or as the result of the prominence given to STEM disciplines.[2] My view in this study is that these external problems are symptomatic of an internal problem that requires an ethical and pedagogy-based solution. What is called for is not simply a return to the "public good knowledge/learning regime" of the past, with its focus on the morality of learning, but a change in paradigms, including an increase in inquiry-based learning and the expansion of cross-disciplinary studies. As one reads in the Boyer Report of the Carnegie Foundation: "Academic majors must reflect students' needs rather than departmental interests or convenience," and, "Customizing interdisciplinary majors should be not only possible but readily achievable" (Boyer Report, 1995, n.p.). Despite the existence of this and other forward-looking reports, the model of an inquiry-based learning with the promotion of interdisciplinary studies has gone largely unheeded.

According to Robert E. Proctor, academia has witnessed the ascendancy of "bureaucratic rationality":

> The modern bureaucratic manager has a moral autonomy that his or her Renaissance predecessor did not have: the ideology of technical expertise, of the understanding and application of the principles of "scientific" management, has replaced the exercise of virtue as a justification for power and authority.
>
> (Proctor, 1998, p. 133)

Today's academic manager works by fiat; the day-to-day operations of the institution are increasingly influenced by the practices of quantitative optimization and other systems management protocols imported from the world of business. Such practices have the effect of reinforcing the barriers between disciplines while minimizing the fertile relationship between teaching and research.

It is incumbent on any educator who wishes to overcome such difficulties to appreciate the multiplicity of 'languages' that coexist in the academy and sort through their respective interferences and points of agreement with an eye toward integration and harmony. In order to understand the ecology of the learning community one must 'translate' across intellectual and cultural boundaries in order to foster communication among scientists, humanists, artists and administrators. Such an effort will necessarily impart empathy to students and a more resilient understanding of the collective good as a key to biological success. If one has seen the elevation of specialization over integration, of digital modalities over the analogical, of quantitative, data-driven research methods over qualitative ones, of ends-oriented behavior over the pursuit of just means, then what is called for is a pedagogy inclusive of these dichotomies, as foreseen in a broad range of contemporary fields including communication theory, deep ecology, complex thought, systems theory and cognitive science.[3]

As Gregory Bateson puts it, "the solution to ecological issues must be ecological" (Bateson in Harries-Jones, 1995, p. 211). The need for greater respect for diversity and complexity in the academy is reflected by an emerging movement in science studies to question the nature of argumentation, verification and proof. Researchers of all sorts are now motivated to consider the role of aesthetics, taste and judgment in forming satisfactory hypotheses about larger, interrelated systems. As Bateson also wrote, improvising on a citation from Galatians, "The ecological God is incorruptible and therefore is not mocked" (G. Bateson, in Bateson and Bateson, 1987, p. 143). Once dualistic schemes and dichotomies (individual/collective, existential/sociological, mind/body, technology/ humanism) are viewed in their larger ecological context, there arises a new and flexible pedagogy that is rich in its affective and intellective stratifications.[4] Through discourse and dialogue, the above dualities can be integrated and refined in the classroom, whether in the instruction of science, art, language or philosophy. When active predicates are transmitted, relationships established, hypotheses ventured, a positive learning process is underway.

In Chapter 1 I define the predicates of education as the qualities actively sought and obtained by educators to acculturate and train the student; the resolution of questions, tensions and conflicts, that arise during the process; and the process of confirmation and validation that follows up on original hypotheses. I then explore these predicates contextually in the writings of three exemplary educators: Alfred N. Whitehead, Gregory Bateson and Bill Readings. The pursuit of a relational logic of education by these Britons affirms the interactive, creative and aesthetic nature of the educational process and seeks to correct the bias in the academy that favors a dualistic (or Cartesian) logic in the conceptualization of knowledge.[5] Whitehead sees a homology at work between curricular structure and the root character of knowledge and "rejects the doctrine that students should first learn passively, and then, having learned, should apply knowledge" (1968a, pp. 218). His educational philosophy is based on the overlapping of three successive stages – romance, precision and generalization – that take place in the learner, with an emphasis being placed on creativity:

The whole point of a university, on its educational side, is to bring the young under the intellectual influence of a band of imaginative scholars. There can be no escape from proper attention to the conditions which – as experience has shown – will produce such a band.

(1929a, p. 150)

Bateson investigates the relationship between evolutionary process and learning. Beginning with his work in the fields of anthropology, psychiatry and interactive psychology, he publishes seminal work on schizophrenia and double-bind theory, schismogenesis (symmetry and complementarity in cultural dynamics) and the ecology of mind. A participant in the Macy Conferences (1946–1953) who contributed to the cybernetic revolution, he became a pioneer in the field of communication theory, stimulating readers hungry for new cultural and intellectual paradigms. Readings was already an educational luminary before his death in 1994 at age 34. Readings called attention to the historical shift in the internal mechanisms and codes that give structure and meaning to the American university based on its historical models in Germany and Britain. He believed that the best constraints on students are self-imposed and the best antidotes to conformism are conscious choice and willfulness. He questioned how this dynamic pedagogy could occur in the current institutional reality in which corporate strategies have displaced traditional academic values and 'information transmission' is confused with learning. He advocated that educators resist the current "University of Excellence" by devoting themselves to the temporality of learning and honest pedagogy; and he underscored the need for a reinvigorated ethics and a return to a sense of justice in the academy. Like Whitehead and Bateson, he regarded the need for a theory of symbolism to integrate the poles of objectivity and subjectivity, fact and value, history and self in the learning process.

Chapter 2 presents four figures in the development of constructivism as a pedagogical philosophy beginning with Giambattista Vico, whose view of the interrelationship of the arts and sciences sought to reconstitute the classical *paideia*. The Vichian idea that human beings can only know the truth of what they themselves have made has theoretical and practical consequences for Vico's pedagogy and his vision of a restructured university capable of fostering the development of modern science. Vico's ideas on education are extended in the modern period by such thinkers as Ernst Cassirer, Jean Piaget and Gregory Bateson. At the basis of Cassirer's pedagogical philosophy is his theory of the symbol, the symbol being a universal and transcendent modality in culture. The result of this unifying theory is that symbolism, pervasive across the disciplines, provides a moral and ethical means for integrating communication about teaching. Cassirer's thought is compatible with Piaget's, which emphasizes the pluralism of experience and the role of dynamic learning in the construction of meaningful order. Piaget's constructivism assumes that an operational bridge exists to link together the hard sciences, the human sciences and the historical disciplines. This systems view of epistemology is related in the conclusion of the chapter to a number of contemporary thinkers who endorse the organization of knowledge and the university in terms of a heterarchy, or rule within a circle.

Chapter 3 explores the bases for a process theory of learning applicable across the disciplines. First it traces the modern history of process pedagogy beginning with Kant and leading through Cassirer and Whitehead to an array of contemporary approaches that favor the symbiosis of art and science over the lingering Cartesian dichotomy of "subjective" mental processes and "objective" forms of knowledge. Second, it examines the case of science education, specifically as regards habit formation, ethical instruction and qualitative research. Such diverse thinkers as Whitehead, Bourdieu, Serres, Latour and Dewey are seen to oppose the neoscholastic myth of scientific objectivity and favor a language of relations that fosters an "anastomosis" between the disciplines. Lastly, the chapter examines the pedagogical role played by logical abduction, as articulated by Peirce and developed by later scholars. Thus the chapter's four sections – starting with the historical discussion, moving to the field-specific problem of science education and the related debate over consilience, and the discussion of logical abduction – reinforce one another and aim to exemplify the dynamic integration of the general and specific, of mind and nature, that is a goal of process pedagogy.

In Chapter 4 I argue that the art of language instruction provides a paradigm applicable throughout the arts and sciences. I suggest that the way a student learns a second language is analogous to the process of learning a scientific discipline. In either case the teacher's use of dramatistic, performative and narrative modalities open up the classroom to hypothesis formation, risk-taking and adventure. One's goal in learning a language is the mastery of skills which, once assimilated, are phased out of active conceptual thought. Whether in the arts and humanities, the social sciences, the life sciences or the hard sciences, the art of language instruction provides a form of "categorial thought" (Ceruti) that allows students to transform the data of a mechanistic worldview into a broader holistic knowledge.

In Chapter 5 I examine the future of humanistic teaching by looking at its past, noting that the use of analogies was fundamental to the great scientific and artistic discoveries. I argue that if one is to optimize current educational practices, one must examine the linguistic and epistemological gaps in knowledge, as between the disciplines, with the tools of analogical thinking. While verbal language is largely digital, the kinesic and paralinguistic modes are analogic in nature and of vital importance in communicating about human relationships. I present the case of film studies as offering the opportunity to explore the perceptual difference of the knowledge conveyed by sight vis-à-vis that conveyed by language. A variety of epistemological approaches are explored such as cognitivism, radical constructivism and cybernetics, particularly as they impact our contemporary ways of teaching science in a manner not alien to faith which incorporates a strong ethical component. The complex view expressed here is compatible with the tenet of radical constructivism that knowledge is an event or real occurrence that arises only in non-trivial situations, in contrast to reductionism, behaviorism and other anti-mentalist doctrines that boil down knowledge to the elimination of doubt.

In Chapter 6 I examine the interpretations of consensus in the actual academy, as regards professional questions such as the roles of research versus teaching, disciplinary specialization versus integration and general education courses within the curriculum. I examine how information, knowledge and intelligence are construed by educators and incorporated into their pedagogies and curricula. I consider the relation between institutional ethics and the self, distinguishing between the deontological plane of rules and procedures and the plane of ethics, which requires the subject to assume the position of the "Other." To recognize the Other in oneself is deemed critical if one is to address the question of human rights and prepare students to be world citizens. I draw on Lyotard's view that interlocution and dialogue allow a people to surpass the natural level of the nation (*demos*) and attain to the civic order of *polieteia*, the republic and the city. By taking a dispassionate view of the ethical decisions confronting educators and students, I take the view that these are an intrinsic, rather than supplementary, part of the educational experience. By expanding the skills of students to include new ethical conceptions, one can encourage a new candor about the fragility of the human condition. Thus my focus on the predicates of education means to assert the active, qualitative and dialogic role of the educator and the empowerment of the student as a self-inquiring researcher, trusting that what is ultimately learned will coincide with what has been personally felt and ventured forth.

In Chapter 7 I return to the question of a median language of learning by which disparate fields of knowledge might communicate with each other. I pursue this discussion from a perspective that includes a defense of metaphysics as a science of change. Specifically, I explore the notion of deep structures of knowledge as formulated by various scholars in recognition of the changed status of foundations in contemporary thought. I argue that the liberal arts cannot endure, if educators do not care for their survival and development; that to do so one must recover the virtues and moral coherency of a humanistic worldview; and that such care is manifest in the narratives employed in the classroom to knit together "self" and "environment." By exploiting the deep structures that exist in narrative, structural semantics and complex thought, educators can better come to terms with the discursive limits (or terminological screens) of their professional languages and thus work together to heal the current academy.

In the course of this study the term "predicate" enjoys a variety of usages: as qualitative knowledge that is drawn out through a dialogic, Socratic method; as the analogical and dramatistic use of language; as the manifestation of a deeper cognitive and ethical structure underlying the languages of the disciplines; and as the active and dynamic part of pedagogy that focuses on experience and change. It is our conviction that the most effective teachers understand that by plumbing the depths of their subject matter they are also addressing the habits and cognitions of the individual student and guiding them in the practice of virtue. In this way teachers respond to the challenge to instruct about the paradigms that affect our conscious and unconscious minds; by moving from the multiple orders of the particular discipline toward higher forms of learning, they succeed in communicating to students the immensity that is "out there" and "in here," that is, in the experience of the cosmic and universal as it affects them personally and as citizens.

Notes

1 See Nussbaum, 2010; Schrecker, 2010; Côté and Allahar, 2011; Ginsberg, 2011.
2 See Code, 2006; Baez and Boyles, 2009; Arum and Roksa, 2011.
3 See Wilden, 1987, p. 314, regarding "context theory" which "proceeds from the complex to the structures of complexity, including their environments."
4 On an experiential and local level, other dichotomies present themselves: static/dynamic, harm/benefit, same/different, pure/impure, natural/unnatural, reveal/conceal, creation/discovery, synthesis/analysis. This list was provided by chemist Roald Hoffmann at a Charter Lecture at the University of Georgia in February 1998.
5 See Whitehead, 1929a, pp. 92–93: "So far as the imparting of information is concerned, no university has had any justification for existence since the popularization of printing in the fifteenth century."

1 Whitehead, Bateson and Readings and the Predicates of Education

The Predicates of Education

In his 1993 lectures, *Representations of the Intellectual*, Edward Said provides a trenchant approach to the problem of the intellectual in today's University. The problem is seen as one of self-representation – as scholar, thinker, educator and citizen – in an often-hostile climate that subjects one to extraordinary pressures in the name of professionalism. Said recalls the otherwise divergent thinkers Julien Benda and Antonio Gramsci as early warners against the formation of an academic clerisy. Today's intellectual is usually an academic, pressured to specialize in order to advance professionally and avoid the condition of 'exile' – whether actual, as in Said's case, or metaphoric, as in the case of those scholars who resist the call to conformity. By remaining an "amateur" able to cross disciplinary boundaries and to "speak truth to power," such an intellectual is "fueled by care and affection rather than by profit and selfish, narrow specialization" (Said, 1994, p. 82). Said advocates that academics realize the full symbolic and representational impact of their roles in society, and understand that if they oppose the "cult of the certified expert" and resist the "drift towards power and authority" which has seen academic decisions made increasingly by government, not science, that they should expect to be unpopular (Said, 1994, pp. 77, 80).

It is in this context of a crisis in the Academy related to the problem of intellectual self-representation, that I will compare the pedagogical thinking of Alfred North Whitehead, Gregory Bateson and Bill Readings. Born in the years 1861, 1904 and 1960, these English-born and educated scholars brought to their careers in American universities an open distrust for the arid quantification of knowledge and impoverishment of learning that results from the over-specialization of the university. As Whitehead writes,

> Each science confines itself to a fragment of the evidence and weaves its theories in terms of notions suggested by that fragment. Such a procedure is necessary by reason of the limitations of human ability. But its dangers should always be kept in mind. For example, the

increasing departmentalization of universities during the last hundred years, however necessary for administrative purposes, tends to trivialize the mentality of the teaching profession.

(Whitehead, 1968b, p. 5)

Suspicious of autocratic schemes of thought that claim authority on the basis of self-referential judgments (or what Said calls the "Gods that always fail"), Whitehead, Bateson and Readings remind us that even the most objective body of empirical knowledge possesses its own locus of interpretation, and that what is deemed incontrovertible always depends on the definition of a context or logical field (and thus on an 'application' of knowledge).[1] In general these thinkers pursue an ecological epistemology, or philosophy of knowledge, derived not from abstractions but, in Bateson's words, from "actual organisms interacting" (1981, p. 354). Each takes the creative risk of the amateur and seeks to examine, by way of a philosophy of process, the relations between diverse scientific systems. Their respect for epistemological boundaries is expressed in what is typically a spare, economical and aesthetical prose. Thus, it is easy to come upon statements that acquire the value of maxims, such as these from Whitehead's *Aims of Education*: "The introduction to any subject is the process of learning by contact"; "Science [is] almost wholly the outgrowth of pleasurable intellectual curiosity" (Whitehead, 1929a, pp. 100, 69).[2]

Whitehead, Bateson and Readings understand that a symbiosis between humanistic and scientific disciplines is possible only if the experts refrain from privileging pure theory and consent to teach students the methods, and not just the rules of intellectual research. As John Dewey states, "There is a kind of idle theory which is antithetical to practice; but genuinely scientific theory falls within practice as the agency of its expansion and its direction to new possibilities" (Dewey, 1944, p. 269). Dewey also states that humanistic studies must not "base [their] educational schemes upon the specialized interests of a leisure class" or "reduce themselves to exclusively literary and linguistic studies" (Dewey, 1944, p. 268). "Knowledge," he writes, "is humanistic in quality not because it is *about* human products in the past, but because of what it *does* in liberating human intelligence and human sympathy" (Dewey, 1944, p. 269). Whitehead writes in a similar vein:

Knowledge is the reminiscence by the individual of the experience of the race. But reminiscence is never simple reproduction. The present reacts upon the past. It selects, it emphasizes, it adds. The additions are the new ideas by means of which the life of the present reflects itself upon the past. Thus culture, besides involving a criticism of tradition, also requires a critical appreciation of novelty.

(Whitehead, 1968a, p. 202)

In short, the pragmatic and process thinkers I am discussing here are involved in reframing the question of scientific evidence and proof as it concerns education. For them to *prove* is also to *probe* – to muse, to ponder, to mull, to assay. They see in science the great lessons of generalization and abstraction, lessons which each of them sees as having been left by the wayside in their current academic milieu.

In philosophical logic the 'predicate' is what is affirmed or denied about a subject; it may be seen as a quality ruled by a substance, or an action derived from an event. It is also a preliminary assumption, an axiom not subject to proof. Such a breadth of definition allows one to conceive of the predicates of education as: the qualities actively sought and obtained by educators to acculturate and train the young; the resolution of questions, tensions and conflicts, that arise during the process; and the process of confirmation and validation that follows up on original hypotheses. The first definition concerns the tale of subjects interacting with other subjects. The second concerns the phase of correction and adjustment that occurs when we examine those involvements as they perish and become objects, in memory and in the world. The third definition is heuristic as it understands learning as a many-layered and evolving process at once biological, cultural and symbolic that can be developed into theory (but not without the constant relation to practice). The predicates of education thus conceived require that there be personal exchanges and communications via accepted modes of literal and symbolic reference between faculty and students; and that there be a taking of stock, a qualitative evaluation of the individual student not reducible to quantitative measurement. Unlike the materialistic, behavioralist or energy-oriented views of pedagogy, the process, or event-oriented, view holds that the validity of an educational system depends on direct interaction with students who are actively engaged in the creative, imaginative and aesthetic process of thinking.

Whitehead and the Aims of Education

In his 1929 *Aims of Education* – his only complete book on the subject – Whitehead theorizes such a pedagogy, arguing against the superficial or token innovations in curricula that he observed taking place around him. In response to the view among his colleagues that by adding a plethora of numerical graphs to the general tests in mathematics, the curriculum would be improved, Whitehead writes,

> You cannot put life into any schedule of general education unless you succeed in exhibiting its relation to some essential characteristic of all intelligent or emotional perception. It is a hard saying, but it is true; and I do not see how to make it any easier. In making these little formal alterations you [reformers] are beaten by the very nature

of things. You are pitted against too skilful an adversary, who will see to it that the pea is always under the other thimble.

(Whitehead, 1929a, 12)

The "adversary" in this case is the student, wary of the quantified curriculum if only partially aware of its failure to "exhibit its relation to some essential characteristic of all intelligent or emotional perception" (Whitehead, 1929a, 12). Whitehead argues that the problem with generalized testing procedures is the natural spirit and mind of the pupil, alive and malleable, resistant to the passing on of "inert ideas" in the classroom. He rejects the notion of the student's mind as an "instrument" that needs to be "sharpened," and insists that students have a right to be examined by their instructor: "if you are teaching pupils for some general examination, the problem of sound teaching is greatly complicated" (Whitehead, 1929a, 15). The educator rather has the responsibility of integrating general and specific course materials, and to engender style. This is a natural undertaking, the importance of which cannot be overestimated: "Style," writes Whitehead, "is the ultimate morality of mind" (Whitehead, 1929a, 19). How educators represent themselves and their world is symbolic in a manner that exceeds the use of conventional symbols (of science, art, literature, religion or politics). Just so, in transmitting style, the educator must display a comprehensive understanding of the mutual dependency of theory and practice, thinking and acting. He or she must also remember the importance of technical education so as not to overemphasize language in the humanities or specialized modes of data observation in the sciences.[3]

In his book *Symbolism: Its Meaning and Effect*, Whitehead writes, "Human symbolism has its origin in the symbolic interplay between two distinct modes of direct perception" (1985, p. 30). As part of his philosophy of organism he presents a theory of symbolism based on the two major modes of perception: presentational immediacy – the unfiltered acceptance of sensory information and its immediate assimilation and integration – and causal efficacy – the more fateful, heavier, deliberate movement in perception, the persistence of the past in forming present experience. Causal efficacy is not a category or a habit, but a persistence of memory in subjective durations of consciousness.[4] Symbolic reference occurs when these perceptual modes coincide in consciousness, and the immediacy of sense perception combines with "our sense of the withness of the body" (Lowe, 1990, v. 2, p. 209).[5]

As Whitehead wrote in 1944: "Combining Newton and Hume we obtain a barren concept, namely, a field of perception devoid of any data for its own interpretation, and a system of interpretation devoid of any reason for the concurrence of its factors" (1968b, p. 10). The combined viewpoint of Newton and Hume had been accepted by Kant and most subsequent philosophers, but not by Whitehead who claims that "they omit those aspects of the universe as experienced, and of our modes of experiencing, which jointly lead to the more penetrating ways of understanding" (1968b, p. 10). While the common-sense viewpoint of "Nature as composed of permanent things – namely, bits of matter, moving about in space which otherwise is empty" has been rejected by physical science, it has continued to prevail in the human sciences, in the "work-day life of mankind" and "literature" (Whitehead, 1968b, p. 2). As a result, experience and intuition are undervalued and the relations between disciplines relegated to a secondary status when they are not ignored altogether: "The weakness of the epistemology of the eighteenth and nineteenth centuries," writes Whitehead, "was that it based itself purely upon a narrow formulation of sense-perception" (Whitehead, 1961a, pp. 24–25). When the natural sciences are seen as autonomous fields, one fails to see the larger pattern upon which scientific definitions depend. Failure to perceive and appreciate pattern, reciprocity and relation in this epistemological sense leads to the ideology of positivism, a school of thought Whitehead denounces and also connects to Descartes, who understood 'fact' as lying in the instant, not in the endurance.

Whitehead generally renames categories common to traditional philosophy but refutes much of Kant, Hume, Berkeley in the process, attributing more importance than them to the mode of presentational immediacy. His position acknowledges an active intelligence existing in the spontaneous perception of sensory phenomena. Causal efficacy, also a nonconceptual mode, is grosser and able to integrate perceptual sequences of moments of presentational immediacy. (Celestial bodies possess great causal efficacy and no presentational immediacy, and thus do not participate in symbolism.) Our sense of being depends on our experience of events or occasions within durations, or slabs of time. The experience of being depends on the memory of becoming and the awareness of perishing. Unlike Kant and Hume, who saw causal efficacy as a way of thinking *about* sensory perceptions, Whitehead insists on its being a direct perceptual experience unmediated by concepts. Further, he advises that the pedagogical privileging of "the facts" is in error, because it lacks the symbolically conditioned action in the classroom whereby "thought uses symbols as referent to their meanings" (Whitehead, 1985, p. 81). When symbols are not paired with facts, time itself is reduced to the threat of incompleteness. In the course of this denial, the university education renounces its ethical mission.

Symbol derives from a unity, not a duality, of perception. In the symbolic situation or text, symbol is identical with symbolized; it is an association that leads to an identification. In a broad sense, symbol remains the vital quotient in human culture, the identifier of a connection between sensual and non-sensual, material and ideal, secular and divine.

Roberto Calasso has given a consonant gloss of "symbol" that clarifies its role in teaching:

> *Symbolon* means the broken halves of a piece of wood or pottery which come together to reconstitute a smooth and solid surface, barely incised by a transverse wound. More than teaching substitution, to which it must still pay homage, the symbol teaches interpenetration, *the inevitable layering of things.* The symbol is a ghost that enters another ghost, mingles, dissolves there, escapes. It drags behind itself, in a golden chain, everything it has passed through.
>
> (Calasso, 1994, p. 213)

Symbols retain universal meanings despite their varied forms of expression, which might include their encryption or the taboo against their naming. The symbolic word in a religious ceremony, for example, retains its mystery and ambiguity while it refuses to relinquish its precise naming faculty. As I argue below, this sort of bipolar enabling is at the basis of the linguistic and literary practice that teachers and students can employ to communicate without losing track of the primacy of first-hand knowledge. Symbols are not different in this sense from the first-hand knowledge of an experimental scientist:

> First-hand knowledge is the ultimate basis of intellectual life. To a large extent book-learning conveys second-hand information, and as such can never rise to the importance of immediate practice. Our goal is to see the immediate events of our lives as instances of our general ideas. What the learned world tends to offer is one second-hand scrap of information illustrating ideas derived from another second-hand scrap of information. The second-handedness of the learned world is the secret of its mediocrity. It is tame because it has never been scared by facts.
>
> (Whitehead, 1929a, 79)

A symbolic grasp of first-hand knowledge will depend on the cultivation of homogeneous thought about nature. As Whitehead argues in the 1920 *The Concept of Nature*, if one limits oneself to a single definable semantic field, one is engaged in homogeneous thought, whereas if one bridges separate and distinct semantic fields, one is engaged in heterogeneous thought.

We can think about nature without thinking about thought. I shall say that then we are thinking 'homogeneously' about nature.

> Of course it is possible to think of nature in conjunction with thought about the fact that nature is thought about. We are thinking "heterogeneously" about nature when we are thinking about it in conjunction with thinking either about thought or about

sense-awareness or about both. [...] I also take the homogeneity of thought about nature as excluding any reference to moral or aesthetic values whose apprehension is vivid in proportion to self-conscious activity. The values of nature are perhaps the key to the metaphysical synthesis of existence. But such a synthesis is exactly what I am not attempting.

(Whitehead, 1971, p. 3)

By refusing to attempt a metaphysical synthesis here, Whitehead preserves the integrity of his thought and his coherence as a pluralist. Those who fail to distinguish between the heterogeneous and homogeneous modes, he states, engage in the "bifurcation of nature" that has been a common error of Western philosophical tradition. They also fail to see education itself as a process rooted in nature:

Consider how nature generally sets to work to educate the living organisms which teem on this earth. You cannot begin to understand nature's method unless you grasp the fact that the essential spring of all growth is within you. [...] The regular method of nature is a happy process of genial encouragement. [...] The first thing that a teacher has to do when he enters the class-room is to make his class glad to be there.

(Whitehead, 1968a, p. 171)

In practical pedagogical terms, an integrated Whiteheadian process requires a confrontation with the unknown, with mystery, vagueness and error; by the same token, the trivial summarizing of "bodies of knowledge," or the imposition of "doctrine," can be stultifying:

Experience does not occur in the clothing of verbal phrases. It involves clashes of emotion, and unspoken revelations of the nature of things. Revelation is the primary characterization of the process of knowing. The traditional theory of education is to secure youth and its teachers from revelation. It is dangerous for youth, and confusing to teachers. It upsets the accepted coördinations of doctrine. Revelation is the enlargement of clarity. It is not a deduction though it may issue from a deduction. The dictionaries are very weak upon this point. [...] It is well known that education as mere imposed order of "things known" is a failure. The initial stages of reading, writing, and arithmetic should be suffused with revelation.

(Whitehead, 1968a, pp. 216–17)

In *The Aims of Education*, Whitehead outlines various chronological periods of life, from childhood through university education. And while these stages require different emphases – particularly as regards the specificity or generality of subject matter – the student must never be passive, and the knowledge must always be relational:

> This discussion rejects the doctrine that students should first learn passively, and then, having learned, should apply knowledge. It is a psychological error. In the process of learning there should be present, in some sense or other, a subordinate activity of application. In fact, the applications are part of the knowledge. For the very meaning of the things known is wrapped up in their relationships beyond themselves. Thus unapplied knowledge is knowledge shorn of its meaning.
> (Whitehead, 1968a, pp. 218–19)

In his role as one of the founders of the Society of Fellows at Harvard, Whitehead put his pedagogical ideas into practice. He and a few colleagues created this program for a select group of gifted young scholars to research a topic without the interference of standard curricula and other material obligations. They sought to create for the Fellows a means to confront not just disciplinary and interdisciplinary complexity during a concentrated period of study, but also to confront one another, to gain first-hand knowledge in dialogue, for which, Whitehead held, they must be comfortable with vagueness. To work in this immediate, unfiltered way, was, once again, to engage in symbolism by seeing "the immediate events of our lives as instances of our general ideas" (Whitehead, 1929a, p. 79):

> Until mankind understands its own history, intimately as a concrete passage into an unknown future, our culture will never be adequate. We treat our novelties of today as though it were a novel fact that there should be novelty. History is the drama of effort. The full understanding of it requires an insight into human toiling after its aim.
> (Whitehead, 1968a, p. 203)

How symbols can function positively and practically during times of social upheaval is evident in the final chapter of *Symbolism: Its Meaning and Effect*. Here Whitehead compares the destructiveness of the French Revolution to the continuity of institutions through the American Revolution and the English 17th century revolutionary period. He argues that symbolism's great merit in the latter two cases is its permanence amid change: "the heroic aspect of the history of the country is the symbol for its immediate worth. [...] Those revolutions which escape a reign of terror have left intact the fundamental efficient symbolism of society" (Whitehead, 1985, p. 76). Since the life span of any nation is finite, and there is destruction inherent in any change of state system, there is great value in the careful maintenance of the symbolic system. To be mindful of 'precedence,' in terms of the use of symbolic reference, is a key to meaningful evolution.

Gregory Bateson and the Ecology of Mind

Such a conservative paradigm in the maintenance of the symbolic system of an evolving society is an obvious link between Whitehead and Gregory Bateson. Bateson's range and transdisciplinary acumen is demonstrated from his early photographic work in Bali to his psychiatric work with Jurgen Ruesch, to the 1969 classic, *Steps to an Ecology of Mind*, to the late *Mind and Nature: A Necessary Unity*. The son of a famous geneticist, whose work he felt he was carrying forward, Gregory's research in cultural anthropology and interactive psychology, family therapy and epistemology, is supported by his understanding of biology and evolutionary theory, game theory, cybernetics, process and pragmatic philosophy.

Thought is regarded by Bateson as an interactive and communicative act. Mind, or mental process, is viewed as a self-corrective analogical system, the biological extension of which constitutes an "event," as in Whitehead and Leibniz, thinkers for whom the question of learning, and learning about learning ("deutero-learning"), is at the center of philosophy's mission. Dewey went so far as to define philosophy as "the general theory of education" (Dewey, 1944, p. 382). Bateson's diverse and prolific production created an enormous watershed of new theory and applied uses of his otherwise specialized research; for example, his work on schizophrenia and the 'double bind' phenomenon in alcoholics; or his pioneering use of photography in anthropological field work. In his later years he extended his transdisciplinary thought to a reflection (compatible with the Whiteheadian theory of perception and learning) on the opposition and interpenetration of mind and nature. On several occasions he explicated his theory of knowledge in dialogues and 'metalogues' that explored the boundaries between cognitive disciplines.

Whitehead had written in *The Concept of Nature*, "nature is closed to mind" (Whitehead, 1971, p. 4). The knower is forever distinct from the known. One's perception of nature, in order to be homogeneous and not divided between "nature perceived and nature unperceived," "does not carry with it any metaphysical doctrine of the disjunction of nature and mind" (Whitehead, 1971, p. 4). Similarly, Bateson's theory of nature and mind is not tied to terminological absolutes or intellectualist abstractions, but to the perceptual knowledge of organisms about their environment, about the population which shares that environment and the overall patterns of recursiveness that connect the individual to it. For Bateson, learning is a process both conscious and unconscious that occurs at different layers of individual and group experience.

Bateson identifies the following types of learning: the primary process of learning, or Learning I, is understood as "the simple response to a simple problem"; the secondary process of deutero-learning, or Learning II, is "the progressive change in the rate of Learning I," understanding the nature of the context; and Learning III, which involves an understanding of the contexts of Learning II and results in a dramatic shift in one's notion of self and system.[6] As theorized, Learning III "must lead to a greater flexibility in the premises acquired by the process of Learning II – a *freedom* from their bondage" (Bateson, 1972, p. 304). For Bateson, the behavioralist understanding of human perception as passive, automatic or rationalistic was in error; perception *always* requires a decoding, the functions of which do *not* lie within the sphere of consciousness: "while perceptual experiences may indeed be subjective, the processes by which we perceive are not" (Harries-Jones, 1995, p. 203). In order to develop his theory of perception and learning, he suggests a homology between it and the problem of natural selection and evolution. Learning is to somatic change as natural selection is to genetic change. While on their surfaces the natures of genetic and somatic changes are quite opposite, they can be profitably compared as stochastic processes. Bateson argues that the same sort of abduction by homology can and should be applied to the field of education.

The difference between change in the individual and the species, between the phenotype and genotype, is explicated by another adventurous thinker in the area of ecological epistemology, Ivan Illich:

> Culture bespeaks a level of life that cannot be rendered in biological terms; genetic endowment and cultural heritage evolve according to opposite laws. Natural selection operates upon undirected variation that leads into genetic divergence; cultural evolution passes to the next generation traits that the present one has shaped. Biological evolution sprouts new branches that do not cross-fertilize, branches that never again unite once they have become solid. Culture evolves along another route; its form is anastomosis: like a river, its waters divide, meander, and reunite.
>
> (Illich, 1982, p. 140)

While Bateson would no doubt argue that biological evolution is also engaged in 'cross-fertilization,' or significant recursivity affecting the genus, the critical point is that natural evolution occurs on a scale that is beyond the somatic experience of mind and that stochastic processes are essential to meaningful change.

By expanding and modifying Whitehead and Russell's theory of logical types, Bateson proposed a radically immanent epistemology which found in the nature-mind dichotomy fertile ground for reexamining the collective unconscious. The first step in opposing the bifurcation of nature was to reveal the assumptions within our language use that foster it; the second was to create a critical field (we've called it ecological epistemology) in which one could classify contexts of messages across various disciplines. In Bateson's system 'facts' and 'values' are not finally separable, but generate qualitative comparisons, or abductions, between the patterns and forms of life and those of aesthetic expression.

In the language of Aristotle, abduction is the inference of the minor premise of a syllogism from the other two propositions. Abduction is also known as inference to the best explanation. Bateson drew his thinking about abduction from Charles S. Peirce's work on that mode of inference, though he put his own stamp on the term. By stressing the necessarily active nature of perception and deutero-learning, he provided a qualitative and interactive model of the predicates of education. This model introduces abduction and ostensive communication into the classroom. By suspending logical rules, abduction can provide a valuable foreshortening, or sketch, of the context within which reason is situated. Abduction is permitted, says Bateson, by the mutually recognized confusion of logical types, of member and class, that is prevalent in verbal and non-verbal communication. According to Bateson, the mode of abduction (metaphor in its broadest application) is more accessible, more 'comfortable' to people than formal explanation. Bateson's broader idea is that a confusion of logical types inevitably takes place in human communication and that the mental aberrations of the schizophrenic occur when the individual – no longer defined as an individual, but in context, as a member of a 'family' – fails to understand abduction, that is, he fails to understand the consensually validated 'discontinuities,' or mixtures of logical types, that pervade in human communication.

Just as epistemologists and educators have seized on abduction as a means of referring to the deviation from standard logic that advances an argument, poets have long been familiar with the suspension of normal social patterns (of sense, of sequence, of identity), particularly in the use of tautology within rhetorical figures to advance a poetic discourse. And so, Bateson suggests, should teachers (as Whitehead had done with his call for aesthetic, symbolic and technical teaching and curricula). Only by the deliberate confusion of logical types can teachers train students to negotiate the semantic challenges of contemporary life:

> It is in the area of meanings, rather than artifacts and behaviors, where modern society is most demanding. Without overstatement, normal participation in the multiple logics of modern society requires the exercise of volition and cognitive ability that were characteristic only of artists and philosophers in traditional society.
>
> (Cronen and Pearce, 1980, p. 188)

On a professional level the educator who takes a creative risk also risks being ostracized. Kenneth Burke has described the pariah-making that occurs within "rational" institutions as the "bureaucratization of the imaginative":

> Obedience to the reigning symbols of authority is in itself natural and wholesome. The need to reject them is painful and bewildering. The dispossessed struggle hard and long to remain loyal – but by the nature of the case, the bureaucratic order tends simply to "move in on" such patience and obedience. Eventually, sectarian divergence becomes organized (as thinkers manipulate the complex forensic structure, to give it a particular emphasis in one direction). But those in possession of the authoritative symbols tend to drive the opposition into a corner, by owning the priests (publicists, educators) who will rebuke the opposition for its disobedience to the reigning symbols.
>
> (Burke, 1984, p. 226)

Since the opposition to bureaucratic tyranny is forced to mobilize against its will, it can lapse into an imitation of the bureaucratic organization of the authority structure and thus neglect to form its own symbols. The 'forensic' mode of social cohesion is required in order to resist a return to the original alienation (or what Bill Readings calls the temptation to 'critique'). For this reason, the educator-scribe must walk a fine line between a premature irenics and a fruitless and polemical dissent. As Burke states: "A fundamental revolution takes place when men shift from magical notions of authority (authority sanctioned by custom, as with king or parents) to the forensic concept of delegated authority (stemming, we might say, from the 'democratization of peerage')" (Burke, 1984, p. 332). It was in response to such an aggravated need that De Tocqueville wrote:

> I know of no country in which there is so little independence of mind and real freedom of discussion as in America. [...]
>
> If ever the free institutions of America are destroyed, that event may be attributed to the omnipotence of the majority, which may at some future time urge the minorities to desperation, and oblige them to have recourse to physical force. Anarchy will then be the result, but it will have been brought about by despotism.
>
> (De Tocqueville, 1945, pp. 285, 293)

Bill Readings and the University of Dissensus

Education is one of the 'free institutions' of America, and is still threatened by the forces of uniformity recognized by De Tocqueville. How one responds to this crisis and seeks to refresh society is a question confronting educators. The dedication to predicates and process, as opposed to materialism, behavioralism and bureaucracy, must be conceived as a dissemination to a broad demographic stratum, not a hieratic elite. In light of these general principles, I would now like to look, with Bill Readings, at the existing situation in the current transnational corporate university, where, I would argue, one finds only with great difficulty the 'forensic concept of delegated authority' or the 'democratization of peerage.' Readings was a Milton scholar and comparatist, a cultural historian and philosopher several of whose earlier writings on pedagogy and the contemporary university were included in his posthumous volume, *The University in Ruins* after his untimely death at age 34. We will attempt with Readings to apply the same three-part definition of the predicates of education seen above: as the qualities the teacher sets out to impart; as the interactive and dialogic process of dealing with questions and difficulties that arise during the process; and as the subsequent actions taken to encourage a change in state and to participate in a shared consciousness of past, present and future time. Let us briefly recall the common ground established thus far. Whitehead writes, "The teacher has a double function. It is for him to elicit the enthusiasm by resonance from his own personality, and to create the environment of a larger knowledge and a firmer purpose" (Whitehead, 1929a, p. 62). For the purposes of this active and creative purpose, or process of learning based on freedom of choice, ultimately the best constraints on students are those that are self-imposed: Constraints are indeed context. "Freedom and discipline," writes Whitehead, "are not antagonists" (Whitehead, 1929a, p. 47). Bateson says much the same about rigor and imagination; without both one has entropy. Negentropy rather is a sort of grace, complemented in the classroom by humor, ostensive communication and the coping with uncertainties. For this anomalous member of the University of California Board of Regents, the University is not meeting the challenge due to the inherently 'anti-aesthetic' prejudice of current 'obsolescent' higher education practices and pedagogical presuppositions.

When the predicates of education break down and become mandates, in Kant's terms the determinative judgment has been implemented without the deeper guide of the reflective judgment. Such is the case in today's climate of excessive specialization and the isolated self-replication of academic departments. Bateson argues that, thus far, we have no adequate language that considers mind as a self-corrective analogical system, that we have no language of relations. The energy-matter metaphor, he says, is outdated, and not simply in the hard sciences, but in education and epistemology.[7] It is precisely in attempting to derive such a language of relations within the current academic culture that Bill Readings comes into the picture.

Readings' notion of a "University of Dissensus" is based on a mode of resistance by individuals and groups of the pressure toward consensus and the notion that learning is a cataloguing of information. As 'peripheral singularities' in the faculty, these educators project a democratic future and adopt a performative and maieutic approach to learning. They also resist the more common forms of diversity programs in the university, which tend to mimic the pedagogical assumptions of the disciplines they ostensibly diverge from as well as their ideal of an archival organization of all the scientific knowledge of a field. By "resisting the drift toward technologizing levelling" and "unreflective [and] regressive representationalism," the practice of dissensus is itself a performative (rather than "constative") assertion of "radical otherness" (Miller, 1995, p. 131). In Whitehead's terms, such an educator of dissensus as proposed by Readings does not conceptualize otherness, but acts it out perceptually and symbolically, thus resisting the pressure, ubiquitous in today's culture, to transform everything into data.

Readings proposes handling the crisis in the current University by allowing for academic autonomy, respect and cooperation to be recognized as an alternative to the model of consensus; their realization is that consensus remains dedicated (willingly or not) to a patriarchal and constative mode, to the separation of 'facts' from 'values.' Both are finally alien to the world of will, of sensibility. In similar spirit, Bateson, in his 1978 letter to his fellow Regents, writes: "So, in this world of 1978, we try to run a university and to maintain standards of 'excellence'" (1980, 241). Bateson deliberately puts the word excellence in quotes. As Readings summarizes in his *The University in Ruins*, this term, "excellence," has become ubiquitous in writings about the American university (e.g. mission statements), and is in fact a signifier without a referent. In the University of Excellence, the rigorous lack imagination and the imaginative lack rigor. In Bateson's terms,

> Innovations become irreversibly adopted into the on-going system [of the curriculum] without being tested for long-time viability; and necessary changes are resisted by the core of conservative individuals without any assurance that these particular changes are the ones to resist.
>
> (Bateson in Wilder-Mott and Weakland, 1981, p. 247)

Our discussion in this chapter has implicated an academic ethics, as operating against what Said called the new clerisy. Readings defines ethics as a question of *ethos* or custom, not of moralism: "[Ethics is a] mode of *judgement* [...] that proceeds without criteria (such as moral principles) but only as regards the ethos of the judgement, its status as a judgement that claims to do justice" (Readings, 1991, p. xxxi). I would like to remember this definition in the conclusion of this chapter, which addresses the issue of an integrated – aesthetic and ethical – philosophical approach to teaching.

If, as Readings argues, the model of the Humboldtian University has yielded to that of the University of Excellence, in which the faculty emulate, or become, administrators driven by the cash-nexus, and for whom accountability and accounting are synonyms, one is also witness to a general 'dumbing down' of the university, as classes have shorter syllabi and fewer texts, larger class sizes and thus less personal contact and dialogue, less thinking, more orientation toward the multinational marketplace. All this conforms to the university's declared mission, which, invariably, is the goal of 'excellence.'

For Readings,

> Globalization paradoxically undoes the possibility of a single world culture (or a single world history), because the single world market it proposes is no longer predicated upon the relation of subject to state as the point at which the system acquires meaning.
>
> (Readings, 1991, p. 191)

This fundamental change is reflected in the failure of the contemporary university to fully embody the national identity of the country in which it is situated. (Readings' primary focus is the American university, though he also discusses the situation in France.) The change has profoundly affected the institution's position and status within the society. Without entering into the terminological complexity of Reading's theoretical discourse – our own emphasis wishes to be practical – it is sufficient to state that for Readings, the University has lost its authenticity as a locus of the universal or as a place for the convergence of the ideals of a society. This great loss in contemporary culture is what he refers to as the 'University in Ruins.' What this "paradigm shift" requires of contemporary educators is an honest appraisal of what has happened, with a strong dose of disillusionment. In order to face this changed economic and social reality, one must not seek a return to the Humboldtian university of the past – which would amount to nostalgia – or seek a new university in which the broken unity of the past is reknit together by the means of Cultural Studies or interdisciplinary programs. Rather, says Readings, one must ask what the "posthistorical University" might be, and one must remain receptive to "the shifting disciplinary structure that holds open the question of whether and how thoughts fit together" (Readings, 1991, p. 191).

The case of 'excellence' is an example of the phenomenon that Readings refers to as 'dereferentialization': the dereferentialization of culture and of the university's function within it. To wit, what formerly possessed semantic concreteness in the field of higher education and garnered the respect of larger entities in the society – i.e. the integrity and coherence of the university's mission in support of freedom and enlightenment, or the belief that by a rigorous training in the liberal arts one could advance society's most idealistic goals – has now lapsed or has been appropriated by an intervening ideological structure. By Readings' estimation, this is an intervention that has left the university in 'ruins.'

With the advent of semiotics and structuralism, scholars began in earnest to analyze texts as signifying systems or possible worlds; new critical models were employed to exceed or perhaps transcend the welter of motivations explored by Marxist, Freudian and Nietzschean analysis, schools or areas of thought that were incorporated into the sort of meta-commentary and hermeneutical self-reflexivity that led a generation of scholars, ironically, to undervalue the actual accomplishments of these 'masters of suspicion.' The new possibilities themselves were prey to confusion and to a flawed understanding of symbolism as substitution, and a loss of precise lexical meaning as based on context and usage. Much of this confusion was terminological and could be attributed to the failure to distinguish between homogeneous and heterogeneous modes of thought about nature.

It is in recognition of the hypertrophy of the theoretical enterprise in the academy (similar to what Dewey called "a kind of idle theory which is antithetical to practice") (Dewey, 1944, p. 266), and the consequent academic overspecializations, that Readings critiques the current university status quo and refutes what he calls the Saussurean pedagogical model. Such a model tends to emphasize in the classroom situation either the *addressee* (student as free subject), the *sender* (professor as authority) or the *referent* (subject matter as inviolable corpus of knowledge). As against this model, Readings proposes the Bakhtinian model of dialogism, a fact compatible with Bateson's theory of learning, because of their mutual pursuit of an ecological means of approaching the description, or rather 'double description' (or description of description), of 'self' as a social, not a metaphysical notion. Just as *The University in Ruins* presents a vision of a community in which to dwell that allows for the ecumenical avoidance of the commonplace, the cybernetic revolution (with which we still associate Bateson's name) saw not only the emergence of information and systems theory, artificial intelligence and communication theory, but certain advances in interactional psychology, family therapy and new models of cultural anthropology. It is this profound humanism, I believe, that unites Readings, Bateson and Whitehead. They each make the tacit assumption that theoretical and practical activities are mutually dependent; that learning is an adventure; that the learned community is all too easily lured into conformism, losing sight of the community around it. As Whitehead clearly states in a speech entitled "Harvard: The Future," the role of the educator is to preserve in many respects the homogeneous discourse about nature, also as regards the university, its origins and its future:

> Curiously, the withdrawal of universities from close association with the practice of life is modern. It culminated in the eighteenth and nineteenth centuries, and heralds the decay of a cultural epoch.

I am not talking of the theories that men may have held at any time as to university functions. The point is as to the closeness of the relationship of the universities to the life around them – a closeness so natural as hardly to enter consciousness. In the first place, the universities arose out of nature, and were not exotic constructions imposed from above. The Papacy found universities; it did not devise them.

(Whitehead, 1968a, 221)

The extraordinary notion of the university 'arising out of nature' is indeed the antithesis of a clerisy of conventional thinkers, as critiqued by Benda, Gramsci, Said and our three Englishmen.

Notes

1 See Dewey's discussion of the "empiric" as "quack," 1944, p. 225: "The word empirical in its ordinary use does not mean 'connected with experiment', but rather crude and unrational."
2 In Whitehead's case we may speak of an epigrammatic mode, 1929a, p. 205: "Education, in every branch of study and in every lecture, is an art"; 1929a, p. 197: "It is essential to keep in mind, that science and poetry have the same root in human nature. Forgetfulness of this fact will ruin, and is ruining, our educational system."
3 See Whitehead, 1929a, p. 77: "An evil side of the Platonic culture has been its total neglect of technical education as an ingredient in the complete development of ideal human beings."
4 See Whitehead, 1929a, pp. 39–40.
5 See Whitehead, 1929a, p. 78: "I lay it down as an educational axiom that in teaching you will come to grief as soon as you forget that your pupils have bodies. This is exactly the mistake of the post-renaissance Platonic curriculum."
6 See Bateson, 1972, pp. 279–308: "The Logical Categories of Learning and Communication."
7 See Harries-Jones, 1995, pp. 235–42: "Appendix 1: Two Models of Ecology Compared: Odum and Bateson."

2 Constructivist Pedagogy and Symbolism

Vico

As Professor of Elocution and Jurisprudence at the University of Naples, Vico delivered seven inaugural orations to the faculty in the years 1699–1707. These addresses had the function of convoking the new academic year and allowed Vico a forum in which to define his pedagogy. The greatest of these, *De nostri temporis studiorum ratione* (On the Study Methods of Our Time) (1709), is a humanistic manifesto in defense of the interlocking system of the arts and sciences; the oration articulates the need for a positive – practical and theoretical – relationship between the academic disciplines. The ideas of the *De nostri* are continued in *De antiquissima Italorum sapientia* (*On the Most Ancient Wisdom of the Italians*) (1710), an inspired work that includes the following formula, according to which human beings can only know the truth of what they themselves have made:

> The true is precisely what is made (*Verum esse ipsum factum*) [...]. To know (*scire*) is to put together the elements of things. Hence, discursive thought (*cogitatio*) is what is proper to the human mind, whereas intelligence (*intelligentia*) is proper to God's mind.
>
> (Vico, 1988, p. 46)

We cite Vico's assertion in the opening of this chapter as an indication of our intent to tie this Enlightenment figure to the tradition of process thought and epistemological constructivism of the modern educators Ernst Cassirer, John Dewey, Jean Piaget, Gregory Bateson and Mary Catherine Bateson.

Trained as a philologist, Vico's concern was to connect the materiality of texts to a theory of knowledge that included creativity as a dynamic force in historical change. The linkage between thinking and doing, *verum* and *factum*, meant that linguistic signs were not static entities so much as dynamic participants in the ongoing pursuit of knowledge. As linguistic signs achieved endurance over time, they formed a symbolic lexicon that could be read as an historical map of the relationships between knowers and the institutions of knowledge, such as the academy or university.

In one of the most celebrated axioms of his *Scienza nuova* (*New Science*), Vico states: "The order of ideas must follow the order of institutions" (Vico, 1968, p. 78). Not only are human institutions the products of the cultures that form them; they are products of the collective consciousness, as are languages and other symbolic systems. Institutions possess their own internal coherence and virtues; they exercise a critical role in the lives and ideas of those who work within them. If this potential is not supported by the ongoing activity of those served by the institution, it loses its reason for being and brings down the 'order of the ideas.' While Vico was committed to the university's success, he had misgivings about its capacity for change. Innovation and erudition could work together only if one rejected arbitrary authority and recognized the equivalency of social organization and self-organization. Changes in the individual and changes in the academy could and should be interdependent and reciprocal.

For Vico, the university occupied a high place in society and was the guarantor of positive and mutually illuminating relationships between science, ethics and the arts. Since the just institution and the just scholar require one another, it was an error to distinguish, in the pedagogical sphere, "the useful" from "the honorable" (Vico, 1993, p. 99). It was inconceivable that a university driven by political or materialistic motivations could attain its desired goals within the diverse disciplines of study. For the sake of a just education, the professor needed to view knowledge from the standpoint of the learner and not as a static and authoritative corpus.[1] Only in this way could the classical *paideia* be returned to its coherence and unity. The curriculum was not to be governed by Cartesian logic or 'clarity,' but by prudence, knowledge and eloquence, all of which depend on the intense cultivation of language. Thus Vico "opposes the encroachments of the mathematical method on nonscientific fields, and underscores the damage resulting from those invasions" (Gianturco, in Vico, 1990, p. xxxi).

While Vico accepts the idea of the unity of the sciences, his understanding of that unity is different from Descartes', as he is not concerned with the quantifiable sciences alone but with the theory of knowledge, or what we now call epistemology:

> Arts and sciences, all of which in the past were embraced by philosophy and animated by it with a unitary spirit, are, in our day, unnaturally separated and disjointed. In antiquity, philosophers were remarkable for their coherence; their conduct was in full accord not only with the theories they professed but with their method of expounding them as well.
>
> (Vico, 1990, p. 76)

Such a nascent epistemology of process foresaw the endogenous, self-derived nature of educational methods. One could not justify the extrapolation of a method from one discipline to another but needed to excavate within the discipline in question. Such internal probing within the operations and functions of a discipline was dynamic in character and required the learner to appropriate for herself the specific truths to be explored.

The mind-body split that arises in Descartes tends to exclude those aspects of phenomenal experience that are uncertain, ambiguous or otherwise resistant to scientific proof. Cartesian logic acknowledges only deductive proof, denying theories of causation that depend on probabilistic hypotheses: Quantity is deemed as knowable, quality is not. Thus Descartes dismissed much of the experience of the arts, religion and folklore as inconsequential to knowledge.[2] Among the many disciplines relegated to secondary status by Cartesian rationalism was rhetoric, a liberal art reclaimed by Vico together with the 'topics,' poetry and history as the basis of moral science.

Vico's discussion of the patterns and stages of humanistic learning is an early demonstration of a dynamically integrated view of the humanities. "The greatest drawback of our educational methods – he writes – is that we pay an excessive amount of attention to the natural sciences and not enough to ethics" (Vico, 1990, p. 33). Scientific language too was a form of symbolic thinking that grew out of the historical relationships between meanings. As Ernst Cassirer has remarked:

> Giambattista Vico posed the problem of language within the sphere of a general metaphysic of the spirit. Beginning with the "poetic metaphysic" which was intended to disclose the origin of poetry and of mythical thinking, he passed through the intermediary link of "poetic logic," in which he strove to explain the genesis of poetic tropes and metaphors, to the question of the origin of language, which for him was synonymous with the question of the origin of "literature" and of the sciences in general. He too rejected the theory that the original words of language were attributable solely to convention; he too insisted on a "natural" relation between them and their meanings.
>
> (Cassirer, 1953, pp. 148–49)

Vico's critique of contemporary scientism as a sterile form of logic that excluded the temporal theories of causation led him to formulate his new science, in which narrative and poetic logic were concrete means by which knowledge emerged out of the unconscious and was registered in language. This knowledge, or *certum*, emerges out of situations that involve the individual in crisis, discernment and choice. Whether humanistic or scientific, it engenders a symbolic language intrinsic to its involvement in the social and historical reality.[3] Because of the situatedness of the separate knowledges each with its particular terminology and semantic field, it is critical that educators be able to integrate their knowledge with the concept of the whole. Regrettably, writes Vico, the university faculty was comprised of divergent specialists unable to communicate with another, a fact that leads him to advocate for institutional reform: "Students' education is so warped and perverted as a consequence, that, although they may become extremely learned in some respects, their culture on the whole (and the whole is really the flower of wisdom) is incoherent" (Vico, 1990, p. 77).

One of the primary fields in which Vico uncovered human symbolic behavior was myth. Myths could not offer moral guidance but could show one how society and the individual have interrelated over time. The study of myth and folklore requires that one adopt a theory of dialogue by which the teller and the told, the subject and object, are reciprocally disposed within a human context. For this purpose, Vico studied the materiality of texts and surveyed the extant records of 'characters,' a term he used broadly to signify mythic personages, the qualities they embodied and the graphic signs of written alphabets. His synoptic tables of ancient cultures in *New Science* assessed these characters anthropologically, assuming the fundamental interconnectedness of diverse languages, ritualistic practices and religious belief systems. A certain diffidence is called for when approaching Vico's linguistic theories, since he was often inexact or allusive to the point where terms lost their precise meanings. We make no effort, therefore, to explore the specifics of Vico's philosophy of language, preferring to not get involved in questions of the origins of language, cultural variations, theories of etymology or of the existence of a universal mental 'speech' shared by all humanity.[4] Rather we focus on the general values of analogical thinking and hypothesis formation, and the idea of the *verum ipsum factum* – or "knowledge is tantamount to operation" (Gianturco in Vico, 1990, p. xlii) – by which the Neapolitan philosopher anticipates the tenets of process studies and constructivism. Vico asked the following: Does the realm of the imagination and poetry, of history and rhetoric, enjoy the place it is due? Is truth appreciated as something experiential which depends on the perceptions of the knower and observer for its definitive form? Or do educators hark back to hidebound notions of objective clarity? Vico would argue that the exclusive reliance on deductive logic (characteristic of Cartesian rationalism and Baconian empiricism alike) alienated the learner from the cognitive adventure of the cultural group, the common narrative of human history and the *sensus communis*.

Cassirer

In the later 18th century, as scientists are able to collect superior data to that of their predecessors, the sciences acquire their own discrete symbolic languages. In mathematics one surpasses the Pythagorean theory for which the cosmos was ordered in perfect numerical relations; new formulations in chemistry and biology break with past schemes. In this changed climate, epistemology emerges as the study of the relations between the fields of knowledge, no longer under the yoke of philosophy.

While Vico's thought was influential in the 19th century and was a precursor to the historicism that dominated the Romantic period, once that movement had exhausted itself in the modern period, Vico fell into relative obscurity.[5] As Ernst Cassirer writes, while the philosophy of history was revolutionary in its linking of the facts of existence to the facts of the self, of the "thing-configurations" and "I-configurations" to which our "perceptual grasp [...] of the world" is bound, human beings continue to strive beyond those facts and toward an "intelligible cosmos" (Cassirer, 1996, p. 111). This cosmos cannot be described in images: "It can be conceived only in *symbols*, the symbols of language, art, religion and theoretical cognition" (Cassirer, 1996, p. 111). Cassirer has identified symbol as the unifying feature in human endeavor and has summarized the protean forms in which it appears. As a universal and transcendent modality in culture, symbolic thinking exists in tension with the entropy and chaos of the world.[6] Insofar as the languages of science depend on symbolic reference, Cassirer recommends that we expand the concept of objectivity to include what is known and represented in symbolic form. Though a follower of Kant, Cassirer's concept of symbol goes beyond the representational; while retaining the concept of subjectivity, he opposes any form of subjectivism. In his chapter 'Nature-Concepts and Culture-Concepts,' Cassirer carries this discussion beyond the domain of pure logic and theoretical sciences to get to the structure of perception. He discusses the limits of objectivism and subjectivism as well as the narrowness of behaviorism, which lacks a theory of meaning. Behaviorism – also known as "learning theory" – lacks focus on interpretation and is too "associationist" (Cassirer, 1961, pp. 150–51). As these limitations apply generally to learning, so they apply to moral learning.

Cassirer's theory of the symbol is threefold, comprising sign, meaning and use. The defining moment in his formulation comes in the analysis of language. By returning to the actual material production of symbols, historically and cross-culturally, Cassirer aims at distinguishing what is properly human (and, in so doing, advances the work of Vico). If Kant had conceived of a gap between the mentality underlying symbolic production and the symbolic production itself, Cassirer sees these as existing on the same plane. In order to better grasp Cassirer's terminology and his concept of the human, let us consider the example he cites of Helen Keller. In the deaf, dumb and blind woman's learning process one sees the Cassirean distinction between the 'sign' and the 'symbol.' While animals perceive and communicate with signs, only humans have the capacity to form symbols: "In short, we may say that the animal possesses a practical imagination and intelligence whereas man alone has developed a new form: a *symbolic imagination and intelligence"* (Cassirer, 1970, p. 33). Cassirer singles out the case of Keller because her awakening into language, and the discovery "that *everything has a name,"* confirms the three different qualities of symbols: their universality, their variability and their support of relational thought (Cassirer, 1970, pp. 36–38).

Another thinker who studied the linguistic experience of Keller was Walker Percy, whose theories of the symbol are grounded in Peirce and his theory of triads. Percy defends symbolic practice from the reductive treatments that emerge from empirical behaviorism and abstract rationalism, both of which fail to acknowledge the symbol as a social communication and thus as the concrete sign of a relation. Percy (1984) remarks on the discovery by Helen Keller of the signifier 'water' as an act that could not be explained by behaviorists and required a theory of the symbol: By understanding that the letters 'w-a-t-e-r' palpated on one hand corresponded to the sensation coursing over the other, Keller tied the signifier to the signified and the referent. The discovery that this action was repeatable led to a heuristic pattern of learning involving the production of symbols. Keller's accomplishment is remarkable because of her deafness and blindness, factors that discount traditional behaviorist rationales.[7]

Cassirer's approach to pedagogy seems especially valuable in addressing current debates, whether in the sciences, where empirical and sensationalist approaches seem to persist, or the humanities, where the problem of symbolic memory is often idealized instead of being related to ideas concerning humanity's "symbolic future" (Cassirer, 1970, p. 55). It is important to affirm in this regard that a professional empiricism does not exclude the scientist from the moral realm. Scientists must be prepared to step beyond the data of science in order to accomplish an outward movement into society in which the ideas of science assert their morality:

> The problem is to discover and develop a new viewpoint, to set up a new standard which cannot be reduced to that of empirical causality but which on the other hand is in no sense in conflict with it. Ethics demands that human actions are to be capable of and accessible to a double judgment; they are to be determined as events in time, but their content and meaning is not to be exhausted by this determinism.
>
> (Cassirer, 1957, p. 50)

The great relevance of Cassirer's thinking is due to its presentation of symbolism as a cultural and epistemological rather than a metaphysical or ontological problem. As such, it is inevitable that symbolism and the notion of the actual (as opposed to the merely possible) will impact directly on questions of pedagogy. As Cassirer noted in discussing the uniquely human characteristic of 'symbolic space:'

> Not immediately, but by a very complex and difficult process of thought, [man] arrives at the idea of *abstract space* – and it is this idea which clears the way for man not only to a new field of knowledge but to an entirely new direction of his cultural life.
>
> (Cassirer, 1970, p. 43)

Piaget

One can cite a number of thinkers who, by exploring the boundaries between disciplines, exemplify Cassirer's commitment to symbolism as a means to reinvigorate the academy. Emerging from their specializations, they possess the attitude of a double vocation and livelihood. An exemplary figure in this regard is Jean Piaget. Also inspired by Kant, Piaget introduced genetic epistemology as a constructivist theory of learning rooted in psychology and biology. In Piaget's view, knowledge was not to be construed as preexisting in reality, but only came about by virtue of the individual's formulations in response to specific observations and experiences. Herein lies the problem of symbolism, which runs like a common thread through Piaget's studies of the stages of cognitive development of the individual, from the child's earliest manipulation of signs to the mature adult's formation of abstract symbolic reasoning. Piaget also explored the areas beyond his specializations, both in the humanities and the hard sciences.

Piaget, like Vico, considered the concepts of science an invention, a fabrication of man; on this basis he identified epistemological errors within psychology and biology even as he developed a learning theory that had broad applications within the larger academic community. Focusing on the qualitative nature of knowledge, Piaget rejects behaviorism and other quantitative sciences that fail to take into account the nature of evolution, both in terms of ontogenesis and phylogenesis. His constructivism abandons the notion of the passive observer and encourages learners to pose and test new hypotheses in response to new situations. He also questions the established modes of working in the teaching profession insofar as knowledge can not be seen as existing apart from the learner (as a copy or imitation of reality), but is arrived at anew in each situation; thus the principles of adaptation, accommodation and reflection replace the notion of given truths. As long as educators retained a Cartesian model of clarity based on the absolutes, complex thought would be excluded from the classroom. The expanded areas of psychological research are impacted by the changed understanding of consciousness as a stratified and highly varied matter, more nuanced in terms of learning than previously believed: "psychology attempts to explain why the development of intelligence ends, in its necessary form of equilibrium, in the setting up of composable and reversible systems of operations" (Piaget, 1972, p. 81).

Genetic epistemology concerns the sociogenesis of knowledge, thus the development of knowledge over time, according to operative processes rooted in the common sense (here too is a link with Vico). The operations lie at the basis of Piaget's pedagogy, which can be described as processual, actionist, integrative and constructivist.

> [First,] an operation is an action that can be internalized; that is, it can be carried out in thought as well as executed materially. Second, it is a reversible action; that is, it can take place in one direction or in the opposite direction [...]. The third characteristic of an operation is that it always supposes some conservation, some invariant. It is of course a transformation, since it is an action, but it is a transformation that does not transform everything at once, or else there would be no possibility of reversibility [...]. The fourth characteristic is that no operation exists alone. Every operation is related to a system of operations, or to a total structure as we call it.
>
> (Piaget, 1970, pp. 21–22)

Piaget's essays on pedagogy are few, but they tie in to his thinking on the subject of education in a way that is opportune for our presentation (in the next section) of the notion of heterarchy as an organizational principle. By recommending a pedagogy that is actionist and integrative of the disciplines, Piaget expresses discontent over the intuitive method, which is 'receptive' and 'static,' as well as the authority-based method, which does not broach the subjectivity of the individual learner. In contrast to these methods, the active constructivist methods are difficult to employ:

> The heartbreaking difficulty in pedagogy, as indeed in medicine and in many other branches of knowledge that partake at the same time of art and science, is in fact, that the best methods are also the most difficult ones: it would be impossible to employ a Socratic method without having first acquired some of Socrates' qualities, the first of which would have to be a certain respect for intelligence in the process of development.
>
> (Piaget, 1977, p. 712)

The reason constructivist methods are difficult might be summed up by stating that they seek access to an "internal epistemology" (Piaget, 1972, p. 95). This epistemology is always in process; it cannot simply be the study of the state of knowledge today, but must concern knowledge's ongoing development and transformation: "scientific thought [...] is a process of continual construction and reorganization" (Piaget, 1970, p. 2).

Once the facts of knowledge are identified, one can perceive the parallelism between the formation of knowledge and its meaning: "The fundamental hypothesis of genetic epistemology is that there is a parallelism between the progress made in the logical and rational organization of knowledge and the corresponding formative psychological processes" (Piaget, 1970, p. 13). Piaget disagrees with the idea that by learning a 'dead language' one can somehow acquire skills that will be useful to one and 'be transferred to other activities:'

> Supporters of this hypothesis [...] will even go so far as to imply an absolute contrast between this subtle or analytic type of mind (*esprit de finesse*) and the geometrical type of mind *(esprit de géométrie)*, as though the latter were exclusive to the sciences and the former to the literary disciplines, whereas both, of course, are found everywhere...
> (Piaget, 1977, p. 709)

Piaget studied the methodological and curricular changes underway in the lower schools and the universities, on either side of the Atlantic. He was dismayed over the large class sizes and the proliferation of unproven methods, in particular the mechanized ("programmatic") methods and the "current receptive methods" which were "intuitive" in character (Piaget, 1977, p. 712). The problem with these methods – aside from the fact that their effectiveness had not been demonstrated – was their failure to constitute a genuine pedagogical approach to operations. Piaget regrets the confusion in contemporary pedagogical debates that associates the static and 'intuitive' methods with the active methods he himself supports. It is a sign of Piaget's dedication to process, his focus on actions and operations and his conviction that the body of knowledge in a field and the history of that knowledge's development are ultimately inseparable, that he is not tied to any specific pedagogic doctrine.

Lamenting the divide between academic departments in the sciences and the humanities, Piaget writes:

> It would be impossible to exaggerate the harm done by such compartmentalizations, the most evident result of which is the constitution of a sort of a social caste of philosophers, who are called upon to deal directly with the total sum of reality without any personal initiation into what is meant by controlled scientific research.
> (Piaget, 1977, p. 708)

Piaget conceived of the system of the sciences as a cyclic order and not as a linear sequence. As he assesses the changes in this regard during the period 1935–1965, he notes that formerly the scientific community had adhered to a linear sequence but gradually came to adopt the cyclic and integrable relation charted here (Piaget, 1970, p. 83) (Figure 2.1):

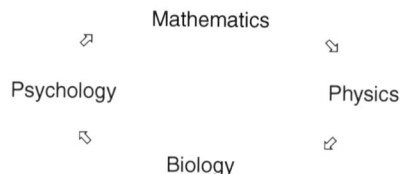

Figure 2.1 The circle of the sciences (Piaget, 1970, p. 83).

About the symmetries and complementarities represented here, Piaget advises as follows: "The circle of the sciences ultimately demonstrates what the analysis of each particular form of knowledge directly emphasizes, but in varying degrees, namely the close interdependence between subject and object" (Piaget, 1970, p. 84). He envisions a future day when the languages of the sister disciplines will be mutually understandable (and not simply those in this chart); but he is also cautious about unexamined assumptions that substantive relations will necessarily be forged across the sometimes great distances separating the human, social and hard sciences. Since he suggests that "the development and the epistemological aspect of all science are essential manifestations of man's activity" (Piaget, 1970, p. 103), it is in this area of researching the mechanisms and operations of knowledge (as notably by recent cybernetic research) that he envisions the most fruitful terrain for future development of interdisciplinary discourse.[8]

Senecan Liberality and Heterarchy

For the constructivist, one of the most valuable things a student can learn is the idea of possibility. Thus, for example, in the science classroom the educator would seek to convey von Humboldt's idea of "science as something that has not yet been and never will be completely discovered" (von Humboldt, 1810, p. 379, cited by Habermas, 1989, p. 109). This is another area where Vico's example remains important, as he vindicated the probabilistic reason and the importance of the *sensus communis* in binding together a cohesive community. Vico reminds us of the complex nature of objectivity as it is formed in the individual subject, a process that begins in childhood and progresses according to certain natural stages and across the broadly integrable fields of practical and theoretical knowledge. In addition, by advocating institutional reform based on the goal of a common intellectual language, Vico was outlining the roles of the university citizen, based on the classic form of liberalism he derived from Seneca, among others.

As Martha Nussbaum notes, it was Seneca who conceived of citizenship as being based on a freedom that does not derive from social class, but from intellectual autonomy and respect. The Senecan liberality depends on the awareness of one's smallness in the larger scheme of things, of the immensity of one's unknowing. As such it fosters humility and respect for the differences of others.[9] Teachers who employ Socratic method in stating curricular goals and institutional exigencies encourage a class-blind cosmopolitanism, challenging students to represent their positions and their histories. Nussbaum, whose analysis is based on her experiences of teaching in a variety of institutions and disciplines, recalls the Stoics' opposition to the classical Roman hierarchies that wished to preserve the academy for 'gentlemanly' (class-determined) education. Today's stoics would oppose the idea of a fixed canon of prescribed texts or the quantification of what constitutes cultural literacy or the fashion of identity politics: "An especially damaging consequence of identity politics in the literary academy is the belief, which one encounters in both students and scholars, that only a member of a particular oppressed group can write well about that group's experience" (Nussbaum, 1997, p. 111).

The particular hierarchies endorsed by constructivist educators are *heterarchies*, or "systemic networks in which the dominant locuses of constraint and control immanent in the system may change place and function – and their relative logical typing – in the overall structure through time" (Wilden, 1979, p. 25).[10] Heterarchy, or "the rule of one's neighbor," is a social and symbolic system based on the recognition of the other; it emphasizes the recursive and self-corrective nature of thought.[11] When applied to teaching, heterarchies engage both qualitative and quantitative means of inference and reasoning; they seek out protocols that connect the internal values of one's discipline to those of other disciplines. The constructivist educator is drawn naturally to such a model as it favors the ability to self-calibrate and discerns between levels of discourse and supports "a double knowledge, in which traditional knowledge and a recognition of the ecology of mind are mutually compared and integrated" (Dal Lago, 1992, p. 163).

Constructivists situate aesthetics and ethics at the center of a dialogue whose purpose is to reframe knowledge and coordinate meanings derived from a plurality of contexts. In this way they adopt the self-reflectiveness of historical humanism: "The Humanist believes in the power of the human mind of investigating the human mind" (Spitzer, 1967, p. 24).[12] This tenet is equally important in the physical sciences, the life sciences, the social sciences, the arts and the humanities. If one is studying Newton, for example, one will learn of the importance of guesswork, hypothesis-making and observation in conducting of empirical research.[13] One will learn how Newton was criticized for the new categories of learning he proposed. If one is studying Vico, one might be reminded that he was led to organize *The New Science* into axioms (*degnità*) in imitation of the systematic use of axioms in Newton's

Principia Mathematica. In other words, the empirical and quantitative constraints of a specialization like mathematics need not limit the moral ideas of the specialist. When Cassirer wrote, "Mathematical laws are the means for knowing dead forms; the means for understanding living forms is analogy. Analogy unveils history's language of forms" (Cassirer, 1996, p. 109), he was not suggesting that we deny the importance of mathematical laws. Rather he was urging that scientists engage in a 'double judgment' in order to preserve the integrity of their moral ideas.

As cognitive psychologist and philosopher of education Jerome Bruner has written, "The very essence of being human lies in the use of symbols" (1966, p. 88). By assembling symbols into social systems and narratives, humans structure their world and "give expression to the group's basic tenets on astronomy, theology, sociology, law, education, even aesthetics" (Bruner, 1966, p. 89). The university, being the principal sanctioner of knowledge in the society, is the symbol-making body par excellence. Yet if one looks at the professional literature on the institution, little is stated about symbol. According to Kenneth Burke, symbolic discussions are averted within bureaucratic structures because such discussions follow their own internal motivational structures rather than those of a legalistic hierarchy: "A study of symbolism is annoying, we must admit, because it requires us continually to be 'off the subject'" (Burke, 1984, p. 191). Certainly if one is interested in exploring the unstated assumptions of educators and the implicit relationships that underlie the official discourse of the institution, a study of symbolism is called for.

Gregory Bateson had the constructivist approach in mind when, as a Regent of the University of California, he advocated the practice of 'paradigmatic conservatism' in the University's practices. Warning against the rapid assimilation by the academy of the ecocidal practices and epistemological errors of the outside world, Bateson criticized the University's quantitative focus: "This enormous emphasis upon the quantitative view and the minimal emphasis on the patterned view is, I believe, the easiest way of descent into hell" (Bateson, 1981, p. 351). Against this direction Bateson advocated for the conservation of an integrated qualitative/quantitative, value-rich, ethical system:

> The total system is a sort of ladder, interlocking settings which are calibrations, which are qualitative, discontinuous, fixed, structural sort of things. And events which are usually quantitative. The tendency of our thinking today, is to think almost entirely on the quantitative side of the picture, and to argue about quantities.
>
> (Bateson, 1981, p. 353)

Such a tendency is leading to unpredictable, perhaps disastrous and global pattern changes; to oppose it in the name of paradigmatic conservatism is to reconnect to an ecological, systems-oriented sensibility that respects eternal verities and the equilibrium of cultural and biological systems. By positing heterarchies, one can situate the individual within dialogical and metalogical structures. According to Bateson, the great oversight of Western humanity lies in its ignorance and avoidance of natural history, and its tacit acceptance of a flawed epistemology originating in the mind/body split:

> First, it is now clear that the medieval view of mind/body relations as a sort of demonic possession is obsolete. Second, although the realm of ideas, information, mind – call it what you will – is immanent in, and inseparable from, the realm of physical appearances, it must be approached with its own special preconceptions and premises [...]. The new science will form around profoundly nonphysical ideas: the nature of the relation between name and that which is named, the nature of recursive systems, and the nature of difference.
> (Bateson, 1991b, p. 157)

The key concepts that anticipate the "new science" Bateson speaks of, are the *"ratio"* named by Gustav Theodor Fechner in the 19th century as the basis of the percept – or the difference that triggers perception – and the concept of "logical types" formulated by Whitehead and Russell in *Principia Mathematica* (1927). This recognition of difference is critical in so far as it presupposes and practices a pedagogy based, as Vico would say, on what human beings themselves have made.

Bateson's call for prudence is a recognition of a societal incapacity to coherently embrace the magnitude of natural and cultural forces in flux due to an addiction to physical metaphors of power and force. In contrast, paradigmatic conservatism entails symbolic thinking that envisions the future of natural organisms and living systems in terms of heterarchy and not under the control of a single entity. To imagine heterarchy is to pursue in concrete terms the true meaning of *education*: to educe, to draw out what is potentially there.[14] When learning is construed as a process of accumulation instead of a drawing out, information is overvalued at the expense of knowledge, and knowledge is mistaken for wisdom.[15] Such a manner of thinking presumes disinterestedness but does so by eschewing symbolism; a trivial certainty is preferred over the non-trivial unknown.

As Edgar Morin writes: "Because we were taught to separate, compartmentalize and isolate learning instead of making connections, the whole of our knowledge forms an unintelligible puzzle. Interactions, retroactions, contexts and complexities, lost in the no-man's land between different disciplines, become invisible" (Morin, 2001, pp. 34–35). If the academic institution is to reconnect to itself and to society, it will make these connections visible, in the symbolic explanations of its role in the advance of knowledge in the society: "To understand means to intellectually apprehend together, *com-prehendere*, to grasp together (the text and its context, the parts and the whole, the multiple and the single). Intellectual comprehension operates through intelligibility and explanation" (Morin, 2001, p. 78).[16] Here one sees fulfilled the pedagogic mission of Vico and the moral investment of the sciences foreseen by Cassirer and the integration of objective and subjective knowledge by Piaget. While symbolic thinking is not always welcome within an institutional structure that prides itself on rationalism and logic, it remains an essential part of academic discourse.

Notes

1 Said, 2000, pp. 89–92, notes the contradictions involved in Vico's forcing the details of language, such as etymology and derivation, back into the physical world, even as he was forcing them into the divine, providential sphere.

2 As Nicholas Rescher puts it, 1996, p. 111: "The fundamentality of psychic process for the constitution of a self was put on the agenda of modern philosophy by Descartes, although unfortunately, he took too substance-oriented a view of a person – as his use of *res* (thing) indicates."

3 See Herrick, 2005, p. 176: "In works such as *On the Study Methods of Our Time* (…), Vico argued that the mathematical proofs of Descartes were just as reliant on symbols as were the orations of the rhetoricians."

4 See Hall, 1941, for a review of Vico's linguistic theories that exposes a variety of inaccuracies and internal contradictions within them.

5 Writing of Vico's philosophy of history and its importance for the formation of the modern "philosophy of culture" and "philosophy of spirit," Cassirer writes, 1996, p. 104:

> No matter how highly we may value the historical achievement of this basic organological view, this cannot distract us from its fundamental, systematic limit. This limit lies in the fact that it too attempts to solve problems concerning pure "meaning" by relegating them to the level of occurrences and so transforms them into problems concerning actual events.

6 Entropy is understood by Bateson, 1980, p. 250, as "the degree to which relations between the components of any aggregate are mixed up, unsorted, undifferentiated, unpredictable, and random. The opposite is negentropy, the degree of ordering or sorting or predictability in an aggregate."

7 One could say that Keller's "seeing blindness" stands as a symbol for deutero-learning, the term defined by Bateson, 1972, p. 167, as the "progressive change in rate of protolearning."

8 See Piaget, 1972, p. 95:

> [T]he most promising interdisciplinary developments are undoubtedly those which can be grouped under the name of cybernetic studies. Cybernetics is itself already interdisciplinary in nature in that it attempts, among other things, to provide a theory and a practical realization of machines which are at the same time programmed and autoregulating, as are living beings. In addition, it achieves this through using models relating to general algebra, logic, information theory, and game or decision theory. Cybernetics is therefore currently the most polyvalent meeting-point for the physico-mathematical, the biological and the human sciences.

9 See Nussbaum, 1997, p. 295:

> We do not fully respect the humanity of our fellow citizens – or cultivate
> our own – if we do not wish to learn about them, to understand their
> history, to appreciate the differences between their lives and ours. We
> must therefore construct a liberal education that is not only Socratic, em-
> phasizing critical thought and respectful argument, but also pluralistic,
> imparting an understanding of the histories and contributions of groups
> with whom we interact, both within our nation and in the increasingly
> international sphere of business and politics. If we cannot teach our stu-
> dents everything they will need to know to be good citizens, we may at
> least teach them what they do not know and how they may inquire. [...]
> Above all, we can teach them how to argue, rigorously and critically, so
> that they can call their minds their own.

10 In tracing the precedents for such a perspective, Wilden, 1979, p. 13, refers
back to Nicholas of Cusa and his concept of God as the "ultimate constraint," "the constraint we now call entropy."

11 See Segal, 1986, p. 135:

> In a heterarchy you rule within a circle [...] McCulloch used the term *het-
> erarchy* to distinguish context-determined value choices from the more
> familiar notion of a *hierarchy*. Heterarchical values, expressed in behav-
> ior, are relative choices, dependent on time and context.

12 Already in the 1960s, the influence of positivism on the humanities caused
Leo Spitzer, 1967, p. 1, to warn against the reductionisms of "so-called
humanists who persist in imitating an obsolete approach to the natural
sciences, which have themselves evolved toward the humanities."

13 In response to the accusation of Newton's adversaries that he was merely
weaving hypotheses, Whitehead, 1929b, p. 52, sums it up nicely: "Newton
was weaving hypotheses." The novel use of symbols had a fundamental importance in the discoveries of Galileo and other revolutionary scientists. As
Latour (1986) argues, scholars are prone to overlook the use of the imagination by mathematicians, a factor that is sometimes dismissed or not
accorded its centrality to the scientific endeavor.

14 See Whitehead, 1948, p. 178:

> the word "education" means literally, the process of leading out. Thus we
> are talking of the way in which all your faculties and capacities should
> be encouraged to expand and unfold themselves. Consider how nature
> generally sets to work to educate the living organisms which teem on this
> earth. You cannot begin to understand nature's method unless you grasp
> the fact that the essential spring of all growth is within you [...]. What
> is really essential in your development you must do for yourselves. The
> regular method of nature is a happy process of genial encouragement.

15 See Whitehead, 1929a, p. 46:

> Though knowledge is one chief aim of intellectual education, there is
> another ingredient, vaguer but greater, and more dominating in its im-
> portance. The ancients called it "wisdom." You cannot be wise without
> some basis of knowledge; but you may easily acquire knowledge and re-
> main bare of wisdom.

16 Morin concludes this particular section by saying, 2001, p. 78: "Understanding,
always intersubjective, demands an open heart, sympathy, generosity."

3 Contemporary Approaches to a Pedagogy of Process

The Modern Process Tradition

In this chapter I explore the bases for a process theory of learning applicable across the disciplines and able to contend with the diverse modes of logic employed in today's academy. In contrast to the persistent Cartesian pedagogy, that juxtaposes mind to body, art to science, man to nature, and separates 'subjective' mental processes from 'objective' forms of social organization and knowledge, I present a process pedagogy that exercises a ternary option in order to mediate holistically between these dichotomies. Specifically, I explore this pedagogy in three areas: the roots of process pedagogy in Kant and later thinkers for whom subjectivity and objectivity were mutually transformable, a development that fundamentally altered the communicative codes and propositional structures employed to assign truth value; the case of science education, specifically as regards habit formation among students and the need to contextualize and generalize scientific instruction; and the educational role to be played by logical abduction, as first articulated in the modern era by Charles Sanders Peirce, whose pragmatic theories have been extended and applied by a number of scholars. Thus, the essay moves from the macroscopic to the microscopic, from the origins and premises of process pedagogy, to the question of institutional practices and learning theory, to the use of hypothesis formation as a shared pedagogical tool across the disciplines.

The modern process tradition is perhaps best exemplified by the work of Alfred North Whitehead. Whitehead's pedagogical philosophy was original and yet compatible with the pragmatism developed by William James, C. S. Peirce and John Dewey. The broad-based and ecumenical pedagogy that ensued laid the groundwork for the development of context theory, complexity theory, and, more recently, edusemiotics.[1] Within the process view, the enactment of educational predicates can only be understood by entering into the particulars of the conceptual organization and self-definitions of the academic disciplines. As Whitehead wrote in the classic volume *The Function of Reason*:

> The claim of science that it can produce an understanding of its procedures within the limits of its own categories, or that those

categories themselves are understandable without reference to their status within the widest categories under exploration by the speculative Reason – that claim is entirely unfounded.

(Whitehead, 1929b, 58–59)

Since Whitehead's day, the need for a language of relations able to mediate between the categorical claims of the scientific disciplines has often gone unheeded.[2] The great expansion of the modern university in the sciences and other areas of specialized knowledge has meant that, in many sectors, quantitative learning has been privileged over qualitative learning. Seeing this re-entrenchment of dualistic thinking as a form of neoscholasticism, process-oriented educators have stressed the importance of the Socratic and humanistic model, finding it to be the soundest basis for a unitive, holistic and liberal education. Esteeming all knowledge to be replete with ethical and aesthetic dimensions, they have rejected the idea of a passive learner and argued for the transformational nature of learning, based on the inherent capacity of students to practice self-inquiry of a qualitative nature.

As process philosopher Nicholas Rescher writes, "the position of process metaphysics is that the interests of a just appreciation of the world's realities call for prioritizing: activity over substance; process over product; change over persistence; novelty over continuity" (Rescher, 1996, 31). Temporality, flux and events (rather than phenomena) are the major concerns of the process thinker:

> The salient idea of process philosophy is that the world consists of – and must, in consequence, be understood in terms of – changes rather than fixed stabilities. But from the time of Pythagoras, various philosophers have taught that while the world's *phenomena* may be ever-changing, the *laws* that govern the comportment of these changes are stable and fixed once and for all. Following the lead of C.S. Peirce, process metaphysics firmly rejects this contention. As it sees the matter, process invades the world's law structure as well; the laws of nature, too, are merely transitory stabilities that emerge at one phase of cosmic history only to lapse from creation and give way to variant modes of operation in the fullness of time.
>
> (Rescher, 1996, p. 91)

Because of its radical dynamism, process thinking – from the ancient mode of Heraclitus and Lucretius, to the Kantian discovery of scientific subjectivity and recursive thinking to the contemporary process mode that moves through Whitehead and Ernst Cassirer – does not fall in place on either side of the opposition between Continental phenomenology and Anglo-American analytic philosophy.[3]

Starting with the Kantian predicate (as expounded in the *Critique of Pure Reason*), one had the framework for a process pedagogy able to mediate between subjective and objective truths. The novelty of the Kantian predicate lies in its allowing for a subject whose knowledge depends on interiority, speculation and reflection as much as on the observation of the external world. What Kant called the analytic predicate is involved in the recovery of data, but the data lies inert until it is animated in a synthesis with the facts of current experience. Subsequently, those facts can be combined with internal values in the individual in order to adapt and shape the future. The stratification of predicates in Kant's system (from the analytical *a priori* to the synthetical *a posteriori* to the synthetical *a priori*) places emphasis on the self, but the self is relational and dependent on practical interactions with others and an active design upon nature.

As Kant writes:

> Metaphysics, even if we look upon it as hitherto only a tentative science, which because of the very nature of human reason, however, is indispensable to us, is meant to contain synthetic *a priori* knowledge. Its main concern is not at all merely to analyse concepts which we form *a priori* of things, and thus to elucidate them analytically, but to expand our knowledge *a priori*. This we can do only by means of principles which add to a given concept something that was not contained in it [...]
>
> (Kant, 2007, p. 48)

After Kant, it was imperative to address the questions of discursive argumentation and logical-experiential proof in a mediated, ternary matter that went beyond the doctrines of rationalism and empiricism and opened the door to qualitative research and the open-ended study of natural systems.[4] Conversely the semiotic code of the scientist or philosopher was subjected to new scrutiny; insofar as it was a communicative act, it was prone to bias and error, ambiguity and distortion. After Kant a new theory of the observer exists that is able to mediate between the opposing epistemological claims of rationalism and empiricism. Kant was

> the great philosopher who first, fully and explicitly, introduced into philosophy the conception of an act of experience as a constructive functioning, transforming subjectivity into objectivity, or objectivity into subjectivity; the order is immaterial in comparison to the general idea.
>
> (Whitehead, 1929a, pp. 180–81)[5]

By envisioning a subject capable of transcendental reason and the faculties of judgment, Kant went a long way toward defining the modern consciousness. As Ernst von Glasersfeld writes:

Kant speaks [...] of a need that arises in "practical life," especially when we want to coordinate our actions with those of others. The thing-in-itself, Kant reiterates in many places, is intended as a "product of thought" (*Gedankending*) that serves as a "heuristic fiction." [...] For Kant, the relation of cause and effect was a "symbolic a priori" category, inherent from the outset in our thinking [...], one of those heuristic fictions that reason needed in order to generate a rational picture of itself as the producer of understanding.

(Glasersfeld, 1995, pp. 40, 42)

Among the heuristic fictions that a self is endowed with is the delimitation of reason by the noumena or the infinite. As Cassirer notes, the Kantian ideal of the infinite is something more and something other than the negation of the finite, and depends for its accurate conception on the facts of communication, relation and process.

After Kant, the status of the proposition and the communicative codes used to formulate the proposition attain scientific value. Thus, modern communication theorists prioritize the Kantian predicates: "By making knowing cooperative, Kant faced the problem of recursivity. How can one know what one knows? Does not the awareness of one's self as a knower contradict the principle? Is self the knower or the known" (Pearce and Cronen, 1980, p. 66). Not surprisingly, the inheritors of Kant's thought go beyond deduction and induction to include abduction (or hypothesis formation) as a critical part of human reasoning.

The elevation of communication and semiotics to the status of sciences – as seen in Cassirer's *Philosophy of Symbolic Forms* – carries with it an understanding of metaphysics as a science of change and function, not substance and being (Verene, 2008). The attractiveness of a relativistic and recursive logic to be shared by the humanities and sciences has led many scholars – since Kant – to advocate for a more heterarchical, tranversal and transdisciplinary organization of the academy into constellations and clusters, rather than the traditional hierarchical separation into specializations, typically under the figure of the 'master.'

Consider the example of Arthur Schopenhauer. Schopenhauer was an early defender of the cognitive importance of hypothesis formation and a caustic critic of the Academy of his day, in particular the German Departments of Philosophy circa 1830. In 'On Philosophy at the Universities,' he converses with the voices of antiquity even as he denounces the near universal enthusiasm for Hegel among academic philosophers, a fact which obscured all those who came before in a dubious fusion of historicism and Judeo-Christian dogma. Schopenhauer elevated Kant, who had demonstrated that God's existence or nonexistence cannot be proved by logical means, a joyous moment that Schopenhauer feels was not experienced by Hegel and his followers. Schopenhauer's objection to the 'chair-philosophy' alleges that cronyism destroys any chance of meritocracy in the academy, especially as regards the selection of course materials and the recruiting of disciples.[6] Schopenhauer's attackers maintained the status quo, which combined the Restoration of monarchy with the regressive side of Romanticism that turned a blind eye to the great historical moment of Kant.

Philosopher David Carr has defended the transcendent philosophy of Kant and Husserl as against those who would confuse it with idealism. What characterizes the transcendental is its 'meaning-bestowing and world-constituting capacity,' its involvement in the empirical as well as the ontological, its refusal to discount or dismiss either tendency as it tends toward the body or the language of man, respectively. Carr reminds us that behind appearances and the veneer of even the most scientific language, reality is simply different from how we might construe it. He shows that Kant and Husserl overcame the realism/idealism opposition and are not part of "the historical sweep of idealism that begins with Descartes, culminates in Hegel, and then is articulated as will to power by Nietzsche" (Carr, 1999, p. 111). Carr is able to reaffirm the importance of subjectivity as a "central philosophical topic" despite the wave of current opinion to the contrary; since the Self or subject is both "subject for the world" and "object in the world," "the transcendental subject is not any kind of thing," but is a "theoretical fiction" (Carr, 1999, pp. 140, 135, 131, 122, 119). In terms of the topic of education, one can say that this honest confrontation with the unknown and the limits of language does not denote a switch away from nominal subjects to verbal predicates, but points to the necessary involvement in both, whenever one is engaged in a cognitive enterprise.

Science Education and the Impress of Habit

The 19th century failed to carry forward Kant's valorization of science's middle path between the rationalism of Descartes and the empiricism of Berkeley and Hume. Whitehead writes of this failure and in defense of Kant's mediation and valorization of science: "Antagonism between philosophy and natural science has produced unfortunate limitations of thought on both sides. Philosophy has ceased to claim its proper generality and natural science is content with the narrow round of its methods" (Whitehead, 1929b, p. 61). By opposing himself to such sectorialized thinking, Whitehead anticipated the development of constructivism and complex thought, and their focus on the polycentricity of knowledge and the retention of metaphysics as the science of change: "If the doctrine of science as the quest for simplicity of description, be construed in the sense in which it frees science from metaphysics, in that sense science loses its importance" (Whitehead, 1929b, p. 55).

Whitehead anticipated the development of science studies, advocating for the instruction of the general context of the sciences, the need for creativity and encouraging hypothesis formation from first-hand experience:

> In the teaching of science, the art of thought should be taught: namely the art of forming clear conceptions applying to first-hand experience, the art of divining the general truths which apply, the art of testing divinations, and the art of utilising general truths by reasoning to more particular cases of some peculiar importance.
> (Whitehead, 1929a, p. 81)

Acknowledging the multiplicity of the sciences, and the difficulty of understanding even one or two, he stressed the critical importance of generality:

> It is essential that the generality of the method be continually brought to light and contrasted with the speciality of the particular application. A man who only knows is own science, as a routine peculiar to that science, does not even know that.
> (Whitehead, 1929a, 82)

Whitehead compared the isolationism among the disciplines to the scholasticism of the Middle Ages, which grew because of its excessive systemization and turning away from the natural world.[7] Not coincidentally, the neoscholastic current today tends to repudiate nature and the body as a site of mediation between the humanities and natural sciences.

One aberration of the neoscholastic doctrines is to consider the possible mediation between the humanities and sciences in terms of the Nietzschean attempt to reconcile Apollo and Dionysus. In the realm of aesthetics, the Nietzscheans ignore the value-inherent, ethically and socially contexted nature of the work of art, and the fact that the creation of art is independent of and prior to its reception. Such an oversight is characteristic of the anti-humanism of the present "age of theory," in which "deconstruction negates any stability or plenitude of sense within enunciatory acts and forms" (Steiner, 1989, p. 99). To stand against the neoscholastics is to recover the value of a temporized, historically integrated view of the arts and sciences.

Pierre Bourdieu has denounced neoscholasticism for its separation of the universities into bunkers where practical thinking is denied and theory is exalted. A corollary of this denial of practical interaction with the world is the attitude Bourdieu calls "scholastic epistemocentrism":

> Imputing to its object what belongs in fact to the way of looking at it, it projects into practice [...] an unexamined social relation which is none other than the scholastic relation to the world.

Taking various forms depending on the traditions and the domains of analysis, it places a metadiscourse [...] at the origin of discourse, or a metapractice [...] at the origin of practices.

(Bourdieu, 1997, p. 53)

Bourdieu includes in his critique "the intellectualism of the structuralist semiologists who treat language as an object of interpretation or contemplation rather than an instrument of action and power [...] and [...] the epistemocentrism of the hermeneutic theory of reading" (Bourdieu, 1997, p. 53). He opts rather for the constructivist integration of objectivism and subjectivism. Such a perspective does not limit symbol production to the sphere of logic and consciousness, but finds it in the bodily knowledge and *docta ignorantia* of those who rely on symbols to define social reality. To speak of objectivity, therefore, one must speak of relations, otherness and marginality, but in so doing one must be supported by concrete historical, linguistic and anthropological information. Similarly, one cannot speak of subjectivity without considering the "abstract schemes of morphology" (Whitehead, 1929b, p. 73) generated by speculative reason. In order to grasp how objectivism and subjectivism can be complementary in this way, it is essential to recognize the importance of habit and the hard wiring of behavior patterns in the learning process.

Teachers are responsible for the formation of symbolic networks in students' minds; such 'mental pictures' are generated from patterns of interference, like holograms. They presuppose actional modes and patterns of behavior that relate to habitual material. In contrast to behaviorism, which undervalues habit-formation, complex thought views it as an essential tool: If tasks are learned and assimilated, they free up the attention span and efficacy of the conscious mind to undertake new tasks. By the same token, if habitual, hard-wired material is deemed harmful or undesirable, the educator will attempt to change it by altering pedagogic practices. As Whitehead suggests, science education

> should train the pupil to relate general ideas to immediate perceptions, and thereby obtain exactness of observation and fruitfulness of thought. I repeat that primarily this acquirement is not an access of knowledge but a modification of character by the impress of habit.
>
> (Whitehead, 1961b, p. 164)

Bourdieu discusses at length the issue of *habitus* as an ignored category of sociological and philosophical analysis.[8] The French sociologist often viewed academe as an aberrant example of just human economies; scholastic man, he ventured, neglects the constitutive nature of *habitus* and habitats in determining the ways of society. The blind trust of *homo academicus* in rationality blocks him from valuing other factors, such as the conditioned and often unconscious reactions to events that constitute decisions. The world of power is seen to depend on mediocre complicities, of time regarded as capital, just as institutions prosper perversely by generating anxiety among their workers. To oppose this, one must temporalize the logic and language of the exact sciences so as to inject reasonableness and sensibility into the arguments and methods of the academy.

Bruno Latour points to a post-Kantian negotiation of the problem enunciated by Bourdieu, replacing the subject/object opposition with that of human and nonhuman. Latour employs Whitehead's terms 'proposition' and 'event' to bestow historicity on the human and nonhuman elements of scientific experimentation. In this way he provides a scientist's perspective on the interrelationship of the disciplines, refuting both the philosophy of history and the philosophy of language, the latter of which assumes "there is a gap between world and words that reference aims to bridge" (Latour, 1999, p. 69). Instead, says Latour, there are small gaps between the "formal" and "material" aspects of reference, so that gradual systems of exchange and articulation occur as an event moves outward from a representational center in both directions, such as "mediations from matter to form" (Latour, 1999, pp. 70, 73). Latour invokes William James to support his idea of 'circulating reference,' of translation and mediation: "Instead of the *vertical* abyss between words and world, above which the perilous footbridge of correspondence would hang, we now have a sturdy and thick layering of *transverse* paths through which masses of transformations circulate" (Latour, 1999, p. 113).

To better describe the transverse paths across and through scientific thinking, Latour speaks of anastomosis or the cross-articulation of discrete epistemological systems, each of which requires 'translation,' since all philosophy and pedagogy are partial.[9] Evolution itself has been understood as anastomosis, a crossing over and fusion of evolutionary lineages, or what Konstantin Maroshovsky called 'symbiogenesis.'[10] In his defense of science studies as a bridge between the subjectivist humanities and the objectivist 'cold war' sciences, Latour defines translation as a means of mediating between codes of meaning and reference:

> Instead of opposing words and the world, science studies, by its insistence on practice, has multiplied the intermediary terms that focus on the transformations so typical of the sciences; like "inscription" or "articulation," "translation" is a term that crisscrosses the modernist settlement. In its linguistic and material connotations, it refers to all the displacements through other actors whose mediation is indispensable for any action to occur. In place of a rigid opposition between context and content, chains of translation refer to

the work through which actors modify, displace, and translate their various and contradictory interests.

(Latour, 1999, p. 311)

Latour's call for the integration and cross-pollination of the disciplines is echoed by Michel Serres, who laments the posterity-fixation of humanists and the up-to-date myopia of hard scientists. Against these contrasting types – each closed off to the future – Serres recommends in *Le Tiers-Instruit* (*The Troubadour of Knowledge*) the model of a versatile and flexible, itinerant educator, an 'Instructed Third' who aims at a mediation between extremes, acknowledging the diverse methods and temporal relationships employed by philosophers, scientists and artists.[11] It is precisely because of the radically different approaches to knowledge that the mediating role of the *Tiers-Instruit* is essential. The troubadour of knowledge is an active agent of the logic of the included third or *tiers inclus*. Such an educator sees in the history of science a "complex" that exists as a "combinatorial topology, a systemic knot" that "cannot be observed: neither seen nor known" (Serres, 1997, p. 20). What such an educator confronts are strong institutional forces of resistance. As Serres wrote in his 1995 book, *The Natural Contract*, "Cartesian mastery brings science's objective violence into line, making it a well-controlled strategy. Our fundamental relationship with objects comes down to war and property" (Serres, 1995, p. 32).[12]

In the book *Conversations on Science, Culture, and Time* with Bruno Latour, Serres adopts the concept of anastomosis to refer to the educator's responsibility to put on display the interrelationships between only seemingly opposite forms of knowledge:

> What is required of the principals is a crossing of boundaries, an *anastomosis* or convergence of previously divergent paths, guided perhaps by a purposeful iconoclasm that leads one back to the twin centers of knowledge, as they are apprehended and transmitted.
>
> (Serres with Latour, 1995, p. 183)

In this figure of the reunification and integration of diverse paths of learning, one has a synthesis of the challenge faced by a teacher who would encourage the formation of new hypotheses in the classroom. Such a teacher must allow for the interaction of two contrasting modes of thinking, the meditative and calculative, and two types of reason, the speculative and practical. These interactions are not without tension and risk, but the greater risk is to deny the potential of scientific and humanistic studies to fruitfully interact.

It is opportune at this point to turn to John Dewey, who while formulating the principles for an educational science a century ago ventured into the problems of science education. Commenting on "the relative defect and backwardness of science teaching," Dewey advocated for a change in focus on "*what* we do [in science education], and not merely about *how* we may do it most easily and economically" (Dewey, 1964, pp. 189, 192). In addition, he elevated the importance of habit to scientific learning and the need to convey that factor to the other disciplines:

> the future of our civilization depends upon the widening spread and deepening hold of the scientific habit of mind; [...] The problem of problems in our education is therefore to discover how to mature and make effective this scientific habit.
>
> (Dewey, 1964, p. 191)

Consilience

As a corollary to the emergence of science studies, the notion of 'consilience' – a term coined by William Whewell (in his 1847 *The Philosophy of the Inductive Sciences, Founded Upon Their History*) as a way to discuss the great theories of science in their moment of formation – has been taken up again by modern scholars. Whewell observed that the testing of hypotheses in different types of inductive or empirical situations generates different types of facts that coexist – as suggested by the etymology of *con* (concurrent) + *silient, siliens* 'jumping' – in a confluence of facts that can only be explained by the existence of a larger truth: "Such a coincidence of untried facts with speculative assertions cannot be the work of chance, but implies some large portion of truth in the principles on which the reasoning is founded" (Whewell, 1967, v. 2, p. 64). Consilience is the name given to the practice of conceptualizing this larger truth, a practice that has historically formed the emergent verities of science, such as the 'Theory of Electromagnetic Forces,' or the 'Oxygen Theory.' In our own day one thinks of the accepted truths of Gödel's theory of incompleteness or Einstein's theory of General Relativity, or the Laws of Thermodynamics that lie at the basis of the study of dissipative structures and entropy by Prigogine. Whewell's book considers the history of scientific thought going back to its foundations in the Athens of Aristotle and Plato and the Florence of Pico della Mirandola and Marsilio Ficino.

Following Whewell's definition, consilient thinkers not only assume there is an optimal means of approaching any intellectual problem, but they assume this optimum depends on the particular hypothesis that is formulated and the identity of the formulator. Consilience is this idea of optimizing one's epistemological tools. As Thagard writes, "a theory is said to be consilient if it explains at least two classes of facts. Then one theory is more consilient than another if it explains more classes of facts than the other one does" (Thagard, 1992, p. 78). And, as Robert S. Brumbaugh writes, "practice, if it is to be realistic, *must* take place in a certain way" (Brumbaugh, 1991, p. 75).

In a recent tome, sociobiologist Edward O. Wilson defines consilience as the unity of all knowledge. While Wilson's scientific research is unexceptionable, his premises regarding the humanities are overly general and approximate, for example the idea that the humanities first capitulated to modernism and then to the doctrines of deconstruction and post-structuralism. According to Wilson, these ephemeral currents do not stand up under the lights of a properly applied science. Wilson situates the humanities below the sciences in defense of what he labels reductionism. He views humanity today as 'Homo proteus,' a species become overly tolerant to a mechanized, digitalized world: "Restless, getting crowded. Thinking about the colonization of space. Regrets the current loss of Nature and all those vanishing species, but it's the price of progress and has little to do with our future anyway" (Wilson, 1998, pp. 304–5). Wilson's treatise lacks the depth of a proper historical reflection. He speaks frequently of the future, but says little about it that is concrete. The leads Rorty to write as follows: "The main trouble with [Wilson's] argument for consilence is that we get no account of what the more integrated culture that its author envisages would look like" (Rorty, 1988, p. 35).

Viewed within the area of pedagogy, Wilson's idea of consilience is monolithic and not an optimalization of epistemological tools. His proposal of a unified-field theory of knowledge – by which he means scientific knowledge – ignores the historic definition of consilience which favors heuristic investigation and reinforcement in research and teaching. Wilson assumes that the arts oscillate between cool, rationalistic periods and passionate, romantic ones, irrespective of geographical and cultural distinctions. He sees this dyadic pattern in our literary culture in the passage from the coolness of the New Criticism to the irrationality of postmodernism:

> In the 1950s the New Critics insisted on drawing out the full meaning of the text, without much concern for the personal history of the author. [...] In the 1980s the New Critics quite suddenly gave way to the postmodernists, who argued the opposite approach. Search, they said, for what the text does not control, and explain the entirety as a social construction on the part of the author.
>
> (Wilson, 1998, p. 235)

Wilson assumes that interpretation in the arts has developed willy-nilly, by the mass adherence to popular trends, and that creative artists are historically determined in their aesthetic and ideological orientations, and thus not free to express themselves individually. His approach to creative and critical works is often second-hand and simplistic, as when Paul Valéry and Stephane Mallarmé are situated on the Dionysian / romantic / irrational side (as opposed to the Apollonian side) of a Nietzschean dichotomy; or when T. S. Eliot is labeled a British poet; or when one reads, "A stanza, which in Italian is a public room or resting place, has been appropriated in English to mean the roomlike set of four or more lines separated typographically from other similar sets" (Wilson, 1998, pp. 239, 234).[13] The fact that *stanza* already possessed its poetic definition in Dante's time eludes Wilson, who relied on a cohort of researchers and was content not to address human knowledge prior to the Enlightenment.

Among Wilson's critics is Wendell Berry, who argues that Wilson's consilience denies the possibility of the very global knowledge it seeks by espousing a purely mechanistic science, and that he rejects the mysteries and ambiguities of the ancient wisdom traditions. While arguing for exploration, innovation and originality, Wilson does not contextualize these processes and procedures with the necessary propriety:

> The question for art, then, is exactly the same as the question for science: Can it properly subordinate itself to concerns that are larger than its own? Can it judge itself by standards that are higher than its own? Can it judge itself by standards that are higher and more comprehensive than professional standards? The issue is the old one of propriety. Is every artist and every scientist to be "free" to work as if his or her discipline were the only one, or the dominant one? Or is it possible to see one's work as occurring within a larger and ultimately a mysterious pattern of causes and influences?
>
> (Berry, 2000, pp. 88–89)

Once again one is talking about operational closure. Berry's approach is Vichian – "We can begin (and we must always be beginning) only where our history has so far brought us, with what we have done"; like Vico, he looks to the organicity of the various disciplines that share a common history and deep structure (Berry, 2000, p. 4). In contrast, Wilson views epistemology as a mechanical problem to be broken down into solvable parcels and considers the free will to be a necessary illusion, placing his trust in a high science of the future that will come to unify the frayed ends of knowledge. As Richard Rorty sums it up: "[Wilson] thinks it is a mistake to think there are many kinds of 'explanations appropriate to the perspectives of individual disciplines.' It is a mistake because, he asserts, 'there is intrinsically only one class of explanation'" (Rorty, 1998, p. 30). For Berry such a trust in a singular method and proof is cynical and only serves to distance the researcher from the specificity of phenomena; rather Berry proposes a curriculum of reconnection with the familiar. His holistic sense of propriety demands that courses across the curriculum be integrated, with an emphasis placed on the framing and future adaptability of knowledge and the creation of better world citizens. The moral issues at stake depend on one's vision of the distinction between reductionism and process theory, as between dualistic (behaviorist) and triadic (Piaget-like) systems. Only the latter incorporate feedback and recursive functions into the learning process, intrinsically and extrinsically.

Consonant with the viewpoints of Berry and Serres is that of Stephen Toulmin, a scientific historian who uses the term 'phronesis' in like manner to our use of consilience, as "the ability to spot the action called for in any situation" (Toulmin, 1996, p. 207). This practical wisdom is the goal of 'participatory action research' as it is of other disciplines in which experimental conditions are not exactly replicable and within which the researcher acknowledges that "the problem of objectivity is the problem of countering our own biases" (Toulmin, 1996, p. 220). Toulmin assesses the claims to objectivity of the hard-science elitists of our day – such as Wilson – who dismiss the efforts of those in the human sciences as failing the objectivity test and thus failing to be science: "Elitism then consists in following the Platonists of our day, who refuse the titles of *rational*, *science* or *research* to fields that depart too far from the High Science model of theoretical physics" (Toulmin, 1996, p. 224). As against those scientists who insist on detachment from their subject of study for the sake of objectivity, Toulmin exposes the need for researchers to be involved in the activities their subjects are involved in, as in the empathy of an ethnographer or psychoanalyst. Furthermore, the problems associated with scientific method translate into problems of social organization: The more elitist the epistemological self-definition of a disciplinary faculty, the more elitist the governance structure of the institution will be. (I return to Toulmin in Chapter 6, where I discuss his advocacy of the teaching of values.)

Complexity theory and complex thought reject claims of a totalization of knowledge. Instead of sweeping solutions or declarations of the end of metaphysics, or claims that philosophy can stand apart from history, complexity theory requires linkage, integration, modesty, responsibility, dialogue. It requires familiarity with the local and acknowledgement of the singularity of nature. It asserts that we must refocus our attention to the 'natural' basis of learning and social cohesion, and away from outdated notions of 'mastery':

> We must add to the exclusively social contract a natural contract of symbiosis and reciprocity in which our relationship to things would set aside mastery and possession in favor of admiring attention, reciprocity, contemplation, and respect; where knowledge would no longer imply property, nor action mastery, nor would property and mastery imply their excremental results and origins.
>
> (Serres, 1995, p. 38)

Among the reductionisms I allude to above, and among the current schools of pseudo-humanistic thought which refuse to 'set aside mastery and possession,' is the trend of neoscholasticism, with its positive understanding of historical nihilism. It has been stated that the danger for phenomenology came when its critical method required more technical work than it could justify with its results. The nihilist finds the only truth to be an inward truth, a pride in having confronted nothingness and survived, rather than an outward affiliation to a social grouping and a socially validated ontology. Nihilism is a case of epistemological hubris and loss of boundaries. It supposes that the task of the philosopher is not that of pluralist but rather of a hieratic tender of the flame of intellectualist abstraction, the central figure of a sectarian wisdom cult. The difference between a process thinker like Bateson and a nihilist like Heidegger is therefore critical:

> Bateson *seems* to share some perspectives of contemporary philosophy, for example those discussed by the late Heidegger – with the difference, however, that the Heideggerian reliance on a *selfness* of consciousness would seem to Bateson the obstinate insistence upon a traditional and bankrupt epistemology. Analogously, Bateson never attempts to translate the essence of poetry (or the essence of religion) into philosophical truth.
>
> (Dal Lago, 1998, p. 160)

It is critical that Bateson leaves the firewall intact between poet and philosopher. For him the self is informed by an abductive structure, like a hypothesis awaiting verification. To rely on the 'selfness of consciousness' would be to reify a dualistic conception of identity. Instead if one relies on a logic of relations, any proprietary notion of consciousness must be rejected as denying the dialectical relation between the multiple systems and codes of scientific analysis. The integration of theories relating to consciousness and the self requires great discretion and an aesthetic sense of proportion in order to integrate potentially conflicting terminologies and arrive at the appropriate mixture of the particular and the general.

Learning through Abduction

As I suggested in the first section of this chapter, the specific mode of thought that has routinely been overlooked by educators is logical abduction, a mode that entails the formation of probable hypotheses as the first step toward logical proof. As seen in the context of Bateson's thought in Chapter 1, abduction is known as inference to the best explanation. Within an institution where deduction is the rationalist's standard of proof and induction is most highly valued by empirical researchers, the lifting up of abduction as an essential tool for fostering an academic culture of inquiry can be problematic. As Whitehead writes in *The Function of Reason*, the importance of final causation as the basis of hypothesis formation and the formation of purpose has too long been overlooked by academicians.[14]

Michael Bybee argues for abduction's importance as a means of proof that has erroneously been "dismissed as irrational, intuitive, or speculative," a logical mistake that has historically "eliminated large tracts of discourse from consideration, e.g. scientific discourse and exploratory essays" (Bybee, 1991, p. 298). Bybee establishes that "Most current critical and pedagogical theories are either incomplete [...] or mistaken [...]. Future rhetorical studies, then, must acknowledge the extent to which discourse partakes of inferential elements, and abduction must be numbered among those elements" (Bybee, 1991, p. 298). Our discussion of abduction here is limited to its applicability in the classroom, especially as regards hypothesis formation by the individual student and as a positive factor within the group.

Charles Sanders Peirce formulated his theory of abduction in several phases. As a form of 'ampliative' inference, abduction is like induction in that its conclusion provides more information than is supplied in the premises of the classical syllogism. In deduction, or explicative inference, the conclusion of the syllogism follows by necessity from its premises. But Peirce felt that one could arrive at any of the three propositions of a syllogism provided the other two were present and the conditions were adequate for proof. These adequate conditions include "pragmatism" and "economy" (Fann, 1970, p. 47). Pragmatism concerns the hypothesis' availability to experimentation so as to determine success, that is, verification of truth or falseness. If this condition is met, the testing is done by induction. Economy concerns the cost and value of testing hypotheses, given the need to select from an abundant number of them. In the real world of finite resources, Peirce maintains, it is important to test the simpler, more likely, and more instinctive hypotheses first, also because instinct is a part of nature and should be given its due. But this latter criterion is useless without the necessary tact that orders the scale and generality of hypotheses to suit the problem at hand. Against the extremes of rationalism and empiricism, Peirce submitted that what was missing in scientific logic and theory-formation was abduction. For him the proper understanding of abduction depended on the shared assumptions of an interpretative community. Indeed, abduction was deemed to be pointless without the logical framework that enables deduction and induction. As Peirce writes, "It must be remembered that abduction, although it is very little hampered by logical rules, nevertheless is logical inference, asserting its conclusion only problematically or conjecturally it is true, but nevertheless having a perfectly definite logical form" (Peirce, 1998, p. 231).

For Peirce, abduction is critical to human reasoning, due to the generality of perceptions and the need to act on acquired knowledge. Neither deduction or induction is able to satisfactorily cover this cognitive trajectory (between initial perception and eventual action). Since "abductive inference shades into perceptual judgment without any sharp line of demarcation between them" (Peirce, 1998, p. 227), the subject requires an economical way to sort through new ideas, in order reject the unclear ideas and render the distinct ideas more clearly. This aspect of reasoning and the 'logic of relations' it comports, was receiving short shrift in the institutions of higher learning, perhaps because of its intrinsic difficulty.[15]

Within Peirce's semiotics, the 'interpretant' was understood as the relationship between the referent and the sign. As Moriarity states:

> Interpretation means that every interpretant, besides translating the immediate object or the content of the sign, also increases our understanding of it in new ways. Peirce called this the criterion of interpretability and explained it as a two-step function that involves both translation and extension, a process that leads to an infinite chain of signification.
>
> (Moriarty, 1996, p. 177)

Within this cognitive view, abduction is especially effective for the interpretation of non-verbal and visual communication:

> Visual and verbal communication differ in the interpretive processes because language interpretation is more involved with manipulating a conventionally learned code, and visual communication involves observations that lead to hypotheses about meanings. Visual interpretation, like the interpretation of semioticians, is more appropriately described as abductive beginning with observing clues in the visual (perception) and moving to a conclusion by hypothesizing about relationships and patterns (cognition, convention) through massive parallel processing to arrive at a unified gestalt.
>
> (Moriarty, 1996, p. 185)

The particular stumbling block one is inclined to find in the academy is the assertion that aesthetics has a place in the humanities but not in the sciences, and that the sciences can ignore the "massive parallel processing" Moriarty writes of. Yet who if not a scientist cannot benefit from the formulation of hypotheses concerning harmony, elegance, and formal and structural economy that originated in a direct observation of nature?

Jarrett Leplin has argued in this vein that abduction contributes to a more practical and concrete means of scientific proof than is allowed for by the positivistic, behaviorist and strictly quantitative methods. Leplin's theory of 'minimal epistemic realism' supports abductive and inductive inference equally: "We are warranted in inducing [...] only if we are warranted in abducing" (Leplin, 1997, p. 114); "The point is to establish a mutual reliance between generalization and explanation, not to regiment their cooccurrence or collapse them into one another" (Leplin, 1997, p. 116); "Traditional empiricism gives the priority to experiment. More recent philosophy of science, by emphasizing the theory-ladenness of observation, has created the presumption that theory comes first" (Leplin, 1997, p. 117).

Noam Chomsky writes of the hope for an eventual Peircean 'logic of abduction,' and the reasons why it has not been successfully formulated. In the due process of intellectual evolution, he states, it is unrealistic to assume the realization of this project, which seeks to ascertain "the limits and capacities of human intelligence," until other localized researches are accomplished:

> Speculating about the future, I think it is not unlikely that the dogmatic character of the general empiricist framework and its inadequacy to human and animal intelligence will gradually become more evident as specific realizations, such as taxonomic linguistics, behaviorist learning theory, and the perception models, heuristic methods and "general problem solvers" of the early enthusiasts of "artificial intelligence," are successively rejected on empirical grounds when they are made precise and on grounds of vacuity when they are left vague.
>
> (Chomsky, 1972, pp. 92–93)

With respect to Chomsky's prediction, it is evident that behaviorism and empiricism still dominate in the fields of psychology and linguistics and that many AI programs still concentrate on technological problems such as computer simulations and robotics. When confronted with the abductive theory, such scientists typically respond with some form of the 'correlation is not causation' argument, even though they employ abductions continuously in their work.

The so-called weak abduction is known historically as 'dormitive explanation,' an expression named after a scene of Moliere's *Le Malade imaginaire* (*The Imaginary Invalid*) in which a patient asks his doctor why opium puts people to sleep and the doctor replies that it contains a 'dormitive principle.' In Peirce's logical theory this is an example of the attributive error of 'disposition.' In effect, by reifying a phenomenon the observer is ignoring its relation with other phenomena, bestowing on it a solidity it does not possess; but as Bateson writes: "About three-quarters of all the hypotheses in the behavioral sciences are fundamentally dormitive principles. 'Anxiety' is a dormitive principle" (Bateson, 1991b, pp. 170–71). Such explanations are very common in human communication and useful in science, provided one acknowledges them as tautological.[16] Viewed as essential components of logical predicates – entities of the reason and not of the truth – they relate directly to the question of efficacious activity, *habitus* and learning. The question of habit and the assimilation of tasks is also one that deeply concerns psychotherapy and other sciences of mental process, such as evolutionary theory and human ecology.

Learning theory was Bateson's way of linking these disciplinary areas, which standard epistemology considers to be disparate. While tautology drives abduction, it is itself barren of the causation inherent in process. Despite the logical error of the dormitive explanation, it allows one to organize large bunches of heterogeneous information:

> the dormitive explanation actually falsifies the true facts of the case but what is, I believe, important is that dormitive explanations still *permit abduction.* [...] This will give us, albeit inaccurately and epistemologically unacceptably, handles with which to grab at a very large number of phenomena that appear to be formally comparable.
>
> (Bateson, 1980, p. 95)

If the errors are consistent among members of phenomena for which the same dormitive explanation applies, then even as one abandons the explanation (as one would disassemble a scaffolding or throw out a first draft) the result is a positive one. As Bateson scholar Walter Fornasa explicates,

> *Ex-ducere* (to bring out) and *ad-prendere* (to grasp in the chaos by giving form and sense to the event) are processes epistemologically and relationally opposite the customary instructional modalities of *in-ducere* (to insert something within insofar as it is lacking) and *in-segnare* (to impress a form from outside) – as every schoolchild knows...
>
> (Fornasa, 1998, p. 204)

It is this recognition of cognitive difference that Bateson is addressing when he writes:

> Mind always operates at one remove away from matter, always at one *derivative* (dx/dt) away from the "external" world. The primary data of experience are *differences*. From these data we construct our hypothetical (always hypothetical) ideas and pictures of that 'external' world. [...] A *report of difference* is the most elementary idea – the indivisible atom of thought".
>
> (Bateson, 1991b, p. 188)

These hypothetical ideas are means of evaluating the past, formulating present experience and establishing expectations or probabilities about the future. Though prone to error, the abduction is a major component of the communicative processes that foster transdisciplinary work and academic freedom; it is comparable in this sense to Kant's heuristic fiction. As Bybee writes, "An abductive argument makes a very weak modal claim, namely, that if the premises are true, then it is *possible* that the conclusion is true" (Bybee, 1991, p. 288). Nevertheless, abductions gain in probability as the number of constraints provided for in their premises are increased.

Paul Thagard has clarified the importance of abduction to scientific reasoning ("abduction is pervasive in ordinary and scientific reasoning"), distinguishing the formation of hypotheses from the inferential process of determining the "best explanation":

> Abduction only generates hypotheses, whereas inference to the best explanation evaluates them. All we should expect of abduction, therefore, is that it tend to produce hypotheses that have some chance of turning out to be the best explanation.
>
> (Thagard, 1988, p. 143)

The ability to formulate coherent abductions that draw together the results of deductions and inductions is a vital means of reinforcing the knowledge of relations at the common basis of both science and art. Such an effort will recast what is understood by scientific proof in a way that includes and increases the portion of inferential thinking, hypothesis formation and abduction. In his chapter 'Generalization and Abduction,' Paul Thagard writes,

> The computational study of abduction is still in its infancy and much remains to be done to increase our understanding of how explanatory hypotheses are formed in science and ordinary life. One important question is the extent to which the formation of hypotheses is tied to their evaluation.
>
> (Thagard, 1992, 54)

The probabilities of learning lie in experimentation and creativity, in venturing out amid the vagaries – that is, among the eventual precisions – of definition. The conventional educator is one who never sets aside the pursuit of precision, of finding one (and only one) answer to every question. This falsely sets up rationalism as the equal of reason, and ambiguity as its enemy. But, as Thagard argues, children and scientists have more in common than one might think, since each needs to cultivate their powers of inference and guessing to successfully negotiate their way in the world. There is humility in this open-endedness; problems will always remain, along with hope and the spirit of industry.

Inna Semetsky has considered this same question of Peircean abduction and the dichotomy of creative versus precise learning in her book chapter entitled 'The paradox of inquiry.' Given that abduction is the "mode of inference that triggers the hermeneutic process" (Semetsky, 2013, p. 274) and encompasses insight, imagination and intuition, it is seen as the appropriate mode to employ when responding to the paradox of inquiry as posited by Plato in the dialogue *Meno*. Socrates' idea that there cannot be new knowledge since one must know what one is looking for in order to discover it, leads him to predicate the theory of recollection, i.e. that "we already possess knowledge unconsciously" (Semetsky, 2013, p. 274). Semetsky carries forward this discourse into the thinking of Dewey – seen to be a forerunner of the science of coordination dynamics – and his promotion of epistemological complexity and Whitehead's metaphysics and specifically his notion of learning process as prehension. Both of these latter thinkers are seen to support the critical importance of abduction as the intensified perception capable of resolving in a non-trivial way the paradox of inquiry in our current day.

A comparable understanding of abduction's role in the creative process, or lying in potential in the unconscious mind, was recommended by Roland Barthes in his analysis of narrative. For Barthes, the exact *name* entailed by the abduction exists prior to one's analytical pursuit of it; it is waiting to be discovered within the temporality or sequence of events that constitute narrative. This name possesses an authenticity and truth value within the narrative texture of language equal to that obtained by scientific procedure:

> Narrative is an activity of language (of signification or of symbolization) and it is in terms of language that it must be analyzed: *to name* is then for the analyst an operation as well established, as homogeneous with its object, as measuring for the geometrician, as weighing for the chemist, as examining through a microscope for the biologist. Further, the name which we find for the sequence (and which constitutes it) is a systematic witness, it proceeds itself from the vast activity of classification of which language consists; I call a certain sequence *Abduction*, it is because the language itself has classified, has mastered the diversity of certain actions under a unique concept which it transmits to me and whose coherence it thereby authenticates; the *Abduction* which I constitute starting from snatches of actions scattered in the text then coincides with all the abductions I have read; the name is the exact, irrefutable trace, as solid as a scientific fact, of a certain *already-written, already-read, already-done*; to find the name is therefore not at all a whimsical operation, left to my mere caprice; to find the name is to

find that *already* which constitutes the code, it is to assure the communication of the text and of all the other narratives which make up the narrative language, for the linguistic or semiological work must always consist in finding the *passage* which joins the anterior of language and the present of the text.

(Barthes, 1988, 141)

What Barthes is postulating is a kind of universal lexicon of narrative, a deep structure or paradigm in which the rudiments of scientific (semiotic, linguistic) knowledge are allowed to affect aesthetic device just as the world of the imagination is enlisted in order to envision ulterior scientific possibilities.

In presenting a foreshortened history of the development of process pedagogy in the post-Kantian era, I have focused on and the reciprocity between the arts and sciences, as was variously articulated by Peirce, Whitehead, Dewey, Cassirer, and later by thinkers like Bateson, Serres, Bourdieu and Latour. Process pedagogy acknowledges the need, across the arts and sciences, for direct observation of nature accompanied by complex and speculative thought. It does not perceive a contradiction therein but rather, by endorsing the arts and sciences of communication, strives to apprehend the emerging and enduring characteristics of the disciplines in order to foster symbiotic relations between them. Whether it is a math or astronomy professor who includes writings on aesthetics and cultural history in her syllabus, or an Italian professor who includes lessons on Leon Battista Alberti's mathematical ideas or Galileo's cosmology in his literary survey class, the goal is to contextualize knowledge and provide students with a pragmatic awareness of the systems of thought and habits of learning they will require in order to act responsibly as world citizens and not simply be the passive recipients of what has increasingly and euphemistically been called knowledge.

Notes

1 Wilden, 1987, p. 314: "Context theory is a strategic reorientation of that network of theories [...] variously called information theory, communications theory, cybernetics, kinesthetics, semiotics, and systems theory."

2 This was the subject of C. P. Snow's celebrated volume, *The Two Cultures and the Scientific Revolution* (1959).

3 See Verene, 2008, for the inherent similarity of Cassirer's philosophy to Whitehead's process metaphysics.

4 Pearce and Cronen, 1980, p. 65:

> For Kant, there are three types of true statement. The first type is analytical and *a priori*, needing no help from experience. [...] The second type of truth is synthetical; that is, the predicate is not contained logically in the subject, but adds something to it *a posteriori*, out of experience, by observing facts in the world and generalizing about them. [...]. A third

type of truth Kant calls the synthetical *a priori*. Here the predicate adds new knowledge, but the knowledge does not come from outside, from the unreliable world of experience.

5 As Whitehead goes on to state in this early section of *Process and Reality*, Kant's discovery was not immediately grasped as both empiricists and idealists failed to '[conciliate] philosophical conceptions of a real world with the world of daily experience' (Whitehead, 1957, p. 181). This latter task will be assumed by the philosophy of organism and, symmetrically, by Cassirer and his philosophy of symbolic forms, both directions in philosophy that contribute to the educational philosophy whose development in the 20th century is explored in this volume.

6 As George Steiner states in his 2001–2002 Norton Lectures, 2003, pp. 112–13: "There inhabits teachers of the order of Montaigne and Schopenhauer a singular 'gaiety' [...]. Schopenhauer's quest for discipleship had been frustrated; almost to the close of his life, his philosophic *magnum opus* had lain unread."

7 Whitehead, 1929b, pp. 44–45:

> The medieval movement was too learned. It formed a closed system of thinking about other people's thoughts. In this way, medieval philosophy, and indeed *modern philosophy*, detracted from its utility as a discipline of speculative Reason by its inadequate grasp of the fecundity of nature and of the corresponding fecundity of thought.
>
> (My emphasis.)

8 Regarding Pierre Bourdieu, Katha Pollitt writes, 2002, p. 10:

> His key concept of habitus – the formation and expression of self around an internalized and usually accurate sense of social destiny – tends to make ameliorative projects seem rather silly. Sociology, he wrote, "discovers necessity, social constraints, where we would like to see choice and free will. The habitus is that unchosen principle of so many choices that drives our humanists to such despair."

9 Whitehead, 1961b, p. 204: "In human experience, the philosophic question can receive no final answer. Human knowledge is a process of approximation. In the focus of experience there is comparative clarity."

10 See L. Margulis and D. Sagan, 2002, p. 12: "Long term symbiosis that leads to evolutionary change is called 'symbiogenesis'."

11 M. Serres explicates the difference between the philosopher's epistemology and the scientist's in terms of the presence or absence of the experimental method, 1997, 88:

> Philosophy devotes itself to anticipating future knowledge and practices on a global scale. A scientist discovers or invents in the lacunae of a method, the failures of experiments, the incompleteness of results or the toppling of a theory, but the philosopher has neither theory nor experiments nor method, thus even less their gaps or their flip sides.

12 The cited lines by Serres are preceded by the following, Serres, 1995, p. 32:

> Mastery and possession: these are the master words launched by Descartes at the dawn of the scientific and technological age, when our Western reason went off to conquer the universe. We dominate and appropriate it: such is the shared philosophy underlying industrial enterprise as well as so-called disinterested science, which are indistinguishable in this respect.

13 In poetic and metrical terms, the dwelling place is the stanza. As Dante writes in *Literature in the vernacular* (II, 9, 2), 1981:

> that in which the whole art is contained should be called *stanza*, a capacious mansion or dwelling-place of the whole art. For just as the *canzone* is the womb [*gremium*] of the whole thought expressed, so the stanza contains the whole art; (...) The stanza of which we are speaking will be the collection into one unity [*congrematio*] of all those elements which the canzone acquires from art.

14 Whitehead, 1929b, p. 26: "Provided that we admit the category of final causation, we can consistently define the primary function of Reason. This function is to constitute, emphasize, and criticize the final causes and strength of aims directed towards them." And Whitehead, 1971, p. 40:

> What then is it that science is doing, granting that it is effecting something of importance? My answer is that it is determining the character of things known, namely the character of apparent nature. But we may drop the term "apparent"; for there is but one nature, namely the nature which is before us in perceptual knowledge. The characters which science discerns in nature are subtle characters, not obvious at first sight. They are relations of relations and characters of characters. But for all their subtlety they are stamped with a certain simplicity which makes their consideration essential in unravelling the complex relations between characters of more perceptive insistence.

One could easily substitute the word abduction for final causation and lose nothing of Whitehead's argument; for indeed, those who effectively practice abduction first know the effect and set out to determine the cause.

15 Speaking at Harvard in 1903, Peirce was critical of the apparent lack of logic in the education offered there, 1998, p. 527: "I cannot but think it deeply lamentable that true, modern, exact, non-psychological logic, which ought to form the background of a liberal education, does not receive attention here to be at all in evidence."

16 Latour, 1999, p. 309, defines "predication" as

> a term of rhetoric and logic meaning what happens in the activity of definition when, to avoid a tautology, a term is necessarily defined through the use of another term. This entails for each definition a translation, the one being obtained through the mediation of the other.

4   The Art of Language Instruction as Interdisciplinary Paradigm

The Unity of Language and the Phases of Education

In this chapter, I examine the art of language instruction as a paradigm of learning applicable across the academic disciplines. 'Language' is understood broadly so as to encompass second languages, the languages of the arts and crafts, the notational systems of the sciences and those of experimental technologies. To learn a language one must absorb content on a variety of levels, from concrete to technical to abstract, and do so by integrating a variety of cognitive functions. To learn any language properly, including the languages of gestures, pictures and other signs, is to acquire another culture, to accept and employ a host of new gestalten which, as Goethe suggests, alters one's vision of oneself: "The man who knows no foreign language knows nothing of his mother tongue" (Goethe in Cassirer, 1970, p. 148).[1] Furthermore, to learn a language is to gain awareness of the nature of language *as such*. I suggest that this concept of language is lost on some educators who ignore the importance of the median or relational languages that connect the disciplines.

As Ernst Cassirer writes, language is the essential tool that humans possess to negotiate around common obstacles:

> There is such a thing as "language," something like the unity of the infinite variety of languages. This is decisive for me. It is for this reason that I start with the objectivity of symbolic forms because, with them, we possess in *fact* what, in thought, seems impossible. It is this which I call the "world of the objective spirit."
>
> (Cassirer, 1970, p. 220)

With this notion of the objectivity of language in mind, one can assess the art of language instruction as a paradigm applicable across the disciplines.[2] The radical novelty of Cassirer's assumption, backed up by his extensive research into historical linguistics and the philosophy of symbolic forms, is that it declares the actuality of a median language that unifies the myriad languages of humanity. With this realization comes the vision of a language of learning that contributes to a communicative convergence between the arts and sciences.

The arts and sciences today are strange bedfellows. They are often viewed as a kind of Hegelian polarity, symmetrical and oppositional, each possessing its balance of cognitive 'force'. But the metaphor of force and territoriality is outdated. If one considers the arts and sciences as a diversified whole comprised of elements imbricated in one another, then one might better conceive of a method of teaching the language of any disciplinary system as a manifestation of language as such. In reality, the qualified language teacher is always pursuing a language of relations, since he or she occupies a position both internal and external to the world of the expert or initiate. In order to better understand the stages of learning a language, I cite Whitehead's three phases of education from his classic work *The Aims of Education*. The phases are cyclical and overlapping and depend for their effectiveness on a rhythm established by appropriate interchanges and borrowings. In Whitehead's conception the initial phase, of 'romance,' yields an idealized and mythic representation of life. In it the student experiences the beauty of nature and the nobility and oneness of humanity. We learn our first language in this protective climate and it is altogether appropriate to learn second languages in that way as well: As Whitehead makes clear, the phase of romance does not terminate with youth. As Vico writes, "There is no discipline which needs reason so much less and memory so much more than language…. There is no other age better than childhood for learning languages" (1993, p. 135). The second phase, of 'precision,' is naturalistic in character and opens the classroom to narrative and the diverse perspectives of all persons involved. It yields detail and scope, and reveals the poverty of deterministic explanations of complex phenomena. Discipline and rigor are essential to this phase as the student learns the essential vocabulary and grammar of the field. In the third phase, of 'generalization' (or 'satisfaction'), one returns to the simplicity and elegance of the phase of romance, but, armed with the increased knowledge gained in the phase of precision, one develops judgment and ethical values. The three phases are consecutive and interpenetrating, allowing for the fact that students progress diversely in different disciplines. While language is the earliest of disciplines to be addressed – "The romantic stage of language begins in infancy with the acquisition of speech, so that it passes early towards a stage of precision" (Whitehead, 1929a, p. 59) – the study of a second language typically comes much later, and thus serves as a case analogous to the sciences in which the romantic stage comes later in the life of the student. Even after the stage of romance is completed, romance continues as the 'background':

> It must be fostered for one reason, because romance is after all a necessary ingredient of that balanced wisdom which is the goal to be attained. But there is another reason: The organism will not absorb the fruits of the task unless its powers of apprehension are kept

fresh by romance. The real point is to discover in practice that exact balance between freedom and discipline which will give the greatest rate of progress over the things to be known. [...] Furthermore, I hold that the only discipline, important for its own sake, is self-discipline, and that this can only be acquired by a wide use of freedom.

(Whitehead, 1929a, pp. 54–55)

The art of teaching for Whitehead lies in the ability to blend the three stages, to possess "rhythmic sway" (Whitehead, 1929a, p. 54) as the learning proceeds.

As a foreign language educator, I can attest to the fact that each of these phases is present in the L2 (second language) classroom. Because of the multiplicity and variety of tasks undertaken in the language classroom, the need for mediation between levels and types of instruction is always a concern. Mediation is best achieved in an atmosphere of equanimity and support for dialogue. Such a milieu leads to the acceptance of risk-taking, the promise of aesthetic enjoyment and the expectation of intellectual growth. Teaching a foreign language involves experimentation and dramatization, choreography and spontaneity. It is useless to wrap the language lesson in grammatical rules unless those rules are enacted.[3]

One such way is through the positive regression of role playing, an absorption in the phase of romance. By the same token, the phase of precision requires the memorizing of tables and tenses, rules (and exceptions), lists and catalogues. The language instructor is faced with a paradox: Is language to be taught as a 'natural' phenomenon akin to L1 or as a 'cultural' set of matrices, in the manner of the traditional instruction of the dead languages, Latin and Greek? Veteran teachers know that neither option is appropriate, but that an integration of the spontaneous approach and that of rote learning can exploit the phase of romance in such a way as to optimize the phase of precision. This leads in time to the deeper, more intuitive phase of generalization in which "the precise study of grammar and composition is discontinued, and the language study is confined to reading the literature with emphasized attention to its ideas and to the general history in which it is embedded" (Whitehead, 1929a, p. 3).

Traditionalists in the field of language instruction rely on grammatical paradigms and rote procedures, batteries of exercises and tests. Orality as a key to literacy in L2 is not seriously considered. In contrast, many immersionists stress orality to a fault, exempting students from the onus of rigorous grammar tests. Being 'student centered,' they frown on error correction and ignore the grammar-based techniques of the past. The divide between these poles is bridged by those communication-based teachers who combine the order of the traditionalists with the spontaneity and naturalness of the immersionists. One such teacher is

Claire Kramsch, who has adopted the notion of 'third places' and 'third cultures' in order to refer to the 'boundary' between the "culture [...] of our past and that of our present":

> [W]e have to view the boundary not as an actual event but, rather, as a state of mind, as a positioning of the learner at the intersection of multiple social roles and individual choices. The stories of such border crossings and of the "conversion" that leads a person to realize she is no longer the person she imagined herself to be are told over and over again by those who have lived them.
>
> (Kramsch, 1993, pp. 234–35)

Kramsch relates the experience of language acquisition to the recognition of cultural differences and the development of interculturality. By accessing popular cultures in the classroom, teachers and students can surmount the 'uncommon subordination and powerlessness' that accompanies the task of learning a foreign language. Third places are situations to be created in the classroom by means of a well-organized yet spontaneous integration of 'instructional discourse' – such as grammatical and lexical lists, paradigms and drills – with 'transactional discourse' that deals with them in context, as cultural content and usage, and finally with 'interactional discourse,' including 'functional and situational role-play, simulation activities, and also stylistic exercises.' A third place is rich because it recognizes the fictional, ludic and artificial aspect of the classroom environment – neither first culture nor second culture – as its own culture of becoming. Kramsch proposes a set of efficient and pragmatic tools so as to stop from stifling students of language and culture with overtly grammatical priorities:

> An educational philosophy that stresses only doing things with words runs the risk of helping maintain the social status quo; it has difficulty dealing with the teaching of culture, because cross-cultural competence, unlike pragmatic competence, is predicated on paradox and conflict and on often irreducible ways of viewing the world.
>
> (Kramsch, 1993, p. 240)

The progression in the classroom from an instructional to a transactional to an interactive language also reflects the ternary rhythm outlined above in Whitehead's three phases.

Literature, Humanities and the Cognitive Sciences

How the denial of third places is manifest in the institutional culture is apparent now as it was in 1925 when Whitehead wrote of 'two evils' concerning the 'training of professionals': "one, the ignoration of the true relation of each organism to its environment; and the other, the habit of ignoring the intrinsic worth of the environment which must be allowed its weight in any consideration of final ends" (Whitehead, 1925, p. 196). Whitehead insisted that the fields of knowledge a university student could be expected to cover were very limited; thus the number of academic subjects required in the undergraduate curriculum should be reduced to a number that suits the phase of generalization: "When we have rid our minds of the idea that knowledge is to be exacted, there is no especial difficulty or expense involved in helping the growth of artistic enjoyment" (Whitehead, 1929a, p. 90). By reducing the number of specialized subjects, one promotes the acquisition of physical intimacy with working systems and languages. Howard Gardner has stated that today's students find themselves in a "shopping mall of the disciplines" (Gardner, 1999a, p. 54) asked to choose between increasingly narrow and professionalized fields; such an entrepreneurial approach to learning devalues third places and allows the arts to lapse amid the general neglect of the environment of learning.

Robert Scholes has written recently on this same matter:

> a few texts well-pondered may be more valuable than many texts consumed thoughtlessly. [...] What we need is a greater variety of courses, with a constant and prevailing emphasis on the process of reading, along with whatever constraints on choices that a given faculty thinks appropriate for the best results.
>
> (Scholes, 1998, p. 39)

Scholes defends the study of rhetoric and reading, which currently occupies a low rung on the teaching hierarchies. Concerning the 'how' of learning, Scholes suggests we discard outdated practices in the teaching of writing in the academic disciplines:

> For too long, we have designed curricula in order to do justice to what we perceived as our subject matter. What I am suggesting is that we stop thinking of ourselves as if we had a subject matter and start thinking of ourselves as having a discipline which we can offer our students as part of the cultural equipment that they are going to need when they leave us.
>
> (Scholes, 1998, pp. 36–38)

What is suggested by the above critiques is that a careful focus on language and reading in a broader range of courses, all of which focus on environmental awareness and the enjoyment of knowledge, could have a positive impact on the structure of curricula and degree programs. Scholes, for example, proposes that the current 'canon of texts' in the field of English be eschewed for the sake of a "canon of methods" (Scholes, 1998, pp. 105–9). Such would provide teachers with more direct interactions with students, who could be engaged analytically and in terms of their imagination as they experiment and test new hypotheses. To adopt such a canon of methods would require that educators be flexible and responsive to student needs, that they blend 'tight' or causal thinking with 'loose' or intuitive and inferential thinking.

Roland Barthes urged something similar, recommending that literature professors reorient themselves to their field so as to correct the pervasiveness there of 'tautology' and 'alienation.' Specifically, Barthes advocated the adoption of three principles:

> The first would be to reverse classico-centrism and to "do" literary history *backwards*: instead of envisioning the history of literature from a pseudogenetic point of view, we should make *ourselves* the center of this history. [...] Past literature would be dealt with through present-day disciplines, and even in present-day language. [...] Second principle: to substitute *text* for author, school, and movement. [...] The text must be treated not as a sacred object (object of a philology), but essentially as a space of language, as the site of an infinite number of digressions; [...] Finally [...] at every opportunity and at every moment to develop the polysemic reading of the text, to recognize finally the rights of polysemy, to construct a sort of polysemic criticism, to open the text to symbolism.
>
> (Barthes, 1989, pp. 22, 27–28)

Barthes' remarks reflect the stimulating atmosphere of the 1960s when semiology and related linguistic studies achieved wide intellectual currency. This sense of aperture and freedom reclaimed the validity of language and symbolism as against the 'pseudo-genetic' hierarchy that placed literature over language studies at that time. Such an opening frees one from the categories routinely used to classify authors, works and genres, and enables one to propose new predicates of education. With the text construed as a "space of language" one is free to reject the "antinomy between literature as practice and literature as teaching" (Barthes, 1989, p. 27). As Barthes states,

> every reading derives from trans-individual forms: the associations engendered by the letter are always caught up (sampled and inserted) by certain codes, certain languages, certain lists of stereotypes. The most subjective reading imaginable is never anything but a game played according to certain rules. [...] There is no objective or subjective truth of reading, but only a *ludic* truth.
>
> (1989, p. 31)

If one is to "play" with language one must know the rules! To construct a "space of language" with the kind of freedom Barthes suggests requires the supportive climate of a dynamic classroom in which one's actions make a difference. As John Dewey wrote in *Democracy and Education*, the "three R's" constitute an overly narrow pedagogical focus that ignores free choice and the ethical goals of a democracy: "[many educators] are aesthetic but not artistic, since their feelings and ideas are turned upon themselves, instead of being methods in acts which modify conditions" (Dewey, 1944, p. 135). The idea that language instruction is an art applicable across the disciplines is a profoundly humanistic idea. It implies a reinvestment in rhetoric and linguistic anthropology. The modern founder of this school of thought is Giambattista Vico, who argued for the symbolic and spontaneous view of language as a concrete manifestation of the spirit and affective intelligence. Not surprisingly, a commentator on Vico's educational philosophy has seen him as anticipating the ideas of Dewey: "There could be no more explicit rejection of the adjustment theory of behaviorism; no more outspoken support, with two centuries of anticipation, of Dewey's conception of the dynamic process of learning" (Gianturco, in Vico, 1990, p. xliii); for Dewey feels there is an "*intellectual* factor in the more spontaneous play and work of individuals – the factor that alone is truly educative" (Dewey, 1991, p. 62). Indeed, dynamically inclined teachers of language across the disciplines recognize this educative faculty in the student and thus promote the corresponding activities. As Dewey writes: "The natural or psychological activities, even when not consciously controlled by logical considerations, have their own intellectual function and integrity; conscious and deliberate skill in thinking, when it is achieved makes habitual or second nature" (Dewey, 1991, p. 62). Thus for Dewey, "Discipline of mind is [...] a result rather than a cause. [...] Discipline represents original native endowment turned, through gradual exercise, into effective power" (Dewey, 1991, p. 63).[4]

In his cogent analysis of the situation of education in the humanities today, Robert Proctor notes how classical studies have been eclipsed, leaving a void: "Classical education may be dead, *but we have found nothing to replace it*"; and "we must take the death of the Renaissance humanities seriously" (Proctor, 1998, pp. 143–44). He presents the pertinent works of Petrarch as they initiate and provide a point of reference to future humanists and educators. If for the great humanist Petrarch, "the ultimate purpose of study was not to become learned but to become good," in our day educators are "[obsessed] with technique," so that, in the case of deconstructionism, one finds a "total intellectual permissiveness," "a new kind of scholasticism" in pursuit of a career that is an end in itself:

> most of the current methodological fads in our universities today, such as quantitative analysis in the social sciences and the latest

literary theories in the so-called "humanities," are of such limited application that having these techniques in one's head can often be an impediment to serious thinking.

(Proctor, 1998, pp. 147–48)

Proctor critiques those administrator-managers who do not guide by moral example or aspire to virtue and wisdom. When colleges and universities fail to select administrators who are respected academics, the space of learning is usurped by managers whose lack of preparation in the humanities leads them to avert any contact with the language and method of self-examination common to Cicero and Augustine, Petrarch and Goethe.

Proctor has asserted in his study of the humanities that for many academics, blinded by quantitative thinking and the preoccupation with technique, 'the past is dead.' Despite paying lip service to the humanities, such scholars view the humanities from the perspective of an isolated personality or mind, an 'intensive self.' Such a view of the self sees knowledge as fragmentary and disconnected, adjectives that also describe many curricula and programs of study that have left behind the liberal arts tradition in favor of the 'utilitarian' and 'capitalist' traditions. Proctor writes,

By looking carefully at how the Renaissance humanists read a modern self back into the ancients, we discover another kind of self, the ancient extensive self, with its ideal not of autonomy and radical freedom, but of harmony and unity with the whole world of being.

(Proctor, 1998, pp. 173–74)[5]

Denouncing the 'great collective amnesia' occasioned by the 'death of the past' in our universities, Proctor urges the implementation of an aggressive and integrated four-year undergraduate liberal arts curriculum that will reestablish the sense of wholeness, of human connectedness with the cosmos through history, and the practice of contemplation of the divine. Such a curriculum can be applied to science majors as well as humanities majors and will require the student to ask the larger and more general questions concerning one's place in the world. Proctor treats the Renaissance as a kind of hinge or point of arrival of the ancient world. At the genesis of this rebirth is Petrarch, who provides a model of dynamic self-inquiry and a critique of scholasticism and its detriment of the life of the soul. Indeed, Petrarch serves as a model for teachers of any era who seek a common language of learning. Without such a language one cannot ask those questions that guarantee the rigor and validity of the disciplines by contextualizing them holistically.

To engage in self-inquiry, therefore, is to espouse the 'ancient extensive self' that sees the individual as part of a cosmic whole; it is also to partake of the unity of all language enunciated by Cassirer. It is also to endorse the cited view of Whitehead that the only proper discipline in education is self-discipline; and it supports the idea expressed in the title of Hans-Georg Gadamer's 'Education is Self-Education,' where the philosopher emphasizes foreign language learning as an intrinsic component of self-education. Gadamer urges that language educators not adopt the traditional reading-oriented approach to L2, but promote active conversation:

> I am firmly convinced of this point: that far too often we view the learning of foreign languages as a one-sided relationship and not as an understanding of each other.
> [...] The most important feature in my own view is to be able to answer when one is asked, to be able to formulate questions oneself and to be able to accept corresponding answers.
> (Gadamer, 2001, p. 533)

A major obstacle to such reforms is the territorial representation of knowledge referred to above. Curriculums are devised that leave students little choice; courses involving creativity are distinguished from those demanding intellectual rigor. While students cover the basic areas with stadium-style introductory courses, these courses do little to teach them about what is good, true or beautiful. Subliminally, students are taught that professors haven't the time to scrutinize their writing and that good test-taking skills are the key to success. What is lost in the process are the linguistic abilities that are the claimed goals of coverage requirements: flexibility, adaptability, the communication of relational knowledge. These are lost because students are not asked to blend concrete, abstract and technical skills in a dynamic and non-trivial way. The stadium classes tend to rely on rote instruction. Tests are often not returned to students and can be the sole source of one's final grade. Viewed in terms of the art of language instruction, such practices and curricular patterns tend to trivialize the radical novelty of L2's emergence in the subject's life and thus the adventure of language. The cybernetic alternative ('cyber-' from Greek, *kybernan* to steer, govern) to such a course is an educational dialogue in which the teacher uses the multiple languages of the discipline to direct and orient, to steer and constrain the students, so as to engage them in a learning conversation with the Other: "Far too often we view the learning of a foreign language as a one-sided relationship and not as an understanding of each other" (Gadamer, 2001, p. 533).

As Heinz von Foerster alleges, we are suffering as a society from an epidemic of perceptual disorder, in particular as regards our perception of the *future*; he argues that the one "common denominator that would identify the root of the entire syndrome" is the tendency to only ask trivial questions, and the tendency "if we encounter non-trivial machines, to convert them into trivial machines" (where the term machine "refers to well-defined functional properties of an abstract entity") (von Foerster, 1984, pp. 201–2):

> Wouldn't it be fascinating to contemplate an educational system that would ask of its students to answer "legitimate questions" that is questions to which the answers are unknown. Would it not be even more fascinating to conceive of a society that would establish such an educational system?
>
> (von Foerster, 1984, p. 203)

It takes courage to affirm that information is not a commodity but the sign of a relation; that knowledge is not information but the awareness of a cognitive difference that begets complexity; that wisdom is not knowledge but a simplicity that stands above complexity; and that the two-pronged approach of a strict specialization shored up by area requirements is obsolete.[6]

When such an archaic model persists, student choice is restricted and the work ethic imparted has little to do with individual motivation or the challenge to be an ethical person. When L2 is brought under the control of L1, one remains essentially monolingual. One is acculturated without being asked to define what one's culture actually is. Educational culture surrounds one in the academy, yet it is hidden; to seek out this culture the younger educators must inquire of their elders. It is often only in speaking that the unwritten lore and practice of the older members of the profession is revealed. A practical issue that arises is the need of younger faculty to communicate with senior faculty about the art of teaching; yet the mentoring relationship can easily be overlooked:

> It would be congenial [...] if the missions of schools could be stated clearly in terms of roles, values, notational skills, disciplinary knowledge, and an understanding of the true, the beautiful, and the good. However, we often fail to state what is intuitive or self-evident to us. Moreover, much of the most important curriculum is hidden – rarely spoken about, conveyed instead by the behaviors and attitudes of the older individuals in the environment.
>
> (Gardner, 1999b, p. 113)

As Gardner suggests, the intuitive awareness of older faculty constitutes a valuable resource that is often ignored by younger faculty. What these masters tell us is that to gain competency in a new language, or a new worldview, generates satisfaction about something one has made, something communicable that carries one's signature and the cadence of one's actions.

To speak of the unstated truths of successful pedagogy is also raise the issue of affective learning. Affective knowledge depends on the individual's active involvement in assessing and defining environments, objectively and also in terms of subjective relations. It asks individuals to

"read" and put into perspective the conceptual foundations of their own culture. [...] This decoding process, when viewed in terms of the mounting evidence of ecological disruption caused by modern technology and cultural values, requires the teacher to consider whether the patterns of thought being shared with students contribute to a greater sense of social and ecological interdependence. This now seems to be the primary educational issue that should frame our notion of cultural literacy.

(Bowers, 1993, p. 122)

Bowers' idea of cultural literacy, therefore, is quite unlike the widely known model of E. D. Hirsch. To define cultural literacy in the manner of Hirsch, in terms of lists – of events or individuals the knowledge of which is deemed essential if one is to be properly civilized – strikes one as arbitrary at best (Dante is required, Petrarch is not).[7] Bowers instead insists on a cultural literacy founded on the student's learning about *how* culture is formed, and thus on the awareness of one's built-in cultural constraints and the dangers of ethnocentrism.

Classroom Narratives and the Convergence of Knowledge

One of the most valuable tools available to the language instructor is narrative. As Galal Walker and Mari Noda write concerning the use of narrative in the foreign language classroom:

The flow of social life occurs in a sequence of *performances*; discrete frames of specified times, places, roles, scripts, and audiences. [...] The implications of this concept of performed culture for language study is that no one really learns a foreign language. Rather, we learn how to do particular things in a foreign language; and the more things we learn to do, the more expert we are in that language.

(Walker and Noda, 2000, pp. 189–90)

The authors conclude, "The question confronting those of us in foreign language study is, Which culture is associated with the language being taught in the foreign language classroom – the target culture or the base culture of the student?" (Walker and Noda, 2000, p. 190). Too often, the 'saga' that is repeated in the classroom finds the teacher playing the part of the teacher and the student playing the part of the student. But if one resists, one may bring the performative function into focus, and along with it the world of will. The defense reaction of students and teachers is to act out their lowest expectations and not to aspire to change what they assume they cannot. What does work are stories that students can enter into and assimilate, scenarios they can imagine. Role playing means accessing the imagination, inventing situations and not accepting those already formulated. It means using ambiguity and taking risks, as occurs in the world when two people combine their partial knowledges of a subject to form a greater knowledge. The language teacher's use of dramatistic, performative and narrative modalities for the sake of opening up the classroom to uncertainty, risk-taking and adventure, has the additional effect of training students to respond to contingencies. In this respect the best class is the one that does *not* flow but pauses over ambiguities, ponders the suchness of language and labors over the rephrasings that students undertake when they appropriate the normative. This principle is applicable to the languages of other disciplines as well. Whether in the humanities, the social and human sciences, information technologies or hard sciences, the use of role-playing (e.g. in the formation of hypotheses) allows students to appropriate the disciplinary language in a non-trivial way and transform the data of scientific experimentation into actual knowledge. If the teacher is successful in stimulating such activity, it will be an art, since a still coarse instrument is being used to cultivate observation, reflection and contemplation of knowledge.

Language teachers know that language learning is doubly rewarding: To begin with, one learns to communicate in L2. But just as remarkable is the change that comes about in one's person: As one appropriates L2, one gains objectivity toward L1. This change provides the subject with positive feedback about the transformative nature of language itself. The complexity and subtlety of language resides in the fact that it is both product and event, code and utterance, *langue* and *parole*: Language is something made and something that happens. In language teaching, this duality is often communicated by means of analogy: For example, a teacher may start with lists of cognates between L1 and L2, revealing a taxonomy of prepossessed knowledge of L2; as students experience more and more patterns and strings of language, they can perform more tasks in L2; in this process the language that was consciously *made* becomes the language that simply *happens*. The habits that attach to linguistic identity loosen and, as a result, one learns better how to learn. The lesson of deutero-learning leads in turn to an awareness of metacognition.[8] The student is constantly receiving new information and translating it into the language of the already known; the process can be thought of in terms of an ascending spiral as linguistic tasks are hard-wired so as to eventually become second nature.

Let us consider the ear's ability to sort through speech in which there are no pauses between words, in order to intuit where one word ends and another begins. This mechanism operates universally in children and adults alike, as the auditory intelligence parses the rhythms of speech according to predictable patterns, benefiting from constant exposure, systematic repetition and recitation of ever longer units of speech. Recent research has shown the unconscious nature of this assimilation of auditory patterns. Rhythm is critical, since our bodies and sensoria assimilate patterns only through repetition and conditioning, which 'wiring' in L2 prepares us to improvise, to create, to converse. Through rapid transitions and recombinations of examples from the multiple strata of the language paradigm one can achieve syntheses that blend clarity and complexity. This 'division of labor' in the sensory reception of language would seem to confirm another insight of Whitehead's:

> It is a profoundly erroneous truism, repeated by all copy books and by eminent people when they are making speeches, that we should cultivate the habit of thinking of what we are doing. The precise opposite is the case. Civilization advances by extending the number of operations which can be performed without thinking about them.
>
> (Whitehead, 1958, pp. 41–42)

There are fundamental differences between the languages of the humanities and the sciences, but there is also a deep commonality. For scientists as for humanists the rhythms of education and deutero-learning focus on actuality and narrative, becoming and perishing, environmental awareness and the pursuit of reasonableness. Clearly the sciences are based on the amassing of general rules or laws based on the rational conclusions that are drawn from controlled experiments repeatable by other experimenters at other times; it is easy to juxtapose the metaphorical procedure of literary minds and artists to this procedure and to conclude that scientists and humanists are worlds apart. But such would be to confuse the techniques of particular *métiers* with the broader conception of knowledge that is the goal of a liberal arts education. It is only in the neglect of this goal that some scientists feel compelled to extricate facts from values. As Stephen Toulmin writes:

> In the Academy, human scientists as much as natural scientists are expected to treat the contrast between facts and values not just as a distinction, but as a downright separation. Yet how can we do factual work in our scientific theorizing, while recognizing "values" in all our practical activities and relations?
>
> (Toulmin, 2001, p. 45)

This syndrome has led to a compartmentalization of the disciplines and a call from many sectors for a reform of the academy:

> Tremendous obstacles that hinder the exercise of pertinent knowledge have accumulated right within our education systems.

These systems make the disjunction between the humanities and the sciences, and the division of the sciences into disciplines that have become hyper-specialized, self-enclosed.

(Morin, 2001, p. 33)

The nature of these obstacles is linguistic and concerns the failure to formulate a language of relations. As one of the great practitioners of complex thought, Morin provides an idea of the road yet to be traveled before cybernetics and related sciences grow into their full potential of a liberating knowledge and knowing.[9] The simplification of cybernetics into a utilitarian machine-science is seemingly based on the attempt to reduce the cyclicity of informational systems to a technology. This immobilizes a field whose very essence is dynamic. A more fully recursive understanding of cybernetics' interrelationships with the physical and biological sciences is called for.

In that spirit, Lynn Margulis, the ecologist known for her explication of the Gaia hypothesis, has written a series of books about speciation, genomes and 'symbiogenesis,' defined as "the origin of new tissues, organs, organisms – even species – by establishment of long-term permanent symbiosis" (Margulis, 1998, p. 6). An important concept that emerges in her studies is anastomosis, the union of parts or branches – as of streams, blood vessels or leaf veins – so as to intercommunicate: "Biologists call the coming together of branches – whether blood vessels, roots, or fungal threads – anastomosis. Anastomosis, branches forming sets, is a wonderfully onomatopoetic word. One can hear the fusing" (Margulis 1998, p. 52). Models of convergence such as symbiogenesis and anastomosis are vital in allowing scholars to negotiate and compare the diverse languages and logical fields of their specializations. How the languages and codes of the disciplines interrelate is analogous to how the individual learner absorbs and organizes data and conflicting hypotheses in order to construct knowledge. Mary Catherine Bateson has written of Margulis's theory that the Earth is a vast, self-regulating organism as follows:

The Gaia hypothesis pulls the data together, but it goes further by offering a metaphor for organizing awareness of the interconnections. Beyond that, it proposes empathy as a way of knowing and imagining connections about which we cannot yet be explicit.

(M. C. Bateson, 1991, p. 140)

Empathy or the language of the heart is a means of confirming the importance of the indefinite; while the experimental sciences usually gauge success by the predictability and repeatability of results; in today's global community, the pragmatic realities of life are often pervaded by uncertainty and vagueness. It is so in the world at large but also in the relationships developed within the academy. As scholars confront unique and concrete situations, language itself evolves in ways that are unpredictable.

Unpredictability is a common problem to the arts and sciences, negotiated diversely and with contrasting methodologies; by the same token, predictability and convergence of systems is a shared epistemological and pedagogical goal. Because of this, communication studies about the systematic means available to identify such processes of differentiation and analogy are necessary skills to the scholar. In his chapter "Convergence of Science and Psychiatry" (in Bateson and Ruesch, 1951, pp. 267–75), Gregory Bateson predicts a convergence between these fields based on shared emerging trends, which include a focus on larger gestalts, on group interactions and on relativist over absolutist approaches to knowledge, and thus on a less quantitative attitude taken toward the nature of experimental variables. As sciences benefit from research in psychiatry and alter their narrow, quantity-based self-definitions, and as psychiatry becomes a more interactive and humanistically informed field of study, the humanities too benefit. As Peter Harries-Jones has written, summarizing Gregory Bateson's notion of co-evolutionary processes:

> Predictable processes are *convergent* processes. Convergent processes are contrasted with divergent processes, processes which in time can never be predicted. Thus the relation epigenesis/tautology can be compared with the relation somatic adjustment/learning; as convergent processes, they can be contrasted with their opposite, divergent processes.
>
> (Harries-Jones, 1995, p. 253)

Some scholars have paid the price for pursuing such convergences between fields of knowledge in a scientific community unreceptive to nonconformists. Candace Pert is a neurochemist who has specialized in receptors, making a fundamental discovery concerning opiate receptors. She continued her NIH-sponsored research on neuropeptides (which constitute the vast majority of the 'ligands' that attach to receptors, inducing change in the cellular structure – along with neurotransmitters and steroids) by becoming an authority on the importance of emotion in neurochemical process. Pert explores the boundary between the conscious and unconscious 'bodymind': "It could be said," she writes, "that intelligence is located not only in the brain but in cells that are distributed throughout the body, and that the traditional separation of mental processes, including emotions, from the body is no longer valid" (Pert, 1997, p. 187). One sees in Pert's initiatives (and those of like-minded scientists) an awareness of the associational nature of mind and a dedication to reformulating the scientific language of neurochemical processes to account for observable convergences of somatic processes and learning. Pert's research extends into the area of learning and the proper reformulation of the language of learning adopted by scientific educators in order to acknowledge the current change in paradigms; thus one thinks of her consonance with the scientists, humanistic thinkers and language educators cited above: Norbert Wiener, Scholes, Barthes, Kramsch, Whitehead. Pert is inspired by Gregory Bateson and shares his estimation of the importance of information theory in the recasting of our views about health and sickness, and about the curing role of the physician and the abilities that patients under the proper guidance can possess to insure their own good health and happiness. Pert battled with the NIH grant establishment and lost, in particular as regards work on one ligand, 'Peptide T,' as an AIDS treatment. She also worked with her husband Michael Ruff on early cancer research in the emerging field of psychoneuroimmunology (which they call psychoimmunoendocrinology). For our purposes it is critical to note Pert's insistence that interdisciplinary work in the biological sciences, along with the change in the language of research and teaching to allow for the "bodywide communication system," has emerged as a new paradigm replacing the "old paradigm insistence on the separateness and autonomy of the individual disciplines" (Pert, 1997, p. 174). The thinking and decision-making that should be at the heart of higher education is compromised when, disengaged from creativity and risk, the scholar is limited to a narrow specialization or a diluted interdisciplinarity.[10] As all good teachers know, successful teaching depends on students who choose to learn. When language loses its vibrancy and student choice is diminished for the sake of a standardized final product, one loses the lesson of empathy.

Another positive instance of the phenomenon of convergence in scientific language is found in strategic psychotherapy, a discipline which takes a stand against traditional psychotherapy, asking the therapist to get involved with the patient and not be a detached authority figure. This is not to deny the professional know-how of the therapist, but to deemphasize the hieratic position of the expert who examines the patient, identifies the malady and attempts to induce proper actions by changing misshapen ideas. The strategic therapist enters *into* the problem, which is conceived as something that concerns all those the patient comes into contact with. The initial definition of the problem is essential and must not be rushed. Steps and procedures must be selected in the proper sequence and at the proper levels of difficulty and must be gauged according to the situation, not repeated from a preestablished list. A small positive change should not go unacknowledged. The patient's expectations should guide the therapy since the very act of formulating expectations effects change. By being a good listener so as to ensure the involvement of "Other" and "world" in the therapeutic context, the therapist can respond to symptoms reported by the patient. To summarize, the strategic therapist engages in four "heresies": Choose Probability over "Truth," Focus on How Rather Than Why, The Therapist is Responsible and Change Comes *Before* Insight (Nardone and Watzlawick, 1993, pp. 17, 20, 22, 28).

It is apparent that these four premises also apply to the teachers of language. Language teachers eschew abstract versions of the truth, favoring the probable; they assume responsibility for learning and look for how, not why it is accomplished. In language teaching one discovers that the ability to produce in L2 is preceded by comprehension, an activity which is silent but not passive. Effective teachers invent activities that put language to use in rhythmic sequences and not as isolated, trivial, data; such interactive work also benefits the group dynamic and *esprit de corps*. The student is a collaborator whose creative imagination depends on the integration of mechanisms and sensations that converge toward the production of a work. This is part of the 'how' of change: it involves constant, direct exposure to the materials of the language – letters, sounds, words – as teachers create concrete and technical exercises that allow the language to emerge in its own inherent rhythms.

This notion of group activity and improvisation was highly regarded by Gadamer, who in highlighting the critical importance of foreign language instruction focused on phonetics and the accurate sounding of the language so as to promote conversations. Just as the acquisition of L1 depends on game-playing and ongoing experimentation, so do the learning of L2, and the maturation of the *forma mentis* generally. In Gadamer's view, one cannot separate out the learning of languages from the overall Bildung or cultural formation of the individual. This is a process that depends on the mystery and strangeness, the 'alien' nature, of L2. It is this sense of otherness that motivates one in a social setting to mimic L2 so as to appropriate it and penetrate its sense of otherness. As Gadamer writes:

> To seek one's own in the alien, to become at home in it, is the basic movement of spirit, whose being is only return to itself from what is other. Hence all theoretical Bildung, even the acquisition of foreign languages and conceptual worlds, is merely the continuation of a process of Bildung which begins much earlier. Every single individual who raises himself out of his natural being to the spiritual finds in the language, customs and institutions of his people a pre-given body of material which, as in learning to speak, he has to make his own.
>
> (Gadamer, 1975, p. 15)

Gadamer's remarks confirm – in the spirit of Goethe's aphorism cited at the start of this chapter – that the state of alienation is inevitable until the individual confronts it by learning another language.

It was in pursuit of similar humanistic goals, including the training in a median language of scholarship, that Whitehead and three other colleagues formed at Harvard, in 1931, the Society of Fellows. The objectives of the Society were stated as being comparable to those of Trinity College in England:

> Not the all-round man but the man who can open new paths is particularly wanted. Lines of work between disciplines today well established are the most promising for tomorrow's investigation. As Whitehead pointed out, *new advances are made by working within present experimental error.* The conventional fields are blanketed by fellowships that take better care than the Society can of the man who should get right to work on his final job.
>
> (Brinton, 1959, p. 25)

Even the most gifted candidates, if disinclined to invention and experimentation, were not appropriate fellows. The rarer 'geniuses,' more vulnerable to the institutional categories of the University, were favored, because better prepared to cross-pollinate – to converge – with the ideas of other fellows. A comprehension of this creative process requires that one have the ability to recognize the events and relations that foster it. The Society was formed as a means of establishing an antidote to the strictures of the departmental system. Diametrically opposite such efforts as those to recast the German University in an authoritarian and Fichtean mold, the Society fostered the growth of such figures as Robert Lowell, W. V. Quine, B. F. Skinner, Renato Poggioli, Allen Mandelbaum and Martha Nussbaum, intellectuals who outgrew the parameters of the departments and saw the traditionalist-progressivist gloss on educational techniques as a cliché. In the colloquy at Harvard one found the true glow of the humanities. Key aspects of this ongoing program are the freedom given the Fellows to do research unimpeded by formal requirements, the informal and convivial sharing of their work and the concern for knowledge at the boundaries of current disciplines. It was the idea of the Society of Fellows that each individual has a discrete potential. Thus it

> [encouraged] the development of each man (*sic*) in his own way, toward his own personal and independent achievement, as the result of his own private initiative. To establish such a condition in an American college would be to work a revolution.
>
> (Brinton, 1959, p. 49)

A critical issue in this regard is the training of teachers. Graduate students are the future professors, but is it advantageous to assign them heavy teaching loads while they are still completing their coursework?

Are admissions standards actually lowered in some cases to enable large departments to increase their number of low paid teachers? Scholes has advocated a reduction in the number of graduate students in the humanities and a dramatic increase in the years of commitment a university offers the candidate in support and training, so as to allow future educators to hone the craft of teaching as well as the scholarly treatise. This idea is not new. In 1950, Norbert Wiener argued for making the PhD dissertation a more challenging and decisive intellectual step forward and culmination in the student's life:

> In view of this great bulk of semi-mature apprentices who are being put on the market, the problem of giving them some color-able material to work on has assumed an overwhelming importance. Theoretically they should find their own material, but the big business of modern advanced education cannot be operated under this relatively low pressure. Thus the earlier stages of creative work, whether in the arts or in the sciences, which should properly be governed by a great desire on the part of the students to create something and to communicate it to the world at large, are now subject instead to the formal requirements of finding Ph.D. theses or similar apprentice media.
>
> (Wiener, 1950, p. 133)

The great cybernetician adds in conclusion a personal note:

> What sometimes enrages me and always disappoints and grieves me is the preference of great schools of learning for the derivative as opposed to the original, for the conventional and thin which can be duplicated in many copies rather than the new and powerful, and for arid correctness and limitation of scope and method rather than for universal newness and beauty, wherever it may be seen.
>
> (Wiener, 1950, p. 135)

It would seem that the culture of the academy – in Wiener's day and our own – makes it difficult to present novel and creative works in one's early research, and that it compounds this difficulty by treating graduate students as employees first, and scholars second.

Ventures such as the Society of Fellows are called for today, given the diffusion of distance-learning models, the capital-intensive quantification of 'output' and teaching performance, the erosion of the Arts and Sciences model for the sake of lucrative institutes, the outsourcing of teaching jobs, and the earmarking of research by corporate sponsors. The tendency is to reify education by reducing possible choices and roads of academic diversity. An unfortunate corollary to this is a trivialization of L2; at many colleges and universities today there is a rapid increase of short-duration study abroad programs; while ever more students are studying abroad, far too few of them are prepared in the languages of the host countries.

In the world of scientific research one has seen the persistent practice of earmarking by funding entities. Such criteria are able to skew results or render their objective monitoring impossible, so that when official reports (for example, on climate change and global warming) go against the policies of the funding agency, the U.S. Government itself may be seen to practice 'denialism,' that is a systematic ignoration of the science. The obvious problem with earmarking is that it short-circuits scientific research. One cannot simply place blind trust in technology as a substitute for the dialectical methods of the sciences. To do so is to view the entire academic endeavor primarily in economic terms. Such was the error of the 2006 Spellings Commission, which asserted the need to establish predetermined earning levels for the future graduates in diverse academic disciplines.[11]

The Art of Categorial Thought

One's goal in learning a language is the mastery of skills which, once assimilated, are phased out of active conceptual thought. Mauro Ceruti writes in this regard of the complementary views of a system provided by internal and external observers:

> The point of view inside the system is the point of view of the autonomy, organizational closure, maintenance, and reproduction of its own identity. The disturbances are not instructive inputs, but simple priming indices integrated into the organizational dynamics of the system according to the reproduction of this same organization. The point of view of an observer external to the system is the point of view from which the problem of the integration of the system in a metasystem is posed, the point of view of the transformations and evolution of the system.
>
> (Ceruti, 1994, p. 102)

Ceruti actually provides a good working definition of the transdisciplinary, a kind of map of the boundary areas between disciplines.[12] Without forcing a sameness of the languages of the arts and sciences, I envision a mutual respect for the pattern that connects, a language of polity to reflect the human ecology of the university. This means adopting a categorial thought that is constructive, though its various sublanguages – of philosophy, chemistry, linguistics, etc. – are fragmentary. As Ceruti writes,

> Categorial thought, understood as constructive thought which gives form to the matrices of knowledge, finds its roots in [a] sort of

principle of more general complementarity [...] in order to account for the relationships between the *results of knowledge* on the one hand and the explanation of their *epistemological condition* on the other. This principle can be found in the general mechanism whereby knowledge, in a stage of its acquired, organized development, perpetuates the greatest covering up of its true, genetic constitutive matrices.

(Ceruti, 1994, pp. 74–75)

This fact of 'covering up' is critical to the argument I am proposing concerning probity, modesty and the recognition of gaps in learning.

The language and logic usually attributed to the exact sciences is atemporal and insufficient for understanding or adequately theorizing the realm of mind. In his discussion of the need for scientists to reinvigorate their interdisciplinary awareness of other fields, Stephen Toulmin suggests that the 'principle of non-contradiction,' which is a *formal* characteristic of some disciplinary methods, has been mistakenly construed to be a *substance*:

In the twentieth century, too, analytically-minded philosophers continued to prefer fields of experience in which our beliefs could be given a quasi-geometrical foundation to those in which that seemed impossible. Once more, disciplines like Physics came out ahead, and were seen as intrinsically rational, while the rationality of fields such as Ethics, in which no agreed analytical proofs seemed to be available, was called in question.

(Toulmin, 2001, p. 163)

To respect categorial thought is to continue in a tradition of humanistic research that assumes argument by ampliative inferences and novel hypotheses to be critical. It is to reaffirm that art is not simply desirable, but essential to teaching; that creative habits are intrinsic to a systems theory approach which considers the questions of emerging knowledge, deutero-learning and metacognition; and that philosophy is not an arch-discipline but is complementary to the other disciplines. In this way one avoids the error of confusing the vehicle that conveys information with the information itself. Such an error is all too common in the current age of theory, which has seen the emergence in the humanities of an impenetrable professional jargon. In the literary field, George Steiner offers the following critique:

Those who proclaim and apply to poetic works a "theory of criticism," a "theoretical hermeneutic" are, today, the masters of the academy and the exemplars in the high gossip of arts and letters. Indeed, they have clarioned "the triumph of the theoretical." They are, in truth, either deceiving themselves or purloining from the immense prestige and confidence of science and technology an instrument ontologically inapplicable to their own material. They would enclose water in a sieve.

(Steiner, 1989, p. 75)

Erudition (*episteme*) matters little if one lacks the practical ability (*phronesis*) to transmit its complexities. Confronted by the difficulties of learning a new language, students discover how to make their first language more expressive and coherent. As the guide in this process, the language educator is obliged to follow the exigencies of art. As with any art, such a pedagogic practice is effective because it possesses its own intrinsic form. To truly exploit the performative and factual aspects of L2 in the classroom is to collaborate with students in a kind of adventure.

As seen, the art of teaching language across the disciplines requires a radical morality. But there is much satisfaction to be had in the affective knowledge and empathy that one gains by increasing a student's awareness of language as such. There is also, if one is lucky, a daily confirmation of Kenneth Burke's intuition that, "[T]he future is really disclosed *by finding out what people can sing about*" (Burke, 1984, p. 335).

Notes

1 "Wer fremde Sprachen nicht kennt, weiß nichts von seiner eigenen."
2 See Whitehead, 1968a, p. 205:

> The function of art is to turn the abstract into the concrete and the concrete into the abstract. It elicits the abstract form from the concrete marble. Education, in every branch of study and in every lecture, is an art.

3 See Hamrick, 1988, pp. 242–43:

> One new aim of education must then be to resist imitating the incomparably more interesting and vivid electronic media to distinguish what goes on in the classroom from time-compressed, disjointed, non-sequential presentations of subject matter. Rather than being entertainers for immediate pleasure, we need now to emphasize stability instead of novelty, order instead of change, and constancy in place of instancy.

4 See Whitehead, 1968b, p. 1: "Philosophy is the product of wonder. The effort after the general characterization of the world around us is the romance of human thought."
5 Proctor cites the following books as models for his work: Toulmin, *The Return to Cosmology: Postmodern Science and the Theology of Nature*, Becker's *The Denial of Death*, Bateson's *Steps to an Ecology of Mind*, and Bellah, ed., *Habits of the Heart*.
6 See Whitehead, 1929a, p. 58. "In a sense, knowledge shrinks as wisdom grows: for details are swallowed up in principles."
7 This point doesn't concern the particular content per se (Dante over Petrarch, clearly an uninformed choice by Hirsch) but the idea itself of a list of required texts/authors.

8 See Gardner, 1999a, p. 113:

> It might have been true that the mastery of Latin and Greek a hundred years ago, or of calculus twenty years ago, was the mark of the individual ready to step out into the world; but today problem-solving, or metacognition, or familiarity with the changing workplace, or mastery of specific intelligences might be a much more valuable attribute.

9 I refer to Morin's major work *La Methode*, of which I cite vol. 1, *Method. Towards a Study of Humankind. Vol. 1: The Nature of Nature.*

10 See Dewey, 1944, p. 192:

> The notion that the "essentials" of elementary education are the three R's mechanically treated, is based upon ignorance of the essentials needed for realization of democratic ideals. Unconsciously it assumes that these ideals are unrealizable; it assumes that in the future, as in the past, getting a livelihood, "making a living," must signify for most men and women doing things which are not significant, freely chosen, and ennobling to those who do them; doing things which serve ends unrecognized by those engaged in them, carried on under the direction of others for the sake of pecuniary reward.

11 See Perley, 2007, p. 134.

12 See Ceruti, 1994, p. 102:

> If […] the observer external to the system can formulate the problems of the transformation and evolution of the system, problems – which are rather insignificant from the point of view within the system – on the other hand it does this exactly on the basis of its ignorance of the detail of what occurs within the system from the point of view of the system itself.

5 Gaps, Faith and Analogical Thinking

Analogy and the Truth

When learning is construed as a process and not a product, education can emerge as an art aided by judgment and fostering dialogue. To view learning in this way is to invite analogical thinking into the classroom. The importance of analogy is perhaps obvious, but in the digital age one feels it necessary to reaffirm the nuances of creative expression that come about as a result of analogical thinking. Unlike digital coding, distinguished by a binary switch, analogic coding contends with continuous gradations of variables. Analogic means are suitable for the negotiation of variable systems – including ecosystems – characterized by broad arrays of differences. Naturally, digital and analogic coding exist side by side in our culture and are mutually reliant for ascertaining the 'truth' in communication. Yet insofar as we are surrounded by the digital world, our analogical means and sensibilities are vulnerable to erosion or atrophy. In this chapter I consider the importance of analogical thinking in terms of the gaps that occur in knowledge and consciousness, in teaching and the institutional structure. What I hope to demonstrate is that analogical thinking provides an optimum means for navigating over gaps that are resistant to digital thinking and that by cultivating analogy teachers can increase receptivity to contingencies and produce a more humane educational climate. As Kenneth Burke writes, analogy has a "role in the discovery and description of 'the truth'":

> metaphor tells us something about one character from the point of view of another character. [...] If we are in doubt as to what an object is, for instance, we deliberately try to consider it in as many different terms as nature permits.
>
> (Burke, 1969, pp. 503–4)

While analogies are ubiquitous in our daily language and culture, there is a tendency to gloss over them and endorse rationalism over reason:

> Analogical thinking, as I describe it [...] in the methods of semiotics, in collaborative knowledges, and in interpretation, brings different

objects or levels or orders together in order to illuminate particular aspects of each momentarily. As Wittgenstein says, analogical thinking begins to "light up an aspect" of what it examines that was not perceived before. That is, analogical thinking is not reductive, or at least not reductive once and for all. Instead, it presents momentary or emergent insights by noting similarities, rather than identities, that suggest trajectories to pursue rather than resting places to inhabit.

(Schleifer, 2000, p. 24)[1]

In order to demonstrate how analogies work in ordinary discourse, I will present a few of them used to describe the university and consider their aptness or truth value. The expression 'ivory tower' suggests an elevated place isolated from the rest of the working world, a calm retreat for undisturbed intellectual labor and reflection. The term may also be used ironically to suggest elitism and aloofness. Writing in the 1940s, poet Wallace Stevens claimed that place had lost its legitimacy:

> There was a time when the ivory tower was merely a place of seclusion, like a cottage on a hill-top or a cabin by the sea. Today, it is a kind of lock-up of which our intellectual constables are the appointed wardens.
>
> (Stevens, 1951, p. 121)

As Stevens glosses one analogy with another – the prison – he suggests that the goal of a disinterested place for thinking and reflection has lapsed into the presumption of a privilege, the claim of a right rather than the exercise of a responsibility. Paul Zumthor described academia with the analogy of the 'ghetto,' designating thereby a place bereft of its former distinguishing characteristic of passionate idealism:

> Still apparently enthroned in the center of our horizon, but in fact marginalized, the Institution, or what is left of it, is little more than a ghetto now, and refuge for those among us who are the least gifted with an aptitude for communication, therefore the least apt to respond to the needs of a changed world. [...] Humanist ethics have become as foreign to our universe as the economic structures of the eleventh century. We have lost that utopian desire that led our forebears to lay claim, in their every enterprise, to the world of tomorrow by evoking the world of yesterday.
>
> (Zumthor, 1986, pp. 18–19)

Michel Serres has adopted a number of memorable analogies for the academy. One of these is the battlefield: "To call the site of universities a campus, what literal luck, since this world formerly designated the entrenched camp set up in the evening by Roman soldiers before an attack or for defense" (Serres, 1997, p. 134).

What is connoted by the analogies of the prison, the ghetto and the battlefield is that the site of education is susceptible to degradation and corruption. The cautionary images used by Stevens, Zumthor and Serres are immediately understood by the reader; they appeal to our common sense, specifically by suggesting that a certain idealism associated with the university is at risk, and that one must struggle to retain the concept of knowledge as something involving the whole person and possessing a spirit of harmony rich in the affective life and immune to that extent from intellectualist hubris and ideological control.

Writing in the 1950s, poet-physician William Carlos Williams warned against the devaluing of language skills by educational institutions that overemphasize the 'science-philosophy.' Williams urged the infusion into the curriculum of works of imagination and poetry:

> Finding no "purpose" in study [the young] quite correctly conclude that a life of action outside of academic walls is preferable to continued purposeless amassing of data within, which, unless clarified, are an impediment to the intelligence rather than an aid.
>
> (W. C. Williams, 1974, p. 3)

Speaking in defense of the pluralism of experience, Williams suggested that many professors are working in the wrong field, pursuing the wrong objectives and misconstruing the nature of proof:[2]

> [The pluralism of experience] is opposed by the pinching academy which tries to relegate it to paleontology, to the "crude beginnings," to an earlier condition. But it is as new – so new, that it will shortly be the newest, most pregnant motivation of thought and life in the world. It is decentralizing in effect as opposed to the merely opportunistic tendencies (due to the surrounding barbarism of the world) of centralization – in the sciences, arts, etc.
>
> (W. C. Williams, 1974, p. 149)

Again one sees effective analogies used to criticize the capacity of the university to stifle learning. (As Antonio Gramsci wrote, the educator can be a figure of great inertia and an obstacle to positive change.) Williams contrasts the use of language in the world of letters to its use in other disciplines, in a short piece entitled '(A Sketch for) The Beginnings of an American Education':

> The use of language by science and philosophy is an expedient because of which strong limitations are put upon its range of effectiveness. It must never, as a means, either in science or philosophy or the other correlated modes (such as history, religion, and the

legislative uses – also journalism and common speech) transcend the idea which it is put forward to represent.

It is in these modes a symbol without reality of its own. Thus it has no reality apart from the thing, movement, event, which it is put to represent.

But in letters the complement of this use of language exists. Words and their configurations become preeminent and (precisely as the manner indicated above) ideas, movements, facts, are the symbols which it uses (or escapes them when it will).

In this case words and their configurations are the reality and the full use of language realized. The only use that can be scientifically and philosophically sanctioned, is that of letters.

(W. C. Williams, 1974, p. 147)

By stressing the need for discreetness and circumspection, Williams reminds us of the limitations of the specialized languages and their dependency on a universal lexicon in which letters and literature enjoy a heightened status because of their ability to embody the reality they symbolize. It is precisely this use of language that we risk losing today as the humanities lose ground to the STEM disciplines.

Scientists rely on analogical thinking as a tool. Students of historical linguistics know how often language changes are said to have occurred by 'analogy' with earlier linguistic forms: "Saussure [...] criticized the turn-of-the-century linguists who saw in analogy an 'irregularity, an infraction of an ideal norm', since analogy constitutes in fact the device by means of which languages 'pass from one state of organization to another'" (Ducrot and Todorov, 1979, 125). Ancient languages are compared by analogy to one another.

As the digital age has progressed, the rich interference of feedback loops within digital circuits has led a new generation of scholars to envision digital and analogical thinking as existing together within a dynamic heterarchical relationship. I have touched on this matter in Chapters 3 and 4 and will return to it later in this chapter, but here I simply wish to reaffirm that as the sciences progress there are constant demands on the scientists to reimagine their disciplines and reconfigure their epistemological assumptions. Undoubtedly these assumptions will continue to differ from those of humanists; thus Cassirer points to "irreconcilable differences between the meaning of this term ['truth'] in the sciences and in the humanities" (Krois, 1987, p. 123). Nevertheless, this should not be a problem: "It is essential to keep in mind that science and poetry have the same root in human nature" (Whitehead, 1968a, p. 197).[3] What is problematic for poets and scientists alike is the failure to recognize the gaps or aporias in and between their vocabularies (or terministic screens) and to allot the necessary space for them in one's epistemological assumptions. This is of vital importance if scholars are to communicate the value of their field-specific findings to the larger learning community.

I am speaking of the "discontinuities, leaps and thresholds" (Ceruti, 2018, p. 134) that exist between fields; these have become fertile areas of research of great interest to complex thinkers. If scientific thought continues to show a bias toward the hard sciences over and against the soft sciences, such thinking is increasingly out of step with reality. According to this standard, the life sciences are weak and immature, still developing, purifying their object of study, while mathematics, physics, chemistry are strong and mature, their laws are known and research is conducted according to a singular authoritative scientific method.[4] The very assumption that there is a single scientific method is anachronistic and fails to recognize the polycentric and heterarchical organization of the sciences that emerged in the 20th century.

We live in a digital age with more information at our fingertips than ever before; yet our knowledge is also more fragmentary, due to our inability to understand the patterns connecting object and subject, nature and mind. During the early days of cybernetics there were debates over whether the brain functioned digitally or analogically; it eventually became clear this was not an either/or question but a both/and question. Nevertheless, the subsequent development of Artificial Intelligence has remained a largely digital enterprise rather than becoming what von Foerster theorized as 'An Epistemology for Living Things.'[5] Such an epistemology would differ from the "concept of an 'ultimate science,' that is an objective description of the world in which there are no subjects (a 'subjectless universe')" primarily because it includes a theory of the observer, of the observing subject, based on the understanding that "life cannot be studied *in vitro*, one has to explore it *in vivo*" (Foerster, 2003, p. 258).

Analogical Thinking and the Cinema

Merleau-Ponty's reflections on the visual as the basis for cognition stand at the advent of a phenomenology of perception that paralleled emerging developments in psychology, philosophy and the arts. In his more topical studies of film he defends the viewer's capacity to spontaneously comprehend the forms, behaviors, emotions, facts and ideas of a film and to interrelate them coherently, respecting the film's rhythms and ambiguities.

> Movies [...] always have a story and often an idea [...], but the function of the film is not to make these facts or ideas known to us. Kant's remark that, in knowledge imagination serves the understanding, whereas in art the understanding serves the imagination, is a profound one. In other words, ideas or prosaic facts are

only there to give the creator an opportunity to seek out their palpable symbols and to trace their visible and sonorous monogram. The meaning of a film is incorporated into its rhythm just as the meaning of a gesture may immediately be read in that gesture: the film does not mean anything but itself.

(Merleau-Ponty, 1964, p. 57)

In developing his theory of visual knowledge, Merleau-Ponty opposes both empiricism and intellectualism. If empiricism boils down the act of vision to a passive reception of external stimuli, an act of observation, intellectualism interiorizes the visual within the subject who produces or 'constitutes the world' on the basis of speculation. The dichotomy is reflected in the sociological approach to cinema on the one hand, and the purely formalistic approach on the other. As an alternative to empiricism and intellectualism Merleau-Ponty locates in the visual and other senses a potential 'union of mind and body' that benefits from the perception of groups, gestalts and configurations.[6] This alternative does not support the outdated views of classical psychology (including behaviorism) or speculative philosophy, but seeks to consider the film as a perceptual object that guides the sensitive viewer to its meaning.[7]

The psychologist James J. Gibson has researched the visual sense as a perceptual system in a manner compatible with Merleau-Ponty:

When the senses are considered as perceptual systems, all theories of perception become at one stroke unnecessary. It is no longer a question of how the mind operates on the deliverances of sense, or how past experience can organize the data, or even how the brain can process the inputs of the nerves, but simply how information is picked up.

(Gibson, 1966, p. 319)

As we view a film, we engage a range of automatic receptors that are positively inclined to be used in the direct processing of images and impulses; from this we derive an actual reality. The analogy of camera movement to body movement is central to Gibson's 'ecological' approach to cinema. Francesco Casetti has summarized Gibson's views as follows:

First, perception means retrieving some invariable structures that are present in the constant flux of shifting stimulations called reality. Second, the information necessary for a correct perception is present in the world and only needs to be "collected" by each individual through the senses, without relying on previous knowledge, mental models, or interpretive schemes. Third, the analysis of how a person moves through the world is crucial to this "collection."

(Casetti, 1999, p. 103)

In Gibson's view of 'direct realism,' events afford meaning directly without positing a central processing capacity in the mind or brain, like the realm of the *verum* (in Vico's terms) that constructs meaning. This direct participation of human and environment without benefit of man-made memory structures is rather like Vico's *certum* and Santayana's animal faith (Hillman, 1990, p. 240). Gibson asserts, "the possibility of perceptual experience without underlying sensory qualities that are specific to receptors," calling it a "theory of information-based perception" (Gibson, 1966, p. 266). He writes:

> If what things afford is specified in the light, sound, and odor around them, and does not consist of the subjective memories of what they have afforded in the past, then the learning of new meanings is an education of attention rather than an accrual of associations.
>
> (Gibson, 1966, p. 320)

To follow Gibson's views, the cultural baggage of students, their memories and associations, may be of limited value in deciphering the cinematic artifact. What counts is the exercise and training of perceptions, since, according to his theory of insight, the optic nerve and the brain reverberate in response to information. In his chapter, 'The Structuring of Light by Artifice,' Gibson writes:

> The correspondences between surrogates and what they stand for have to be learned. One might guess that the more nearly a surrogate specifies an object by convention, the more associative learning has to occur. The perceiver must learn in any case to distinguish among the objects of the world and must learn to distinguish among the surrogates of his culture; but the added burden of arbitrary associative learning is less for images than it is for symbols.
>
> (Gibson, 1966, p. 235)

Film instructors who are attuned to the visual and perceptual learning, Gibson details, will distinguish between visual knowledge and verbal knowledge, thus detaching themselves from the habits of 'ordinary' discourse. Optimally they will unlearn the associative way of viewing that does not think critically about the medium and they will learn to value for their own sake the basic elements of light/dark, sound/silence, motion/stillness, temporal sequencing and recursiveness.

How Gibson's work relates to other research in visual learning and knowledge is suggested by Jeremy Campbell in *Grammatical Man*:

> For Gibson, invariants in the structure of light reaching the eye correspond to the stable features of the real world: the surfaces and edges of objects, to which the brain pays such alert attention, the

texture of the ground that grows more dense with distance. In spite of the fact that the image of an object on the retina may shrink in size as it recedes, the image is invariant with respect to the texture of its surroundings.

(Campbell, 1982, pp. 205–6)

In comparing Gibson's position to Chomsky's, Campbell adopts the language of group theory, suggesting that visual perception be understood as a field with applications in the areas of neuroscience, behavioral psychology and film studies.[8]

One of the claims of filmic logic is that knowledge of the world is always partial and that the idea of 'mind' as a passive receiver or receptacle of information is passé: "The flaw at the heart of many scientific 'explanations' of how the mind works is the premise, not always obvious at first sight, that there can be direct, transparent ways of knowing the world" (Campbell, 1982, p. 213). It follows that divergent scientific viewpoints may be reconcilable at another level of theoretical discourse.[9] Group theory allows one to go beyond the immediate differences of the specialized theorists, insofar as the invariants of light, shape and form are analogous to the invariants of deep language. By bundling generalities, the seeing mind gains knowledge from partial and fluctuating input. This is true for those like Chomsky who say the brain is constantly testing hypotheses about what the eye sees, as well as those like Gibson who say that all the information needed for perception is outside the brain. For the cinematic educator it (ultimately) doesn't matter if it is the eye or the brain that groups the invariants (images, language, ideas), making sense of them. Moreover, the debate between 'opposing' parties whose conclusions are integrable must speak to the need for a keener approach to visual thinking in the teaching of film.

To grasp how the visual sense works in cognition is to form a model for understanding mental processes and provides an example of "cognitive intelligence, which resides only in its embodiment" (Varela, 1999, p. 60), not in some externally controlled mechanism or abstraction. In place of "the notion that the world is a source of information to be represented" (Varela, 1999, p. 52), perceptive interactions can be recognized as such by the "cognitive self," as "cohering" due to the "surplus of signification" (Varela, 1999, p. 56). That is, when knowledge is embodied, patterns of resonance occur that depend for their coherence on feedback systems that function spontaneously and according to the perceptual organs of the individual.

Varela, Thompson and Rosch use the analogy of a jam session in which the musicians respond to each others' instruments without a script or a leader. Such is the 'neural music' of the cognitive system, and once again the visual sense provides an optimal dehabituating model. The pathways from retina to brain are not the same as those from brain to retina. The ready access to the liberating path away from the habitual grasping of the ego, away from "one's own craving for recognition and self-evaluation" belies the idea of "central supervision" and continuously shows us a perceptual-cognitive system that functions without rules (Varela, Thompson and Rosch, 1991, p. 52). The Western concept of the self is inconsequential (save in its negation) to the cognitive event-realization:

> There is a difference [...] between what we usually mean by "unconscious" and the sense in which mental processes are said to be unconscious in cognitivism: We usually suppose that what is unconscious can be brought to consciousness – if not through self-conscious reflection, then through a disciplined procedure such as psychoanalysis. Cognitivism, on the other hand, postulates processes that are mental but that cannot be brought to consciousness at all. [...] Our pretheoretical, everyday conviction [...] is that cognition and consciousness – especially self-consciousness – belong together in the same domain. Cognitivism runs directly counter to this conviction: in determining the domain of cognition, it explicitly cuts across the conscious/unconscious distinction. The domain of cognition consists of those systems that must be seen as having a distinct representational level, not necessarily of those systems that are conscious. Some representational systems are, of course, conscious, but they need not be to have representations or intentional states. Thus for cognitivists, cognition and intentionality (representation) are the inseparable pair, not cognition and consciousness
> (Varela, Thompson and Rosch, 1991, pp. 49, 50).

Critically, Varela, Thompson and Rosch cite Gibson's research, noting that both of their "approaches deny the representationist view of perception in favor of the idea that perception is perceptually guided action" (Varela, Thompson and Rosch, 1991, p. 202).

Each of the viewpoints I have discussed in this section has its specialistic emphases; but each too pursues a middle way that concludes that neither the objectivist nor subjectivist approaches to vision – which emphasize respectively the world and the perceiver – is valid, and rather that a "mutual specification" of "world and perceiver" (Varela, Thompson and Rosch, 1991, p. 172) is called for.

Such a hypothesis is compatible with the approach to film of educator Claire Kramsch, whose use of discourse analysis in teaching cinema exploits the customary distinction made in film classes between mise-en-scène and montage. The mise-en-scène is presented to the class as being comprised of the shot, frame, focus, angle and sound; montage is said to constitute the "order of narration" and the "transitions from one sequence to another" (Kramsch, 1993, p. 193). Kramsch's simplification is useful as it provides students with the tools for analysis without burdening them with too many terms or theory. In a practical way she supports the position argued above, that the expression of one's visual thinking is a multifaceted and layered operation.

As Sandra Moriarty writes, "visual communication [is] grounded in perception, extended internally through cognition and language, and modified externally through social and cultural frames" (Moriarty, 1996, pp. 167–68). This grounding in perception means that verbal language by itself is intrinsically problematic and inconclusive. Umberto Eco has written, "there is no guarantee that every content of every expression can be verbalized (Peirce never said that the interpretant of a word can only be another word – it can be an image, a gesture, a behavioral habit)" (Eco, 1975, p. 16). The failure to give visual thinking its due is what leads to the textualization of cinema, its reduction to a representationist rather than projective and insight-derived mode of communication.

Cybernetics, Faith and Science Education

> Understanding cannot be digitalized. Teaching the basics of mathematics is one thing, educating for human understanding is another. There we touch on the truly spiritual mission of education: teaching understanding each other as the one necessary condition for the protection of humanity's moral and intellectual solidarity.
>
> (Morin, 2001, p. 77)

There is an ongoing danger of trivializing science education by instrumentalizing its goals and oversimplifying what is understood by 'the scientific method.' As one reads in a position paper of the 1999 Carnegie Corporation Meeting on the state of liberal arts education in the United States, the challenges of the new millennium are apparent:

> Scientists are exploring the fundamental questions – the origins of the universe and our place in it, the nature and creation of life, the nature of consciousness and the relationship of mind and body – that have been central to humanistic learning, and the results they produce will demand our best ethical and political responses. Science must be an integral part of any future conception of the liberal arts and liberal learning.
>
> (Barker, 2000, p. 9)

If one is to integrate the sciences with the liberal arts at a time when the sciences are tackling such expansive questions, it is appropriate to draw on the cognitive force of the intuition in the classroom as it is to revisit the great moments of scientific discovery and invention of the past.

Great discoveries over the centuries have depended on analogical thinking. Franklin, Lavoisier, Darwin, Galileo, Newton, Maxwell and Vitruvius were masters of it. Holyoak and Thagard provide a compilation of such thinkers, detailing the argumentative structures of their 'mental leaps,' assessing the scientific use of analogy historically and pedagogically and recommending teaching strategies that exploit the 'constraints' it presents: "The strengths of particularly good analogies and the weaknesses of particularly bad ones can be understood in terms of the constraints of similarity, structure, and purpose" (Thagard and Holyoak, 1995, p. 200). The bad analogies include references to knowledge as something physical that is delivered, conveyed or disseminated. As the authors write, "Language does not convey knowledge but can very well constrain and orient the receiver's conceptual constructing" (1995, p. 182). In like manner, the Greek word for steering, *cyber*, provides the good analogy, of orientation and constraint, that gives cybernetics its name.

As a science of recursive phenomena, cybernetics reaffirms that in order to be coherent, logical systems must negotiate the phenomenon of noise or entropy. To do so in the classroom is to adhere to linguistic propriety while cultivating an awareness of recursive events and feedback. As Mauro Ceruti writes (summarizing the system of the observer of Henri Atlan), "the creation of information can be achieved only by starting with noise" (1994, p. 99). While noise is a factor that diminishes information on one level, it allows for a gain of information on a systemic level:

> Let there be an organized system composed of a series of subsystems correlated with each other by multiple channels of communication. The ambiguity introduced by noise into the transmission of information in one such channel is considered as a quantity of information with a negative sign, that is to say, lost information. [...] This same quantity results instead as denoted with a positive sign (a gain and not a loss of information) when it is considered from the point of view of the total quantity of information contained in the system.
>
> (Ceruti, 1994, p. 100)

'Noise' is an analogy that has been adopted by scientists to describe interference and feedback that affects changes in systems and their integration. These issues are relevant in the classroom, since the optimum classroom is one in which I/Thou relations develop through dialogue, including what is unanticipated or draws attention to the gaps that exist between ourselves and others, as between ourselves and the truth:

> When academics speak of "the pursuit of truth," they rightly imply that a gap exists between ourselves and truth. But there is a conceit hidden in that image, the conceit that we can close the gap as we track truth down. In Christian understanding, the gap exists not so

much because truth is hidden and evasive but because we are. We hide from the transforming power of truth; we evade truth's quest for us.

(Palmer, 1983, pp. 58–59)

In other words, the gaps present in analogies, as signified by the 'noise' that is accepted within the communicative circuit, are comparable to the gaps present in the learning community, whose members discover a truth in dialogue that is not apparent to them in isolation.

Norbert Wiener is another educator who appreciates the need for students to process negentropic noise. As a cybernetician who advocates for a humanistic understanding of computers, Wiener states that faith is necessary in order to practice science. He opts for an Augustinean view which depends on inductive logic:

> The laws of induction cannot be established inductively. Inductive logic, the logic of Bacon, is rather something on which we can act than something we can prove, and to act on it is a supreme assertion of faith. It is in this connection that I must say that Einstein's dictum concerning the directness of God is itself a statement of faith. Science is a way of life which can only flourish when men are free to have faith.
>
> (Wiener, 1950, p. 193)

The faith Wiener speaks of is discouraged by those "people who have elected communication as a career [who] so often have nothing more to communicate" (Wiener, 1950, p. 135). Unlike the Manichaean view of these practitioners, Wiener's Augustinian view is experiential and situates itself under the sign of the question mark, of ambiguity and the intuition. Faith is first of all an asking and an exposing of one's experience of asking; it is the recognition of a gap and a homage to the unsayable.

A colleague of Wiener's from the Macy Conferences (1946–1953), Gregory Bateson, considered early in his career the measurements of stimulus and response employed by psychologists to chart the progress of learning. Reinforcement was said to be a higher logical type than stimulus and response, since it requires of the learner a recognition of a change in context, a break or gap, and a suspension of the middle term of the logical syllogism. In addition to this meta-difference, reinforcement follows four other criteria:

a.   The event called reinforcement proposes the fact of its own occurrence. It is perceptible.

b.   It proposes certain characteristics ('rightness' or 'wrongness') in the sequential relation between 'stimulus' and 'response' [...].

   c. It proposes that a certain contingency pattern among the three components in sequence is or shall be characteristic of the ongoing interchange.

   d. It proposes the even more abstract notion that the ongoing flow of interactive behavior is, in general, divisible into segments having some sort of contingency pattern.

   e. It proposes that the SEARCH PATTERN of the learning subject is 'right' in the sense that this search pattern will discover this particular triadic patterning (Bateson, 1970, p. 72).

In this sequence of criteria, Bateson introduces a qualitative difference between stimulus, response and reinforcement, such that discrete patterns of behavior can be articulated within a flow that is recursive and heuristic. This flow presupposes the temporality of the learning process, the ultimate sense of which cannot be known by the subject or the observer since it depends on emerging responses to contingencies within the stimulus, response and reinforcement. Here one sees the germ of Bateson's ecology of mind and his later epistemological writings, which examine questions of the sacred along with the role of abduction and tautology in the formulation of sacraments.[10] He is clearly attempting to articulate a set of scientific criteria present in pedagogical situations that depend on analogical thinking. Partly contingent and partly determined, these criteria aim at engaging the learning subject in a reflection that might lead from the empirical to the abstract along the pathway of the virtues and humility. Thus in statements b. and e. above, the 'right' decision is also the moral decision.

Living systems are bound by communication systems – languages, genetic codes, gestures, demarcations of habitat, rules of comportment. In the complex fabric of human culture, semantic fields exist by virtue of the gaps between them. Without the unstated steps taken consciously and unconsciously by communicators, no meaningful change, growth or adaptation can take place. As Bateson writes, "All knowledge has gaps [...]. Mental process includes the capacity to form new connections, to act as what I have called self-healing tautologies"; in addition, these gaps are organized into "gaps of details between details," "gaps between kinds of description" and "[gaps] in the hierarchy of descriptive statements" (G. Bateson in Bateson and Bateson, 1987, pp. 150, 165). Called by Stephen Toulmin the pioneer of "post modern science," Bateson's epistemology was eventually built "around three notions – the necessity for 'multiple descriptions' of all natural processes, a 'circular' conception of causal interconnections, and the role of 'stochastic processes' such as natural selection in generating new modes of adaptation" (Toulmin in Wilder-Mott and Weakland, 1981, pp. 365, 362). As we have seen, Bateson argued that the oversight and error of Western man lies in his ignorance and avoidance of natural history. Based on this premise he developed a context theory of learning that differed from the first generation of cyberneticians, among them William Ross Ashby and Warren McCulloch, who had theorized learning as involving an overall reduction in 'noise' in the interpersonal system and in the individual.[11]

Bateson was himself an effective 'second order cybernetician'; though he did not use that term to describe himself, he was instrumental in advancing the scholarly discussion about recursivity to a point where psychologists, anthropologists, radical constructivists and complex thinkers could find its application useful. A classic example is found in his formulation of the double bind, the reflexive relationship in which a paradox exists between different communicative levels of a hierarchical relationship (imagine a parent screaming while telling a child to relax and enjoy himself). Double binds are characterized by command structures that are mutually contradictory, eventually leading to breakdown of the communicative system. Bateson gives the example of the alcoholic who stops drinking in response to a low self-image, but who upon acquiring a renewed sense of self-control and self-image tires of that and returns to drinking. The drinker is living a paradox because of the radical split between the mind and body, which can ultimately only be resolved by a "spiritual experience" (Bateson, 1970, pp. 330–31). W. B. Pearce cites the alcoholic as an example of a paradoxical reflexive relationship, a "strange loop": "a loop occurs when the contextual force is equal in strength to the reflexive force; the loop is 'strange' when the reflexive force changes the content of the contexts that guided the action" (Pearce, 1989, p. 47).

Bateson explored reflexive loops in relationships that have the capacity to grow in positive and nurturing ways. These involved conflict resolution, mediation and 'working through' the double bind to the point where creativity was generated in the relationship. This direction was pursued by Pearce and V. E. Cronen in their work on 'charmed loops,' which are essentially strange loops whose root paradox the subject chooses to go beyond.[12] Three skills are required to do this:

> First, healthy persons must be skilled in creating or choosing among their own meanings, particularly at the higher levels of abstraction that contextualize others. [...] Second, healthy persons must be skilled in believing their own meanings. [...] Third, healthy persons must be skilled in choosing their referent groups, which may be quite dissimilar to their peer groups.
>
> (Pearce and Cronen, 1980, pp. 311–12)

It is Gregory Bateson's conviction that the 'pattern that connects' living systems has the potential to nurture positive relationships, but only if one has the proper management of meaning and belief in such meaning. Feedback loops exist in time and are not without risks. As one transcends the current context of learning, the subsequent context arrives with its own protocols and requirements:

> In biological evolution, adaptive changes occur during the lifetime of an individual, adjusting him or her to various forms of stress, effort, demands placed upon skill, and the like. [...] They are achieved, however, at a certain cost. What is consumed is entropy, i.e., uncommitted possibilities for change in many different physiological and neural variables and parameters. The uncommitted alternatives (entropy) are lost, eaten up by commitment and by becoming unchangeable parts of patterns (negentropy). Adaptive changes limit the possibilities for future adapation in other directions.
>
> (Bateson, 1991b, pp. 209–10)

When adaptation takes place, discrete linguistic tasks and behavior patterns can be assimilated into the system of habits. In this process the conscious mind eschews complications, heeding the dangers of language itself and recognizing the dimension of the unsayable. This amounts to the expression of faith, which is critical if one is to avoid epistemological error.

"Seeing is believing," writes Bateson, adopting the adage to refer to the gaps intrinsic to perception and the fact that perception patches over the discontinuities of consciousness (Bateson in Bateson and Bateson, 1987, p. 96). For Bateson, the sacredness of reality is a given; the humility required to speak of gaps in epistemology and ontology recognizes that no single system or metalanguage will suffice in framing and communicating the essence of the sacred. A repeated theme in *Angels Fear* (a book co-authored with Mary Catherine Bateson) is that God will not be mocked, whether God is formulated in terms of a Judeo-Christian tradition or as G. Bateson's idea of Eco, being "the pattern that connects" and the composite of all living systems; conversely, "mere purposive rationality [...] unaided by such phenomena as art, religion, dream, and the like, is necessarily pathogenic and destructive of life" (Bateson, 1991a, p. 40). G. Bateson sees religion as a function of faith, not vice versa. Faith is broader and more biologically integral to the organism. Faith is critical to our perceptions and sensations and the reliance on the bridges we construct between them, in reality, as in the determination of causation. When we assert and place our trust in a causation that we cannot understand perceptually, sensorially or cognitively, we are supported by faith, not illusion:

> In the aggregate of propositions that are called "faiths," or religious creeds, it is ultimately not the propositions that that assert indubitable and self-evident truth but the links between them. It is these links that we dare not doubt – and indeed doubt is comfortingly

excluded by the logical or quasi-logical nature of the links. We are defended from doubt by the *unawareness* of the gaps.

> (G. Bateson in Bateson and Bateson, 1987, p. 95)

Mary Catherine Bateson too has discussed the importance of gaps in the learning experience, arguing that there is a latency period that occurs before students are able to acquire new concepts; during this period, they learn to abstract and reflect. Thus teachers are best advised to be aware of the resistance of the learning phenomenon to quantitative analysis:

> Learning is the fundamental pattern of human adaptation, but mostly it occurs before or after or in the interstices of schooling. Preoccupied with schooling, most research on human learning is focused on learning that depends on teaching or is completed in a specified context rather than on the learning that takes place spontaneously because it fits directly into life.
>
> (M. C. Bateson, 1994, pp. 196–97)

M. C. Bateson has worked in the area of education and lifelong learning, and has in recent years taught seminars on the narratives of self. Reflecting on her years of personal experience in Iran, Israel, the Philippines and the United States, she names 'recognition' as 'the paradigm of all learning.'[13]

If one reads M. C. Bateson's summary of the 1968 Conference on the Effects of Conscious Purpose on Human Adaptation, one finds a perfect example of such recognition in the context of a pluralistic experience. The account takes the form of a dialogue in which the various speakers – biologists, ecologists, anthropologists, cyberneticians and systems theorists – often disagree, but never lose sight of the goal of advancing their knowledge on how the human subject learns and grows through positive interaction. Over the seven days of the conference the topics ranged widely, allowing experts to steer discussions in their specific areas. Of particular value as a mediating influence was Gertrude Hendrix (the only other woman besides Bateson), a math teacher who advocated teaching by 'conscious generalization' rather than by 'authority.' Speaking of instructing her algebra students in the distributive principle for multiplication, Hendrix emphasized the awareness of the rule rather than its verbal articulation. The degree to which the correct mental pattern was not consciously articulated worked to the student's advantage: Students learning a technique by induction were more successful in applying it to new situations than were students who learned the concept of the rule and accepted it on authority. Hendrix made it clear that experience-based learning must be followed by verbalization of the principle, which carries with it a sense of detachment because it is abstracted from the initial generalization which engaged learners at "levels of their minds outside of consciousness": "The value of this power of detachment through use of language is [...] on a par with its value for communication. It is the great safeguard against transfer of *unsound* learning" (M. C. Bateson, 1972, p. 112). This combination of heuristic vigor and detachment toward the language of scientific argumentation boded well for the connectedness of the participants in the 1968 Conference.

A compatible school of thought that arose in the digital age was radical constructivism. If as seen in Chapter 2, constructivism was a major school of thought that encompassed the pluralism of experience that responded in the 20th century to the new epistemological reality by seeking to incorporate analogical thinking into the teaching of science, radical constructivism continues in that pursuit. Its aims are to "[give] students the reasons *why* particular ways of acting and thinking are considered desirable" and to allow educators to renounce the "claim of objective truth" (Glasersfeld, 1995, p. 177). For that purpose, it is essential to stress teaching over training, as the distinction between teaching and training corresponds to that between true understanding and mere competency. Glasersfeld takes issue with behaviorism's privileging of rote learning and its disconcern for thinking and understanding. In contrast to the behaviorists, he understands 'environmental stimuli' and 'reinforcement' as part of a larger feedback cycle. The idea that "scientific explanation can take into account only what is directly perceivable by an observer" is in error because it ignores the questions of reference within the observing organism: "The assumption that what observers isolate in their own perceptual fields as stimuli must be the same as what functions as stimulus for an observed organism, is a presumption based on the most naive form of realism" (Glasersfeld, 1995, p. 179). As Glasersfeld puts it, a drawn point on a blackboard is not a geometric point, but is the concept of that point. Similarly, "science is not intended to describe reality but to provide a system for us to organize experience" (Glasersfeld, 1995, p. 186).

Another compatible movement in line with the above thinkers is the new cognitivism. According to Francesco Varela, cognitivism opposes "the computationalist tradition [...which...] postulates that sensory inputs are successively elaborated to reconstitute a centralized and internal representation of the external world" (Varela, 1999, p. 53). Varela disagrees with the computational and behaviorist theory of psychological development with its "input-processing-output" model, to which he opposes a model based on the emergence of a "selfless (or virtual) self" (1999, p. 53), as present in various wisdom traditions – Buddhism, Taoism, Christianity – and based on the practice of compassion. Citing the connection between cognition and ethics, Varela elaborates the three-part nature of the virtual self or soul, and refutes any attempt to localize it in an actual place in the brain; rather it is "a coherent global pattern that emerges from the activity of simple local components" (Varela, 1999, p. 53).[14]

Despite the disciplinary and attitudinal differences that separate the scientific educators I have profiled in this section, they all share an opposition to the traditional epistemology and its practice of deterministic and neopositivistic science. They embrace pluralism and the value of experience in scientific thought and single out the indivisibility of subject and object, observer and the observed, in responsible scientific inquiry. As seen, their positions lead by necessity to a new pedagogy which acknowledges the gaps in representational language and cognition, and the fertile boundary that exists between the conscious and unconscious mind.

Gaps in Literary and Historical Discourse

Poetry is a means of ordering the world. It employs verbal and nonverbal technique, song and silence, rhythm and gesture. As Etienne Gilson has noted, the appreciation of poetry should not be confused with the literal comprehension of its sense:

> The poet does not speak to make himself understood. That which he says may have a meaning, but those who believe they understand his poetry because they have understood that meaning fool themselves as much as they do who, because they do not grasp the meaning, believe that they do not understand his poetry.
>
> (Gilson, 1988, p. 99)

Because of its particular use of analogy, poetry provides the key to a certain pluralism and discreetness of language. In poetry one finds a model of the economy of language as well as its flexibility and varieties of usage. Wallace Stevens stipulates four types of analogy as they arise in poetry:

'emotional analogy,' being the sorts of asides and ironic or lyrical responses and associations that capture a feeling through the spontaneous use of an image;

'analogy of rightness,' based on the appositeness of the image: the imagination as a power that situates one at the very center of consciousness;

'analogy in the personality of the poet,' not an individualistic identification, but a profound involvement with one's subject;

'analogy of involuntary images,' as in the 'music' of poetry, this is a quality that evolves over time in its specific characteristics.[15]

We could paraphrase by saying that for Stevens poems are constructed by means of analogies deriving from emotional spontaneity, vividness, personal authenticity and the intangible quality of words and images. As with Bateson's list above concerning the categories of reinforcement, one presupposes a progression through stages that involve the subject in a self-affirming cognitive process. If with Bateson, reinforcement is conceived as a kind of search pattern that properly orders contingencies, with Stevens, analogy means the poetic consolidation of images that render one's sense of the world in a way intrinsic to one's actual knowledge. Stevens' typology involves the sense of rightness, which connects the appropriateness of an image to its veracity and ethical resonance. In either case, learning takes place across a gap in consciousness.

As seen above, while analogical thinking has been involved in great scientific and humanistic discoveries over the centuries, its practical codification has been lacking.[16] Similarly, in arts education, one still finds the mystification of the artistic process. Many college programs in the arts reduce creativity to an impulse or question of taste, or the gift of talent, genius or inspiration. As James Elkins has written, classrooms in the fine arts are often pervaded by a fundamental irrationalism. Creative writing programs are not known for their study of the great writers; more usually the student compiles a body of work that mimics the styles and idiosyncrasies of one's teachers. As John Fowles has written:

> Americans [...] have a strangely pragmatic view of what books are. Perhaps because of the miserable heresy that creative writing can be taught ("creative" is here a euphemism for "imitative"), they seem to believe that a writer always knows what he's doing.
>
> (Fowles, 1998, p. 25)

What is often forgotten is the role of experience in making art. Given the fact that analogy and metaphor are created in a process that is deliberate, mysterious and internal, it is critical that one inquire what the poem or artwork actually communicates about feelings and relationships.[17] There is a tendency in the academy to treat the work as a precious object or an extension of the artist's ego; in either case the work is torn away from the network of human relations: "The cognitive and subjective orientation toward making art that is learned in a discipline-based art education classroom reinforces the highly restrictive view of art as an autonomous act of creation that should lead to an equally autonomous art object" (Bowers, 1993, p. 132). If the understructured art or creative writing class fosters the idea that spontaneity is the same as freedom, the overstructured class confuses rigidity for rigor. The challenge to the educator is not simply to keep students subjectively self-satisfied or objectively well-informed, but to draw them into heuristic and intuitive relations with the ostensive subject matter.

Professors of literature and history find the same problem. Often pressed for time, by large class sizes or the perceived need to standardize content, they reduce their historical subject matter to an unproblematic continuity. As the medievalist Paul Zumthor has written (concerning his own field),

> the temptation to which many medievalists succumbed, and still succumb [...] was to dissimulate the gaps, not in their documentation, but in that mantle full of holes, history itself; to take some plaster kneaded with their ideology and patch those gaps potentially threatening to their own (good) conscience.
>
> (Zumthor, 1986, p. 43)

By failing to heed the gaps and syntonies between them, historians fail to take advantage of the transformative power of analogy. Early in his *Cantos*, Ezra Pound cites Confucius on the responsibility of historians to think in terms of gaps and to respect the unknown:

> And Kung said "Wan ruled with moderation,
>   In his day the State was well kept,
> And even I can remember
> A day when the historians left blanks in their writings,
> I mean for things they didn't know,
> But that time seems to be passing."
>
> (Pound, 1970, p. 22)

To leave blank spaces where one's knowledge is imperfect is a lesson for the poet, as it is for the scientist and historian. Pound's contemporary, Louis Zukovsky, addressed this concern about the need to leave gaps in the classroom:

> Roger Bacon's *Six Causes of Teaching Ignorance*:
> Unsound Authority
> The Over-Academic
> Lack of Willingness to say *I do not know*
> Saying *I know*
> Pretense to Wisdom
> Fear of, and Catering to the Crowd.
>
> (Zukovsky, 1978, p. 248)

A responsible teacher must always be prepared to state, 'I don't know.' The gap left thereby is a form of empathy. It is pedagogically stimulating to acknowledge the unknown and emerging questions at the boundaries of knowledge, the mysterious workings of creative process and the unconscious motivations of the psyche. Such is the nature of art.

Allow me to cite an example from my teaching. When studying the poetry of Giacomo Leopardi with a class, I focus on the concreteness of the imagery and musicality of the verse. The pictorial and the lyrical aspects of the poetry appeal directly to the senses and contain analogies of the types listed by Stevens. The *incipit* to Leopardi's "Canto notturno di un pastore errante dell'Asia" (Night Song of a Wandering Shepherd in Asia) "Che fai, luna in ciel?" ("Moon, what are you doing in the sky?"), is disarming in its simplicity. When students hear this question made by a nomadic shepherd, they sense its candor and universality and enter immediately into the dialogue. After reading the poem – which Leopardi based on an account of the lives of Kyrgyz shepherds who have the custom of singing to the moon – they grasp the menace and tragedy implicit in Leopardi's view of life. In the poem, in which the poet adopts the voice of the illiterate shepherd, what stands out are the contrasts between the shepherd and the moon, the shepherd and his flock, and the similarities between the flock and the moon – equally indifferent to the desolation of the cosmos – and between the poet and the shepherd, both conscious of their isolation. Musically what stands out is the extraordinary beauty of Leopardi's language. Students learn from this poem that it is only by means of a vague and expansive language that one can one describe the effects of nature, since only these words encompass the dimensions of time and sensory mutability:

> What [Leopardi] requires is a highly exact and meticulous attention to the composition of each image, to the minute definition of details, to the choice of objects, to the lighting and the atmosphere, all in order to attain the desired degree of vagueness.
>
> (Calvino, 1988, p. 56)

Thus the poetry of the indefinite is also a poetry of precision, since only language that is vivid and precise can express the vastness and indeterminacy of nature. Leopardi represents the gap in knowledge that corresponds to "the relationship between the idea of infinity as absolute space and absolute time, and our empirical knowledge of space and time" (Calvino, 1988, p. 64). Students who are introduced to the concreteness of Leopardi's verse in its pictorial and lyrical dimensions are better equipped to appreciate his philosophy and to gain a sense of his importance in the history of Italian letters, as both continuator of the past and as a disruptor of the reigning forms of discourse.

How professors approach the teaching of literature varies widely. Leo Spitzer identified a positivistic, anti-mentalist and behaviorist school of thought that contrasted with his own inductive development of a 'philological circle' of interpretation that depended on the factors of taste, value, intuition and harmony. Spitzer framed the pedagogical debate as being between those who recognize the pluralistic nature of the literary experience and those who cling to an 'agnostic attitude':

> It is the belief in the autonomy of the word which made possible the whole movement of Humanism, in which so much importance was given to the word of the ancients and of the Biblical writers. [...] The Humanist believes in the power bestowed on the human mind of investigating the human mind. [...] A man without belief in the human mind is a stunted human being – how can he be a Humanist? The humanities will be restored only when the Humanists shed their agnostic attitudes.
>
> (Spitzer, 1967, pp. 24–25)[18]

For the humanist, in other words, the intrinsic recursiveness of study and the opportunity to reinforce one's belief in the power of language among an extended community are central components of a valid pedagogy. For the literary agnostic, the text becomes a bearer of ideology without wonder; having lost its autonomy the word is instrumentalized and inserted into a general program suitable for examinations, freighted with isms and concepts.

A propos of this distinction between humanists and skeptics, and in support of the need to promote the enjoyment of literature, Pier Vincenzo Mengaldo criticizes the editors of literary textbooks who overwhelm students with footnotes and cues for the reading of great works:

> In my opinion, one must proceed in the exact inverse order. A minimum of data and a maximum of existential freedom, in the reading, within certain limits of cultural verisimilitude that must be defined on a case by case basis. Also: greater freedom to professors themselves to construct a functional commentary with their students. Never forget that the reading is above all a vital experience.
>
> (Mengaldo, 1991, p. 102)

Mengaldo recommends that the Italian lyceum exam of 'maturity' be eliminated. Certainly, if one is to cherish the experience of reading, one must maintain linguistic propriety and probity. In my experience, this has meant stressing the dialogic component of literature: between writer and reader, speaker and listener, educator and student. His fellow Italianist Romano Luperini would concur with Mengaldo:

> The invasion of the logotechnocrats has helped dry up interest for the life experience that every literary text encloses, and it has distanced young people from the reading, now reduced to an exercise for applying descriptive models. Moreover it has had another, no less negative, result: it has attempted to transform teachers into

technicians, into white-collared specialists, providers of competencies. The teacher had to cease being an intellectual and educator, give up speaking in the name of values [...] in order to provide students with a series of technical tools, described as objective and neutral.

(Luperini, 1998, p. 105)

As a result of the pressures placed on the educator to separate facts from values, literary instruction has been diminished and the emphasis on technical linguistic competency increased. It is apparent from the above remarks that Spitzer, Mengaldo and Luperini support the primacy of students' enjoyment of literature. As Whitehead puts it: "Mere literary knowledge is of slight importance. The only thing that matters is, how it is known. The facts related are nothing. [...] It does not matter what [the pupils] know, but the enjoyment is vital" (Whitehead, 1929a, pp. 88–89).[19] I would suggest that literature is not alone in this mandate to generate enjoyment among students.

Allow me to illustrate this point with a discussion of a short story by Luigi Pirandello. 'The Cathar Heresy' is the story of Bernardino Lamis, a Professor of the History of Religion who (believes he) is in a blood feud with an academic rival, a German scholar whose study of the Cathar heresy was published after Lamis' own study but did not cite him or give him credit. Sensing the need to set the record straight and vindicate his intellectual superiority, Lamis grows obsessed. He ignores his family and moves into a rented room where he does not cook or even sleep in a bed; he survives on pastries purchased at a local café. The culminating moment comes when Lamis has composed a rebuttal of his rival and is set to deliver it in lecture form to his students. It is a rainy day and when he arrives the classroom is empty, but the myopic professor confuses the numerous raincoats and umbrellas that are strewn about on the seats for an audience of listeners. He proceeds to deliver his definitive exegesis of the Cathar heresy. Near the end of the hour-long lecture, students file out of a class next door and come to retrieve their coats and umbrellas from Lamis' classroom, only to be warded off by the one student who has just and wishes at all costs to spare the professor the embarrassment of knowing he has delivered a lecture to no one. As a parable of the lack of dialogue that results from intellectual solipsism, the story engages the metaphor of myopia to capture the notion of academic *hubris* and the pedagogic error of treating students as mere receptacles. The conclusion one draws is that if the languages of scholarship and teaching are to evolve, they must do so together by involving teachers and students in dialogue.

As seen in this chapter, educators who base questions of authority on technical performativity and the application of preordained models of competency tend to ignore the connectedness between learning and the unconscious, as between logic and psychology. It was suggested that educational pretexts, such as rules that encourage passivity and mutism, are counterproductive as they stifle creativity and the natural heuristic desire to learn. By emphasizing the pluralism of experience and the role of intuition, teachers can encourage the self-educating drive within each individual and place into relief the epistemological gaps required for perception of wholes and the construction of meaningful order. Such gaps have been illustrated in the work of historians, in the patterns of stimulus, response and reinforcement of psychologists and anthropologists, in the stylistic choices of poets and in the stages of learning of students of different ages and cultural backgrounds. If the educator, like the Confucian figure of the historian, leaves gaps in the presentation of material to account for what is not yet known, students are more likely to find the adventure of learning compelling and establish the connections between knowledge and experience. In reality, educators do not know the force of their practical and theoretical constructions until they emerge as *habitus*; there is an undeniable element of faith that accompanies any worthy pedagogy. This Emersonian self-reliance depends on one's ability to cope with the heterogeneous and the multiple, with enigma and paradox, much in the way that modern science has learned to integrate within its working methods the recognition of uncertainty, entropy and incompleteness.

Notes

1 Schleifer organizes his study, which ranges over diverse disciplines, in terms of three discrete levels of analysis: a semiotic-semantic level, a relational and collaborative level, and an interpretive level. In the process he touches on several of the themes that I discuss here: translation as cognitive activity; narrative configuration as deep linguistic structure; the gaps between conceptual language and the incommensurable; and visual thinking.

2 See W. C. Williams, 1974, p. 61:

> The laborious processes of scholarship are a bar when they make life futile with a crushing burden of proofs. [...] How in the world can knowledge set up its "scientific," "philosophic" measurements as sacrosanct rigidly, tyrannically above me when everything it does denies them *as a whole*. I assert that the whole is greater than all its parts and that since no one knows anything about it all proofs are invalid – as prohibitions – except relatively to its own set of conditions...

3 See Cocteau, 1988, p. 212:

> Written numbers speak to an inferior level of intelligence. The poet's politeness consists of *not writing his numbers*. The great pyramid expresses itself solely through relationships. The ultimate politeness in art consists of speaking only to those who are able to uncover and measure its relationships.

4 See Ceruti, 2018, pp. 112–40.

5 See G. Bateson, 1980, pp. 123–25, on the partnership of analogic and digital coding in mental and evolutionary processes.

6 See Jay, 1993, pp. 297–327, for a discussion of Merleau-Ponty's positive view of vision, including his film theory.

7 See Morin, 2005, for an anthropological study of the development from the 19th century "cinematographe" to the 20th century "cinema," the latter typified by metamorphoses of time, space and the notion of their representation, in contrast to the relatively simple documentation of reality that is presumed to have been accomplished by the former. Morin's study builds on the work of Merleau-Ponty.

8 See Campbell, 1982, pp. 205–6:

> Mathematicians deal with this process of invariants being preserved under transformations by means of a very powerful, formal system called group theory, which has proved of great usefulness in making intelligible the structure of matter at the atomic level. Group theory is concerned with patterns and relations, with the essential sameness of things concealed beneath their surface differences, in much the same way that Chomsky's work in linguistics that are invariant, even though languages differ from one another in relatively superficial ways.

Campbell also notes, 1982, p. 209, that

> two American psychologists, Robert Shaw and Buford Wilson – both of whom concur with the broad lines of Gibson's theory of perceptual invariants whereby the brain pays attention to the unchanging features of sensory impressions – have proposed that the perspectives of solid objects, the various viewpoints from which they may be seen by an observer, form a group. Shaw and Wilson suggest that, for many objects, a few perspectives only are enough to provide us with sufficient information to specify the whole shape of the object, because some of these perspectives may be generators of the complete group of perspectives.

9 Crick, 1994, p. 77, disputes Gibson's idea, alleging that his work can be boiled down to "the vague idea that the brain simply 'resonates' to the visual input." Crick's disciplinary orientation in constructing a theory of visual awareness and function is neurological and biochemical. Crick dismisses AI research somewhat unkindly, and defines "cognitive science," 1994, p. 272, as

> any discipline that studies cognition scientifically. Its main branches are linguistics, cognitive psychology, and Artificial Intelligence. In Stuart Sutherland's opinion, "the expression allows workers who are not scientists to claim that they are." [. . .] "...Cognitive scientists rarely pay much attention to the nervous system".

In Crick's chapter, "Attention and Memory," one has a useful definition of short-term memory (including the brief "iconic memory" and the somewhat longer "working memory"), and long-term memory, all of which have bearing on visual thinking.

10 The lesson of deutero-learning leads in turn to an awareness of metacognition. See Gardner, 1999a, p. 113:

> It might have been true that the mastery of Latin and Greek a hundred years ago, or of calculus twenty years ago, was the mark of the individual ready to step out into the world; but today problem-solving, or metacognition, or familiarity with the changing workplace, or mastery of specific intelligences might be a much more valuable attribute.

11 Von Foerster, 2003, p. 289, includes himself and Bateson among the second order cyberneticians:

> What is new is the profound insight that a brain is required to write a theory of the brain. From this follows that a theory of the brain, that has any aspirations for completeness, has to account for the writing of this theory. And even more fascinating, the writer of this theory has to account for her or himself. Translated into the domain of cybernetics; the cybernetician, by entering his own domain, has to account for his or her own activity. Cybernetics then becomes cybernetics of cybernetics, or *second-order cybernetics*.

See also Von Foerster, 1995; Heims, 1991.

12 Pearce and Cronen, 1980, p. 311, provide this example:

> From the perspective of a Buddhist who believes that all propositions distort reality and are false, the boxed statement, "All statements in this box are false," is unproblematic, but "All statements in this box are true" is objectionable. The ability to convert strange loops into charmed loops is the key to thriving in a recursive society.

13 See M. C. Bateson, 1972, p. 203: "It is not that we do not value learning that comes as recognition, but that we have despaired of making it the paradigm of all learning"; and 1972, p. 211: "Education creates a malleable and skilled workforce, but also perpetuates elites and creates revolutionaries. It can create xenophobia or cosmopolitanism."

14 This is similar to Ricoeur's concept of the self as other in *Oneself as Another*, discussed in Chapter 7.

15 I paraphrase from Stevens, 1951, pp. 107–30. See also Ibid. p. 118:

> There is always an analogy between nature and the imagination, and possibly poetry is merely the strange rhetoric of that parallel: a rhetoric in which the feeling of one man is communicated to another in words of the exquisite appositeness that takes away all their verbality.

And Ibid., p. 130: "Thus poetry becomes and is a transcendent analogue composed of the particulars of reality, created by the poet's sense of the world, that is to say, his attitude, as he intervenes and interposes the appearances of that sense."

16 Creativity Studies has emerged as a vital field in this regard; one thinks of such scholars as Frank Barron.

17 As Whitehead advises, 1933, p. 370: "The success of language in conveying information is vastly overrated, especially in learned circles. Not only is language highly elliptical, but also nothing can supply the defect of first-hand experience of types cognate to the things explicitly mentioned."

18 A similar viewpoint was registered by Mario Soldati, 1959, p. 224, who describes the professors he met during his two years on the faculty of Columbia University (1930–1931) as dull and unproductive followers of the 19th century philological method in literary criticism which presumed "never to judge" ("non giudicare mai").

19 See also Whitehead, 1968a, p. 171: "The first thing that a teacher has to do when he enters the class-room is to make his class glad to be there."

6 Ethics, Virtues, Rights

A Culture of Consensus?

The cobbler has broken shoes. In the case of the modern educator, the proverb has proved true. One has witnessed a convergence of related problems: the ascendancy of systems-management approaches to administration, increased state support for online for-profit universities, the downsizing and outsourcing of faculty jobs, the exaggerated focus on technology and STEM courses. It is not surprising that many scholars have sensed a diminishment of the traditional goals of the university, especially when funding for the humanities is being cut with respect to other disciplines.[1] Scarcity causes competition, a factor not conducive to educating the virtues. In the final two chapters I assess the *technical*, *ethical* and *epistemological* aspects of this crisis and suggest that a meaningful solution will depend on the integrative approach to these three areas, not viewed in isolation but comprehensively.

The renowned scholar of Judaica, Jacob Neusner, has written of a conformism that has arisen in the academy, converting it from a milieu of lively debate and high achievements to a patronage system whose laws may be unwritten but are known to all:

> Universities have become places of privilege and self-indulgence, in which boredom – the cost of easy tenure based on considerations of politics, not accomplishment – reigns, and energy and commitment to learning defy the norm. Tenure marks not achievement but acceptability. Those who go along get along.
>
> (Neusner, 1995, p. 47)

While one might dispute the extent of this phenomenon, the idea that the admission to rank and tenure is a kind of cultural rite of initiation is well taken. Professors, like other professionals, often decide to work with their disciplinary blinders in place. Yet faculty do not exist in a void. They are dependent on colleagues for practical, intellectual and affective exchanges. Questions of faculty governance are critical to meaningful polity. Ideally consensus be can arrived at in the manner described by Parker Palmer:

> Consensus is not a democracy of opinion in which a majority vote equals truth. Instead, it is a process of inquiry in which the truth that emerges through listening and responding to each other and the subject at hand is more likely to transcend collective opinion than fall prey to it.
> (Palmer, 1983, p. 97)

And yet, a system routinely based on consensus cannot always be trusted to arrive at responsible ethical decisions. Consensus can work to ameliorate conflict, but it can also devolve into the "deliberate evasion of basic conflicts of principle [...] a process in which certain issues were effectively excluded from political argument [...] a bland or shabby evasion of necessary issues or arguments" (R. Williams, 1976, p. 77).

One hears the claim for probity from all quarters in today's university, a fact which should motivate the cultivators of language to investigate the actual predicates – the risks and opportunities – involved in such claims. Alain Badiou has engaged in such an investigation and urged that one resist the brand of negative ethics – or 'ethics of necessity' – that emerged at the end of the 20th century. Unlike the 'ethics of truth' rooted in the pursuit of the Good, this negative ethics is based on claims of necessity made by dominant groups and individuals who, as witnesses to the crises in the world are also the benefactors of the status quo. For Badiou it makes no sense to discuss ethics in general terms insofar as ethics arises only within particular situations: "There is only the *ethic-of* (of politics, of love, of science, of art)" (Badiou, 2002, p. 28). Unfortunately, there is a widespread tendency to invoke ethics as an end in itself; this end is arrived at by means of 'consensus' and in the name of such ideas as 'otherness,' 'human rights' and 'democracy.' The problem is not with these worthy causes in themselves but how they are used to supplant and ignore the realities of concrete situations and put in their place a learning regime characterized by inertia, turning one's back on the not-known.[2]

There are market pressures to favor the hiring of educators who reduce course contents to the already-known, that is a static body of packageable knowledge. This fact leads to the diminishment of the figure of the Master, since the educator can now be replaced by any able disseminator of the packaged material (also by electronic means). The communication of knowledge is elevated to the highest status in this educational climate. By collaborating in the process of streamlining the disciplines – which allows for some disciplines to be relocated to more lucrative sectors of the institution – educators become compliant and estranged from the truth-process.

In Badiou's view, the culture of consensus harmfully reduces education to the dissemination of knowledge and thereby forecloses possibilities of truth-processes. If, as Bill Readings demonstrates, today's university has drifted away from the Humboldtian model – with its emphasis on the integration of "objective science (cultural knowledge) with subjective spiritual and moral training (cultivation)" (Readings, 1996, p. 66) – and toward a corporate and entrepreneurial model, what Badiou provides is a kind of clinical study of the character, motivations and symptomology of this mutation. Thus, once again, stakeholders in the educational enterprise do best to consider what 'consensus' means in any given professional context.

Faced with this situation, Bill Readings recommends abandoning the old idea of consensus, instituted in support of society, and adoption of the idea of dissensus, in support of the community:

> Far from community being the locus of unity and identity, the question of the proximity of thinkers in the University should be understood in terms of a *dissensual community* that has relinquished the regulatory ideal of communicational transparency, which has abandoned the notion of identity or unity.
>
> (Readings, 1996, p. 127)

The practical impact of the changes described by Readings has been to render the disciplines less contextualized and more specialized. In becoming more technical, the liberal arts have lost the humanistic glue that once held them together. While specialization is vital to discovery, it is useless if specialists lose track of the larger context in which their discipline resides. In recognition of this reality, Readings urges the practice of dissensus as a collaborative and symbiotic construction of local learning communities within the institution: "A dissensual community would thus be a development of the social bond as a necessity of sharing, of community. However [...] necessity and community cannot themselves be made the object of a consensus" (Readings, 1996, p. 188).[3]

Writing in the late 1970s, Umberto Eco estimated that over the course of five years in our contemporary civilization, today one would see the amount of changes that formerly occurred over the course of a century. Eco writes of a new Middle Ages in which populations isolate themselves into like-minded clans while certain areas, especially urban areas, are ceded in a process of 'Vietnamization' to the conflicts of today's culture, irremediably altering the university: "Among the replies of authority is the tendency to decentralize the great universities (a kind of student defoliation) to avoid dangerous mass agglomerations" (Eco, 1986, p. 77). Eco's insight is that the American university, said to resemble a medieval monastery, is experiencing a breakdown:

> Our own Middle Ages, it has been said, will be an age of "permanent transition" for which new methods of adjustment will have to be

employed. The problem will not so much be that of preserving the past scientifically as of developing hypotheses for the exploitation of disorder, entering into the logic of conflictuality.

(Eco, 1986, p. 84)

While this decentralization has taken place in diverse ways in diverse locales, it is undoubtedly true that the pace of historical time has quickened and the face of the university has changed, especially as regards the status of liberal thinking. Eco anticipated the unhinging of the disciplines we are witnessing today in the form of a diminishment of the Arts and Sciences model.

Eco's pessimism is shared by Robert M. Rosenzweig, President Emeritus of the Association of American Universities, who has written that the attempts being made to recover the "consensus on values" that the traditional liberal arts curriculum represented are "illusory" (Rosenzweig, 1998, p. 186). Though new interdisciplinary areas are opening up, "the shift away from the traditional liberal arts as the defining core of the education of undergraduates is real and probably irreversible" (Rosenzweig, 1998, p. 186).[4] Rosenzweig's depiction of professors in denial over the sense of entitlement they once felt – due to continuous growth in research funding after World War II – is enlightening, now that such funding and the privileges that come with it are gone. Many professors have concluded that in comparison to the academic ethos they were educated in, the scale has tipped toward the power of influence and away from the power of enchantment. Yet it is also true that already a generation ago American colleges and universities shared a neocorporative alliance with the government and business world. While institutions were committed in the 1980s and 1990s to a kind of social engineering which instrumented reforms in selected areas, such as altering their demographic and racial makeup, the major schools remained fundamentally elitist in their political orientations.

A related problem is the emphasis placed on faculty research over faculty teaching. While it is axiomatic to say that research and teaching are separate activities, such reasoning leads to a sterile dichotomy in which the two are cast into competition. Yet if viewed within a heterarchy, the two activities are interpenetrating: Without research teaching becomes a recitation of the trivial, and without teaching research becomes abstruse. It is research *and* teaching that one must undertake if writing a curriculum, a textbook, a monograph or a lecture; while the dualistic reasoning that separates thought from action, body from mind, is happy to separate teaching from research, for the scholar-teacher who creates an environment in which the aesthetics of knowledge and the hands-on ability to make things is preserved, research and teaching are part of the same symbolic and unitive, natural process.[5]

In *The Postmodern Condition* (discussed in the section 'The Rights of Others' in this chapter), Jean-François Lyotard writes that in the future, universities will continue to value creative research by scholars able to perceive and arrange information in new patterns; however this continuation – the "need [...] to 'imagine' new models" – will come at a price. Teaching (the "transmission of information") will be radically separated from research: "[T]he solution towards which the institutions of knowledge all over the world are in fact moving consists in dissociating these two aspects of didactics – 'simple' reproduction and 'extended' reproduction" (Lyotard, 1984, p. 53). The assumption that researchers engage in work that is imaginative while teachers simply transmit information leads to the idea that learning can be quantified. This in turn leads to the supposition that analytic logic will suffice in the study of complex systems and that a series of general education classes in different specialized areas will provide students with a coherent vision of the whole. Such a view ignores the fact of self-education and the need for students to have mentors who are active researchers. It is worth recalling that Whitehead included self-education (not to be confused with individualism) as a major tenet, as it was only through self-discipline and freedom that the learner progressed.[6] Nor is it a contradiction to say that the limitation of the educator's role to that of stimulus and guide makes the position all the more demanding. Gadamer felt similarly: "[W]e must proceed so that we never forget that we educate ourselves, that humanity educates itself, and that the so-called educator participates in this process only in such modest roles, for example, as teacher and as mother" (Gadamer, 2001, p. 530). We are speaking of the concept of maieutics that was gradually eroded in a university focused increasingly on research to the detriment of teaching in which the division of labor often boiled down to a question of resource allocation.

Hugh Kenner recalls the decline of teaching and candor that came about during the Eisenhower presidency with the rise of the modern research establishment. Kenner skewers the academic bureaucracy's relentless tendency to absorb resources, as it grows more self-important. What results is a mediocre competitive system:

> As for the liberal arts, they were soon subserving Objectives, their capacity for growth and their right to a slice of the enlarging pie connected with their demonstrable ability to further the Whole Student. [...] The Multiversity grew and prospered, and within it sundry Departments grew and prospered, thriving each one on Requirements. Requirements, being interpreted mean: If you will force your students to take courses in my department, I will force my students to take courses in yours. Thus we shall jointly thrive.
>
> (1995, pp. 48–49)

This brings us to the question of general education. Does a humanities concentrator required to take Biology or Chemistry 101 come away from that experience with a rudimentary knowledge of the larger interrelational contexts of those sciences? Do science students required to take courses in literature, history, philosophy or religion perfect their writing skills? Would not the fine arts classroom benefit from a more scientific and analytical understanding of its media? William Paulson has critiqued general education requirements saying "they are not general enough," that what we need are integrative courses that provide students with "a very general picture of what is known about the physical universe, organisms and the environment, forms of human society and culture, and the state of the present-day world" (Paulson, 2001, p. 180). Debates over the role of general education in the curriculum are not new. Whitehead defined the problem in 1925 as follows:

> I do not think that the secret of the solution lies in terms of the antithesis between thoroughness in special knowledge and general knowledge of a slighter character. The make-weight which balances the thoroughness of the specialist intellectual training should be of a radically different kind from purely intellectual analytical knowledge. At present our education combines a thorough study of a few abstractions, with a slighter study of a larger number of abstractions.
> (Whitehead, 1925, p. 198)

Updating Whitehead's language one would say that the ecology of learning depends on learning about ecology, that the healthy educational ethos is one in which the learner's uniqueness and individuality are valued above all.

Today's students bring with them knowledge and motivation, but also engrained habits and expectations, including the expectation to be entertained:[7]

> To me, liberal-arts education is as ineffective as it is now not chiefly because there are a lot of strange theories in the air. [...] Rather, it's that university culture, like American culture writ large, is, to put it crudely, ever more devoted to consumption and entertainment, to the using and using up of goods and images. For someone growing up in America now, there are few available alternatives to the cool consumer worldview. My students didn't ask for that view, much less create it, but they bring a consumer weltanschauung to school, where it exerts a powerful, and largely unacknowledged, influence.
> (Edmundson, 1997, p. 40)

Undoubtedly many professors have yielded to the 'consumer weltanschauung,' not simply by entertaining students but by converting traditional academic materials to the more utilitarian, performative format that aims to insert students into the job market.

As John Fowles wrote in 1964, the economic justification is important, but it is being used improperly to efface the other goals of education:

> There should be four main aims in a good education. The first is the one that pre-empts all present systems: the training of the pupil for an economic role in society. The second is teaching the nature of society and the human polity. The third is teaching the richness of existence. And the fourth is the establishment of that sense of relative recompense with man, in contrast to the other orders of animate life, has so long lost. We need to fit the students for a livelihood, then for living among other human beings, then for enjoying his own life, and finally for comprehending the purpose (and ultimately, the justice) of existence in human form.
>
> (Fowles, 1964, pp. 141–42)[8]

Today the pressures on faculty to guarantee a certain future earning power for their graduates are coming directly from the government. Many faculty employ mass media as part of their curricular design of short-cut paths to targeted job markets. In some cases, recruitment programs are treated as course material. It is not surprising, therefore, that digital media and entertainment have become major subject areas – and not just communication skills – in the technologized university. Mary Catherine Bateson has written:

> As a society, we have become so addicted to entertainment that we have buried the capacity for awed experience of the ordinary. Perhaps the sense of the sacred is more threatened by learned patterns of boredom than it is by blasphemies.
>
> (M. C. Bateson, 1994, p. 56)

As I have suggested above, a culture of consensus is a worthy goal in the academy, but only if that goal is accompanied by a thoroughgoing probity and educational ethics that safeguards the truth, the good and the rights of the minority. For indeed, 'learned patterns of boredom' too can be considered a kind of consensus. How can faculties work to counter such compromises to the educational mission? It is that question I wish to keep in mind in the following section, where I consider relative definitions in the actual educational context of the terms *information*, *knowledge* and *wisdom*.

Information, Knowledge, Wisdom

As the 1998 Boyer Report of the Carnegie Commission states, citing the authority of John Dewey, the old model of information transmission has lost its academic credibility: "learning is based on discovery guided by mentoring rather than on the transmission of information. Inherent in inquiry-based learning is an element of reciprocity: faculty can learn from students as students are learning from faculty" (Boyer Report, 1995, p. 15). Now, two decades later, it is fair to say that many educators continue to rely on the physicalist metaphor of knowledge as something transmitted (or delivered) exactly in the way that information is transmitted. With the educator's status reduced to that of "knowledge provider," learning is little more than the "traffic of knowledge" (Glasersfeld, 1995, p. 195). In contrast, inquiry-based learning stresses the predicative and constructive nature of the learning process and thus the qualitative and dynamic understanding of knowledge.

Let us consider the field of economics. Edgar Morin has described the current practice in this field as follows: "Economics, the most mathematically advanced social science is the most socially, humanly backward science because it has abstracted itself from the social, historical, political, psychological and ecological conditions inseparable from economic activity" (Morin, 2001, p. 34). Economists have yielded in many sectors to the vogue of neopositivism and overspecialization, which ignores the question of epistemological complexity. Stephen Toulmin writes similarly of economics in a discussion of the imperious advances of the methods of the exact sciences. In the wake of Newton's *Principia*, the enthusiasm over a rational method for prediction spread from the paradigm of physics to that of the social sciences. Theoretical economists after Adam Smith increasingly formed mathematical models to explain the performance of markets. And yet, as Toulmin writes, "the human sciences, not least theoretical economics, based their programs not on a realistic account of the actual methods of Physics, but on their vision of a Physics that never was" (Toulmin, 2001, p. 48). This tendency leads to the favoring of certain technical and abstract specializations within the disciplines, such that junior faculty are encouraged to follow only these pathways, and those who do not are weeded out. Moreover, these theoretical models remain so fixed on intricacies that they are not readily explainable to scholars in other (even closely related) disciplines. And though the recourse to such abstract models without reference to intervening cultural factors (such as the differences between developed economies and those of third world countries) has frequently ended in failure, the academy continues to embrace outmoded economic models.

The situation in economics is symptomatic of the tendency in other specializations to ignore their impact on human and other populations. For the sake of the ethical cohesion of the university, Toulmin urges that academics throw off the blinders that have isolated fields from one another under the sign of a strict "rationality" and adopt a more integrative and contextualized practice of disciplinary "reasonableness" (Toulmin, 2001, pp. 21–22). Since there is a tendency for social organizations to reflect in their structures and internal governance procedures the same presuppositions and biases that their members possess within their disciplines, the recommended change to a culture of reasonableness would also presage a more democratic, less elitist academy centered on an inquiry-based approach to knowledge.

When information is the goal of education, neither speculative reason nor calculative reason can benefit. While speculative reason is customarily assigned to the humanities and calculative reason to the sciences, these reasons in fact overlap. They are heuristic and require the formation and testing of hypotheses over time. It is in support of such an inquiry-based understanding of knowledge that Toulmin argues for the need to "abandon the naive cumulativist/preservationist view of knowledge acquisition" (Toulmin, 2001, p. 131). Similarly, the great linguist Walter Ong has written:

> Knowledge itself is not object-like: It cannot be transferred from one person to another physically even in oral communication, face-to-face, or *a fortiori* in writing. I can only perform actions – produce words – that enable you to generate the knowledge in yourself. The concept of 'medium' or 'media' applied to human communication uses an analogy that is useful but nevertheless so gross, and so inconspicuously gross, that it regularly falsifies what human communication is.
>
> (Ong, 1999, v. 3, p. 157)

A mathematician and systems theorist who shares Ong's critique of the objectification of knowledge and also sees this matter in the framework of institutional ethics, is Heinz von Foerster. The Austrian-born cybernetician and participant in the Macy Conferences seeks to explain the current paradigm shift in Western thinking with reference to the ground of the human organism in its communicative interactions: with other organisms, with itself and its psyche, and within the context of a living ecology or biosphere. Von Foerster conceives of ethics as an 'underground river' intrinsic to one's activity and beliefs. This deep structure is supported by two 'sisters,' metaphysics and dialogics. The first of these, metaphysics, concerns the types of questions one asks about life and how one frames them; the second, dialogics, concerns the language of function as opposed to the mere language of appearance. When an entity constitutes a hierarchy that denies participation in the formulation of significant questions, it is unethical: "through hierarchies, entire institutions have been built where it is impossible to localize responsibility" (Foerster, 2003, p. 293). In resistance to such hierarchies, von Foerster offers this metaphysical postulate: "Only those questions that are in principle undecidable, *we* can decide" (Foerster, 2003, p. 293).

These questions are those that allow for freedom of choice since they challenge one to formulate responses to questions about truth, beauty, creation, justice and love. Or as Edward Said writes:

> The goal of speaking the truth is, in so administered a mass society as ours, mainly to project a better state of affairs and one that corresponds more closely to a set of moral principles – peace, reconciliation, abatement of suffering – applied to the known facts.
>
> (Said, 1994, pp. 99–100)

The epistemological breakthrough envisioned by von Foerster drew from the humanistic philosophies of Wittgenstein and Cassirer, and is associated with radical constructivism (discussed in Chapter 5), which sought to reclaim the ethical distinction between information and knowledge:

> The primordial and most proprietary processes in any man and, in fact, in any organism, namely "information" and "knowledge," are now persistently taken as commodities, that is as substance. Information is, of course, the process by which knowledge is acquired, and knowledge is the processes that integrate past and present experiences to form new activities, either as nervous activity internally perceived as thought and will, or externally perceivable as speech and movement. Neither of these processes can be "passed on" as we are told in phrases like "Universities are depositories of Knowledge which is passed on from generation to generation…," etc., for *your* nervous activity is just *your* nervous activity and, alas, not *mine*.
>
> (Foerster, 1984, pp. 193–94)

In other words, dealing in moral codes is telling others how to act, while dealing in ethics is telling oneself how to act. Thus "it is impossible to speak about ethics"; or in the words of Wittgenstein, "It is clear that ethics cannot be articulated" (von Foerster, 2003, p. 290).

A more nuanced way of saying this is that ethics cannot be isolated from the empirical context of scientific research: Empiricism does not exclude the scientist from the moral realm. As Cassirer writes, scientists must be prepared to step beyond the *data* of science in order to accomplish an outward movement into society where the *ideas* of science can assert their morality:

> The problem is to discover and develop a new viewpoint, to set up a new standard which cannot be reduced to that of empirical causality but which on the other hand is in no sense in conflict with

it. Ethics demands that human actions are to be capable of and accessible to a double judgment; they are to be determined as events in time, but their content and meaning is not to be exhausted by this determinism.

(Cassirer, 1957, p. 50)

In *The Devil's Dictionary* Ambrose Bierce defines "Education" as "That which discloses to the wise and disguises from the foolish their lack of understanding" (Bierce, 1958, p. 34). The aphorism suggests that the wise recognize their ignorance, dwell with uncertainty and go lightly in the fields of knowledge, but also that education has the power to illude one, to cover up one's ignorance. Bierce's definition leads us to ask what sort of 'understanding' is at stake. Is it objective or subjective? Or do these poles converge in the 'wise' who understand the extent of their ignorance? As Norwegian philosopher and deep ecologist Arne Naess reminds us, this is fundamentally the problem articulated by Socrates and involves the question of frames of reference: "That which is not known is adequately classified as unknown only by virtue of what is assumed not to be unknown" (Naess, 2008, p. 148). The practical consequence of this verity for the educator is that students need to be guided through a truth-process in which the nature of their unknowing is made clear to them (though such a disclosure can only be an approximation, an adjustment of one's consciousness of frames of reference). The importance of this truth-process is accentuated by the rapid nature of change in our era, dominated as it is by new technologies and new truths breaking through the encyclopedia of current knowledge. In such an epistemological climate, the weaker position is the one that conceives of data and theory as independent from one another for, regardless of the academic discipline, the depth and appropriateness of learning will depend on the integration of abstract reasoning and concrete technical skills. An essential part of this process is the acknowledgement of one's ignorance: "We must seek to do justice to teaching rather than to know what it is. A belief that we know what teaching is or should be is actually a major impediment to just teaching" (Readings, 1996, p. 154).

The position I am detailing is indebted to the pragmatic and process traditions, which emphasize the importance of humility, modesty and constraint as essential criteria if one is to confront the complexity of scientific evolution: "The reality of the situation is that we nowadays find unfolding throughout contemporary science a flourishing project of accepting the world's complexity and devising the cognitive instrumentalities needed to come to grips with it" (Rescher, 1998, p. 207). Dewey, James and Peirce – despite their differences – shared the conviction that people are the agents of their own destinies. In contrast to the reductionist practices of logical positivism, they defended the validity and potential truth of religious beliefs. Their new pragmatic conception of knowledge was impacted by mathematics and logic, evolutionary theory and philosophy, literature and the arts, along with numerous emergent disciplines. Like Whitehead, they saw the new paradigm of knowledge as something to be enacted in a dynamic process that was ultimately unique for each individual learner. It was this paradigm that laid the groundwork for the educational advances represented by the cybernetic revolution. If that paradigm shift is to be exploited in its full humanistic potential, educators will need to adopt a pedagogy of mediation and complexity capable of linking the arts and sciences within a common body of learning that considers in a non-trivial way the future health of the planet.

It is useful here to recall and expand on Bateson's three types of learning. These begin with the grasping of information (protolearning or Learning I) and continue with the learning of the contexts of that learning, deutero-learning (Learning II), which brings about a change in the subject's behavior. While this improved ability to learn is ethically neutral (students in authoritarian classrooms learn how to please authoritarians), it allows the subject to anticipate a higher, more ethically positive level, Learning III, which leads to a "profound reorganization of character" (Bateson, 1972, p. 300). Thus if Learning II presupposes one's knowledge of the cognitive patterns of Learning I, then Learning III concerns the awareness of the patterns of those patterns. This is close to what Whitehead referred to as 'wisdom':

> Now wisdom is the way in which knowledge is held. It concerns the handling of knowledge, its selection for the determination of relevant issues, its employment to add value to our immediate experience. This mastery of knowledge, which is wisdom, is the most intimate freedom obtainable.
>
> (Whitehead, 1929a, p. 30)

Educating the Virtues

In discussing the 'institutional environment' in *Oneself as Another*, Paul Ricoeur relates the morality of institutions to the plurality of peoples and the autonomy of the self. By confronting two definitions of the self, as reflected in the tendencies to remain the same over time (*idem*-identity), or to change by engaging true selfhood (*ipse*-identity), the philosopher provides insights that relate directly to the goal of an altruistic yet practical academic environment. In his discussion of "The Self and the Ethical Aim," Ricoeur addresses respect as a quality that implicates and requires the Golden Rule: "What fundamentally characterizes the idea of institution is the bond of common mores and not that of constraining rules" (Ricoeur, 1992, p. 194). The enforceable pertains to the plane of norms, regulations and morals, while the Golden Rule involves altruism, voluntary goodness and respect towards others, and thus pertains to the plane of the ethical and teleological. How common mores are insured relates to the distinction between two types of justice, as between morality (deontology, rules) and ethics. The former applies to the formalism of the status quo while the latter requires an extension toward the Other with the wholesome intent of respect and solicitude, values guaranteed by the presence of an anonymous third person who is invited to share in the institutional relationship of justice. Ricoeur labels this third party the *tiers inclus*, or included middle. Within an institutional framework, the third person is often left out during negotiations between an 'I' and a 'you.' But when a third person is included, one may see emerge the salutary strength of "power-in-common" as opposed to "domination" (Ricoeur, 1992, pp. 194–95).

The ethical arrangement exists over time and guarantees solicitude and the forthright expression of affect; in contrast, when rules alone dominate there is the risk of violence and humiliation (not least of which self-violence, self-humiliation). In Ricoeur's theorization, humiliation is equal to 'the destruction of self-respect' and the loss of higher moral understanding. Authoritarian bureaucracy is unamenable to the rule of universalization; as such it can lead to the betrayal of friendships and the perversion of collegiality.[9] In discussing John Rawls' two principles of justice, the deontological and the ethical, Ricoeur considers how only the ethical provides the proper discernment of the individual's merits within the institution and thus the proper differentiation of the goods to be distributed. The Golden Rule is only viable in the individual who engages the self as *idem* and *ipse*, implicating the "dialectic of *self* and the *other than self*" (Ricoeur, 1992, p. 3) and not merely *idem* (an unchanging identity over time), for such a person perceives an uninterrupted gradient between enactions of the Golden Rule with oneself, with another person, within a collectivity or an institution.[10] The question thus arises: How is one to optimize these enactments so as to maximize the climate of respect within the scholarly community?

One suggestion is to restore the professor's status as an 'officer' of the institution to whom is delegated the power to determine distribution of goods and resources. As an officer, one has every right and responsibility to work within a vigorously ethical climate of justice and respect. Too often within the academic culture, guidelines and methodologies adopted in the name of rationality actually undermine the goals of academic agency and freedom. As Aldo Gargani has argued, rationality is easily manipulated into "that state in which one finds oneself bound by rules"; in order to correct this abuse, rules must be understood as "a reflection of linguistic practices" so that "chance" can be welcomed into the governing process as "the companion of the research into new languages" and not merely a "mechanical repetition" (Gargani, 1985, pp. vii–ix). Varela writes in a similar vein against the preemptive framing of knowledge by means of rules:

> Positing rules as mental activity is factoring out the very hinge upon which the living quality of cognition arises. [...] Context and common sense are not residual artifacts that can be progressively eliminated by the discovery of more sophisticated rules. They are in fact the very essence of *creative* cognition.
>
> (Varela, 1992, p. 252)

It is apparent that within an ethical curriculum, courses should be integrated with respect to the imagination, cognitive experimentation, variation of points of view and diversity of pedagogical-discursive approaches. To enlist the powers of the imagination in the classroom is essential if students are to comprehend the heuristic nature of scientific discovery and construct their own intellectual and creative itineraries.

David Carr's *Educating the Virtues* examines the falseness of both 'traditionalist' (Durkheimian) and 'progressivist' (Rousseauian) positions about the merits of education and socialization with respect to human beings. In refuting these "crudely oversimplified pictures of human nature, social influence and the origins of virtue" (Carr, 1991, p. 18), Carr shares the diffidence expressed toward them by a moral developmentalist like Piaget and outlines a third way (in the spirit of Ricoeur's 'third included,' Serres' 'third instructed' and Kramsch's 'third places'). Naming Dewey as an educational philosopher who rejected the traditionalist-progressivist dichotomy, Carr argues that educators have abdicated their responsibilities to train by moral example, that many who ostensibly maintain a focus on morality err by reducing it to 'information,' trivializing course content:

> The purpose of practical wisdom in moral matters is less that of establishing what is the morally right thing to do and more that of determining the appropriate form which moral conduct should take for the effective achievement of right moral ends. [...] Moral education and moral understanding *are not appropriately construed on the model of imparting and acquiring information*, but rather more on the model of seeing the point of, valuing and being favourably disposed towards certain forms of positive conduct on behalf of oneself and others.
>
> (Carr, 1991, pp. 253–54, 259)

The challenge enunciated by Carr is not to be met with quantitative analyses or plans which aim to maximize the flow of information. Such plans typically fail to visualize knowledge and yield to the temptation to avoid the moral life, to isolate oneself from its difficulties:

[I]t is not always possible in this hard world to satisfy simultaneously what is required of us by all the virtues – either because of the wickedness of others or because through our own weaknesses we paint ourselves into moral corners. [...] It is anything but the case, then, that aspiring to a virtuous life is the end of moral problems – on the contrary, there is a real enough sense in which acquiring the virtues to any degree or coming to appreciate what they mean in human life *introduces* a range of problems which creatures untroubled by reflection on questions of moral principle could not possibly have – but clearly such an aspiration must nevertheless form the basis of the proper way to proceed for all who wish to create and to contribute to a civilised and decent human society.

(Carr 1991, p. 267)

Carr dedicates his book to "certain conceptual problems or confusions about the nature and purpose of moral education, rather than to considerations about, say, how moral teaching in schools ought to be practically conducted" (Carr, 1991, p. 268).

Carr's use of Kant to support his position is refreshing and reinforces a point made by von Glasersfeld: "Kant's 'transcendental philosophy' (in contrast to the 'transcendent' or mystical), is a purely rational analysis of human understanding and provides a model that is in many ways fundamental to the constructivist orientation" (von Glasersfeld, 1995, p. 38).[11] To reaffirm Kant's importance in our discussion is not to assume the so-called neo-Kantianism, but to update that philosopher's view of cognition in the wake of the scientific discoveries such as quantum physics of the 20th century. For Kant,

the notion of substance expresses that to which all predicates are attributed. Kant held that this category, *substantia et accidens*, characterized the nature of the object of cognition. This was an assumption in physics until Kant's day and it was even inherent in classical logic. Physically, a thing's characteristics define it as a reality. Logically, characteristics are predicated of the logical subject that names the substance or thing under consideration. Reality is the sum total of these determinations of things.

(Krois, 1987, p. 115)

Cassirer's response to the Kantian predicates is to not renounce the notion of substance but to conceive of that

fundamentum as illustrated in the historical character of science: "No particular astronomical system, the Copernican no more than the Ptolemaic [...] may be taken as an expression of the 'true' cosmic order, but only the whole of these systems as they continuously unfold in accordance with a certain context".

(Krois, 1987, p. 122)[12]

Cassirer is mindful of the fact that the steady advance of the sciences and the emergence of new paradigms can never be allowed to displace the need for a certain modesty on the part of the scientific educator, whose job remains in part that of 'educating the virtues.' I will conclude this section with three brief discussions of exemplary scholars who have reminded us of this compelling need, which is coextensive with the need to not view the sciences in a hierarchy or exaggerate the authority of the scientific method.

As stipulated in our Introduction, it is not our intention in this study to enter into the discussions of professional educationalists about such 'external' matters as resource allocation, corporatization or the political relations of universities with the state; we have focused rather on the intensive nature of learning as well as the intellectual organization of the academy. Nevertheless, when discussing the specifically ethical character of a perceived crisis in academia, I have found it desirable to cite here three volumes that have much to tell us about the nexus of science and ethics in today's academy: *The Imperative of Responsibility: In Search of an Ethics for the Technological Age* by Hans Jonas; *The Politics of Inquiry* by Benjamin Baez and Deron Boyles; and *Biology as Ideology* by R. C. Lewontin.

In his 1989 *summa* Hans Jonas makes the case for restoring the centrality of ethics to the life of the university at a time when technology has overtaken the spirit of academia. Jonas advances "a theory of responsibility as a correlate of power"; and he maintains that "a heuristics of fear" is essential if students are to be aware of the perils of the future, notably the prospect of ecological catastrophe; he makes the point that "secular reason must base the normative concept of man on a cogent [...] doctrine of general being," in line with which metaphysics must underpin a philosophy of nature, recognizing that to do so, one "must brave the veto of the reigning analytical theory" (Jonas, 1984, p. x). With respect to our discussion in this chapter of the need to update our understanding of scientific method, Jonas provides a precious reminder of science's limitations: "For natural science it is enough that in the *measureable* regions the quantitative-deterministic accounting always tallies, that is, that its equations each time stand the test of event and its method is rebuffed by none" (Jonas, 1984, p. 72). Recalling the Whiteheadian distinction between speaking about nature 'homogeneously' or 'heterogeneously,' Jonas's remarks speak to the need to see the results of science as existing in time and subject to the conditions of a specific experimental-empirical situation or context: "[S]cience itself, as an occurrence within the universe which it undertakes to explain, is forever excluded from what *it* can explain. Its own existence is indeed its own best corrective" (Jonas, 1984, p. 72). These are the limitations that empower the scientist with ethical responsibility; conversely the lack of recognition or adherence to these limitations enfeebles science – including the purported science of education.

In *The Politics of Inquiry*, Benjamin Baez and Deron Boyles critique the 2002 report, *Scientific Research in Education* (SRE), commissioned by the U. S. National Research Council (NRC). The effect of the report was to reduce educationalism to a science measureable by quantitative assessment; based on such assessments, educators would make recommendations about how to allocate resources for the sciences in the future. To their credit, Baez and Boyles extend their sociological approach into the areas of philosophy and epistemology. This was necessitated, if by nothing else, by the exploitive use of the writings of John Dewey by the NRC, which cited Dewey in support of their position that a science of education exists and requires certain rules of practice. But, as Baez and Boyles remind us, citing Dewey, "[S]cientific research cannot yield 'rules of practice.' Its value is indirect; it consists in the provision of 'intellectual instrumentalities' to be used *by the educator*" (Baez and Boyles, 2009, p. 67).[13] Dewey opposed the 'spectator theory of knowledge' that the NRC perpetuates, the view that the knower is a passive party to knowledge and does not alter the nature of the known. Dewey, of course, espoused the opposite view, that the knower is dynamic, an active agent in the scene of learning and has an impact on how the data is collected and the knowledge is represented. For Baez and Boyles, the widespread adoption of the scientism of the SRE would skew the science of the future, valuing one science over another. The authors choose not to enter into a debate on the merits of the SRE, since that would draw them into the argument under the erroneous terms set forth by the report in the first place. Rather, their intent is to show the effects and consequences of the policies that followed upon the publication and dissemination of the SRE: "The argument that science is concerned solely with investigating 'observable' phenomena is what makes this report scientistic and positivistic..." (Baez and Boyles, 2009, p. 38).

Esteemed geneticist R. C. Lewontin has provided a compelling case against the determinism that persists in certain quarters of the scientific community. Lewontin explores the current ideology of science, for which science itself would be the authoritative guide for the construction of a just and egalitarian society; he reveals the cracks in this edifice by comparing it to earlier dominant ideologies. Biological determinism is just one example of how a flawed understanding of cause and effect can lead to the legitimation of a thought regime that blocks the development of a positive ethics of science. In his Massey Lectures, *Biology as Ideology: The Doctrine of DNA*, Lewontin takes aim at a number of false assumptions about genetics that have proliferated since the discovery of

DNA. He extends his critique to administrators and political persons who base funding decisions on the errors of reasoning of such biological determinists as E. O. Wilson, the well-known sociobiologist. Lewontin reminds one of Jonas in his sounding of a cautionary note. If in Jonas's case it is the heuristic fear concerning the perils of the future that should be instilled in students and educators, for Lewontin it is the monition to not confuse correlation or agency with causation. Lewontin delivers the sort of internal/external perspective on scientific theory that is needed by laypeople: He exposes the 'internal' nature of the scientific logic concerning genetic and evolutionary theory, a logic that can only be situated in time, in specific experimental settings and contexts; and the 'external' nature of determinations and conclusions drawn about the scientific work, and what their consequences should be for the larger society. Since, as stated, it is not our intent to delve into the political and policy areas, we include this argument in a philosophical spirit, in harmony with Dewey's defense of democracy as a process, a process at the center of the educational mission.

The Rights of Others

Since the 1960s such business practices as Human-Capital Theory have made inroads into the academy, impacting how scholars are employed, evaluated and remunerated. One has seen the widespread practice of downsizing and outsourcing, as in other commercial sectors. But unlike those sectors, in education one cannot assume that the results of a quantitative enforcement of scarcity will be only quantitative in nature. Rather the consequences of such measures, which have further fostered the myth of specialization within the academic community, are arguably deleterious in a qualitative sense. By enforcing an ideology of efficiency the neoliberal state has led the academy into an ethical crisis, based in part on its instrumentalist approach to education.

This situation was described by Lyotard in his 1984 study of the impact of new technologies on the sciences, *The Postmodern Condition: A Report on Knowledge Report*. This sociological study commissioned by the Conseil des universités du Québec considers the status of knowledge in the Western postindustrial economy and its tertiary institutions of learning. For Lyotard the academic institutions have fallen under the ethos of performativity and technological efficiency and have lost track of the "grand narratives of speculation and emancipation" (Lyotard, 1984, p. 38). When Lyotard uses the term 'grand narratives' he is speaking technically to refer to Western society's historical vision of national goals and the traditional division of the university into academic disciplines. With the lapsing of these narratives or goals, one finds oneself in the 'postmodern condition,' the scenario of a university given over to the mercantilized and bureaucratized regime of pure efficiency and performativity. In the section of the *Report* that touches directly on our topic, 'Education and its Legitimation through Performativity,' Lyotard predicts the emergence and domination by those disciplines we now refer to as STEM, stressing that universities will be called on to be 'functional' in the creation of 'skills' (rather than 'ideals'); and that the former goal of democracy and social progress will be replaced by technical training in marketable services in a university subordinated to the powers of the state.

Lyotard remains detached from the postmodern condition he describes. What is legitimate in the postmodern milieu, he observes, continues to depend on what is true and what is just, and these determinations depend on the consent of the knowing subject. There is an implicit humanistic question underlying the entire *Report*: Who has acceded to the postmodern condition and who has not? What choices are there for those who would resist the bureaucratic forces instrumentalizing the commercial-informational development of society in the postindustrial period?

> Knowledge is no longer the subject, but in the service of the subject: its only legitimacy (though it is formidable) is the fact that it allows morality to become reality. This introduces a relation of knowledge to society and the State which is in principle a relation of the means to the end. But scientists must cooperate only if they judge the politics of the State, in other words the sum of its prescriptions, is just.
>
> (Lyotard, 1984, p. 36)

If for Lyotard the university has become a corporatized, bloodless institution, those who wish to resist the system can do so by assuming a pedagogical attitude that is 'sublime'; but this is precarious and can amount to little more than an individualistic escape.[14] In contrast to the sublime – the aesthetic of the unrepresentable – the beautiful invites one into a discussion of ethical fairness in the academy. In his writings and seminars on Kant, Lyotard asks how the aesthetic judgment explored in the *Critique of Judgment* impacts the civic community and the phenomenon of justice; he concludes – and here we speak in the most general of terms – that a subject's feelings of pleasure due to the experience of the beautiful contribute to a healthy, just society. His positions on these matters have much to offer to anyone who is concerned about teaching on matters of fairness and justice in society.

In commenting on Lyotard's pedagogy, Gordon Bearn points to the perceived need to affirm beauty over and against the sublime; if the 'University of Beauty' is to emerge, it will be due to the cultivation of 'intensities' and to a certain passionate unruliness among colleagues. Bearn emphasizes the centrality of the imagination to Lyotard's vision, also for students in the hard sciences, social sciences, vocational technologies, accounting and business.[15] In a not dissimilar fashion, Bill Readings has characterized Lyotard's pedagogical thinking as decentered, pragmatic and focused on an ethical practice that places into relief the 'Other':

> That is the lesson of Lyotard's pedagogy. There is some Other in the classroom, and it has many names: culture, thought, desire, energy, tradition, the event, the immemorial, the sublime. The educational institution seeks to process it, to dampen the shock it gives the system. *Qua* institution, education seeks to channel and circulate this otherness so that some form of profit can be made from it.
>
> (Readings, 1995, p. 198)[16]

In a 1996 lecture at my university entitled 'The Other's Rights,' Lyotard asserted that human beings as a species lack certain instincts for which they compensate by 'interlocution.'[17] By exploiting their conversational and dialogic gifts, humans develop civic discourse and succeed in 'interiorizing the Other.' When humans fail to exploit their innate dialogic gifts, they revert to animal-like, instinctive communication, the demotic, which 'seeks to keep the Other out.' It is only by means of the civic tendency that one is able to interiorize the Other, while the demotic tendency actually keeps the Other out: "The discontent from which contemporary societies are suffering, the postmodern affliction, is this foreclosure of the Other" (Lyotard, 1993b, p. 146). In the civic discourse one sees the critical role of recursiveness and constructibility in human language as it is manifest in reciprocity of speech, the parity of interlocutors and the characteristic of justice itself. But civic discourse is not a given, since people veer towards historical heritage, national identity and relations to language which exclude alterity.

As seen in our discussion of Ricoeur, the deontological code concerns rules that belong to a particular concept of the self as the *idem*, an identity fixed in one's unchanging nature over time, in contrast to which the ethical presupposes an understanding of the self as *ipse*, an identity located in that true selfhood, which is always developing. This is the same matter addressed by Lyotard in 'The Other's Rights.' To recognize the other in oneself is critical if one is to maintain one's humanity; human rights depend on a people's ability through interlocution and dialogue to exceed the natural level of the nation and the *demos* and attain to the civic order of *politeia*, the republic and the city. Dialogue and interlocution are not realized spontaneously by human populations; rather a learning process is required if one is to interiorize the Other and eschew demotic discourse, which employs the rule-bound goal of consensus as a substitute for civil discourse. A key role in this process is played by the Master, meaning the educator who is genuinely capable of assuming the figure of the Other. But the Master is resisted by those in power who tend to employ rules without ethics in order to dominate the intellectual and political systems.

The goal of the beautiful is salient in Lyotard's final book, *The Confession of Augustine*, as he speaks with hope of recuperating the Pauline and Augustine tradition. Here Lyotard focuses on the foundational importance of the 'event,' that is of a profoundly diachronic phenomenon, in contrast to the synchronic phenomenologies of Being that gave rise to postmodernism.[18] Lyotard's working definition for the event – reminiscent of Whitehead's 'actual occasion' – is at once philosophical and practical, being focused on the simple act of communication:

> I would like to call an event the face to face with nothingness. This sounds like death. Things are not so simple. There are many events whose occurrence doesn't offer any matter to be confronted, many happenings inside of which nothingness remains hidden and imperceptible, events without barricades. They come to us concealed under the appearance of everyday occurrences. To become sensitive to their quality as actual events, to become competent in listening to their sound underneath silence or noise, to become open to the "It happens that" rather than to the "What happens," requires at the very least a high degree of refinement in the perception of small differences.
>
> (Lyotard, 2000, pp. 17–18)

By focusing on this notion of event with reference to perception and becoming, Lyotard was also discussing educational process.[19] As he saw it, this process of anticipation and willingness to dwell with imperfect predicates as they evolve in the classroom can be compared to the process of translation:

> Communication is a question of translation [...]. One can be translated, one can translate himself or herself. In any case, translation is the transference from one idiom, be it national or personal, to another. This "conveyance" implies many problems on all the "levels" of language: from the phonetic and literal to the most subtly connotative. At bottom, the definition of a language is that it can be translated into another. So that it is irrelevant, I think, to worry about communication, as if its lack were the stumbling block to the existence of human communities.
>
> (Lyotard, 1988, p. 43)

Lyotard opposed the idea of educational performativity as a purely ends-oriented orientation that ignores the full range of the event. It is the comprehension and contemplation of the nature of that fact that distinguishes human beings from other animals. That is what makes narrative communication so decisive, as it connects facts and deeds to hypotheses and relations. Since no narrative is intrinsically superior to any other, one can imagine the cognitive role of diverse narratives self-organizing into networks sustained by mutually corroborating facts, all expressed in a common language. Yet there is resistance to narrative pedagogies in the academy, as they are deemed to be unscientific, intuitive and unsystematic.

In this chapter, I have documented certain problems in today's university. By relating those problems to an ethics, as enunciated in the work of Cassirer, Ricoeur, von Foerster, von Glasersfeld, Carr and Lyotard, I have suggested the insufficiency of merely technical responses to problems involving students and faculty in their creative and intellectual communities. I have argued against the confusion of information for knowledge, and against the saturation of the academic environment with data; in like manner, I have clarified the superiority of ethics to a deontological set of rules. If in this chapter I have sought to connect the technical and ethical reasons for rehumanizing the academy, in Chapter 7, I continue the discussion on the epistemological side of that argument, which also includes a defense of metaphysics as a science of change.

Notes

1 Heller, 2004, p. 37, discusses the impact of the HOPE scholarship and others like it:

> The effect of these merit-aid programs on college access differs substantially from that of need-based grant programs. Merit grants go disproportionately to students who would have attended college even without the public assistance, while need-based programs help those who the research tells us require assistance to enroll in college.

2 See Badiou, 2002, p. 30:

> The reign of ethics is one symptom of a universe ruled by a distinctive combination of resignation in the face of necessity together with a purely negative, if not destructive, will. It is this combination that should be designated as nihilism.

3 It was precisely this possibility that I addressed in Chapter 2 where I posited the benefits to be derived from the formation of faculty heterarchies.

4 See also Rosenzweig, 1998, p. 186:

> [Multidisciplinary] programs can be both engaging of student interests and rigorous, two major requirements for a successful educational experience. The proliferation of such programs, a likely eventuality, hardly foreshadows the death of the liberal arts. If there is further weakening of those fields, especially the humanities, it will occur from within, not from without. It will be the result of the failure of humanists to find a compelling contemporary setting for their work. That is a battle that will be won or lost by the practitioners themselves.

5 Arum and Roksa, 2011, provide a chilling picture of the larger reality that allows this imbalance between teaching and research priorities to persist. Addressing "the limited learning that exists on U. S. campuses" they analyze how for none of the players in the system – teachers, administrators, students,

graduate students – learning is the major priority: "Limited learning on college campuses is not a crisis because the institutional actors implicated in the system are receiving the organizational outcomes that they seek..." (p. 125).

6 See Whitehead, 1929a, p. 55.

7 Recognition of the student's importance in recent years has led in some areas to the development of "student-centered" pedagogy, which stimulates students to shape the course content and give structure to daily lessons. While it is obvious that students must be actively involved in their learning and motivated to assume responsibility for it, when the student-centered method becomes an end in itself the result is an excessive lassitude bolstered by the indefensible suppositions that a talking student is a thinking student or, conversely, that a silent student is a passive student.

8 Fowles also writes, 1964, p. 177:

> Our present educational systems are all paramilitary. Their aim is to produce servants or soldiers who obey without question and who accept their training as the best possible training. Those who are most successful in a state are those who have most interest in prolonging the state as it is; they are also those who have most to say in the educational system, and in particular by ensuring that the educational product they want is the most highly rewarded.

9 As Ricoeur writes, 1992, p. 251:

> A genuinely conflictual situation appears when, digging under the pure rule of procedure, one unearths the diversity among the goods that are distributed which the formulation of the two principles of justice tends to obliterate. As I have said, the diversity of the things to be shared disappears in the procedure of distribution.

10 As seen above, Heinz von Foerster has written similarly of how the validity of an institution's ethics depends on how successfully its members can simultaneously interact with themselves, with others and with the larger environment.

11 Regarding Kant's "practical imperative" ("Act always in such a way that the humanity, in your own as well as in other persons, is treated as end and not just as means"), von Glasersfeld adds, 1995, p. 38:

> Thinking beings [...] are ends in themselves and no other purpose must be substituted for this. Strictly speaking, this is not an "ethical" precept but a prerequisite of ethics. It simply asserts that we have to consider other people's humanity and that we ought not to treat them as objects.

12 Krois is citing Cassirer, *Philosophy of Symbolic Forms*, v. 3. p. 476.

13 Baez and Boyles are citing Dewey, *Sources of a Science of Education*, p. 28.

14 See Lyotard, 1988, p. 44:

> The split between the faculties inscribed in the esthetics of the sublime is the sign of a complication or complexity in sensibility. It is the same with modern and contemporary arts. They require an infinite number of commentaries, each of which has to be taken in turn as a work of art, that is, has to be felt and commented on. The network formed by all these phrases, for which no common code exists, becomes more fragile in proportion to its increasing complexity. It seems to me that the only consensus we ought to be worrying about is one that would encourage this heterogeneity or 'dissensus.'

15 For Bearn, 2000. p. 253, learning occurs due to the passion of teachers and the resultant rhythm of their instruction, "not by efficiency, not by the sublime, but by intensity, intensities of compression and connection": "compression" is the contraction of duration while "connection" is its extension, in the classroom and the learning process generally. And Ibid., p. 254:

> In a University of Beauty, teaching would not be smooth and efficient but rough and rhythmic, inspired both by rhythm's active character to connect otherwise disparate sites of intellectual activity, and by rhythm's passive character to find more and more stimulation from the energy compressed into a single site. [...] Being a person well trained to deliver information as efficiently as possible has almost nothing to do with being a good teacher.

16 As Readings notes, 1996, p. 156, Lyotard singles out three specific "pitfalls" that debilitate the current academy: "the hierarchy that makes the professor an absolute authority and the students so many receptacles..."; "the claim that teaching raises no difference between teachers and students, the demagoguery that suggests there is nothing to learn"; and "the reduction of education to the development and training of technocrats."

17 J. Lyotard, 1993b, pp. 135–48.

18 As Ong has written, 1999, v. 3, p. 156, there is a need for a diachronic phenomenology if we are to be able to understand "the actual history of writing, its growth out of orality."

19 As Pradeep Dhillon notes, 2000, p. 111: "Lyotard's emphasis on the analytic of narrativity persuades us to look again at justice in relation to liberal education."

Deep Structures and Narrative

The university years are for exploration, generalization and the satisfaction of the whole person. The predicates arrived at in this process require for their articulation a median language able to integrate heterogeneous forms of discourse. Educators who cultivate such a language tend to go beyond the immediate content of course materials and beyond the statutory expectations of employers. As John Fowles writes, "What the state or the system considers a good teacher and what is a good teacher are always two different things. A good teacher never teaches only his subject" (Fowles, 1964, p. 148). A gap exists, in other words, between the restricted semantic field of a discipline and the broader usefulness of knowledge as a dynamic predicate in society. It is by accentuating this fact that the educator can lead students to a holistic awareness of their place in the larger community.

While it is true that the operational languages of separate disciplines may have little in common, that realization leads to another form of knowledge that educators can share. As C. A. Bowers writes:

> [Students are] dependent on the teacher's ability to provide a comparative basis for recognizing the root metaphors – or paradigms for representing the deepest levels of the culture's epistemological framework – that frame and give conceptual coherence to the patterns of social life. If the teacher is unaware of the deep levels of the symbolic ecology, such as the assumptions that underlie our view about the nature of work, technology, and individualism, the socialization process may leave students with the ability to manipulate facts and data but not to understand that they are doing it in accordance with archetypal patterns dictated by the culture encoded in the language they have acquired.
>
> (Bowers, 1993, p. 120)

If educators are to awaken students to "the deep levels of symbolic ecology," they will situate their disciplines within a broader integrative epistemology and adopt a pedagogic practice that is more imaginative than the one required of them by "the state or the system." In so doing they are being true to the understanding of pedagogy as an adventure that begins in childhood: "The voyage of children, that is the naked meaning of the Greek word *pedagogy*. Learning launches wandering" (Serres, 1997, p. 8). In that spirit I consider in this chapter the deep structures of knowledge and the usefulness of narrative as a means to gain access to them. Such deep structures or complex gestalts are typically resistant to quantitative measurement.

For the scholar most closely identified with 'deep structure,' Noam Chomsky, the term has a precise scientific meaning: "In the Standard Theory [deep structure] is generated by the base, receives the lexical items and undergoes semantic interpretation, and, finally, is converted to well-formed surface structure" (Chomsky, 1998, p. 170). In formulating his theory of generative grammar, Chomsky devised a system and terminology capable of including the unconscious biological features of human development and language use. Since its inception, 'deep structure' has been appropriated by other scholars and its usage has expanded. Chomsky consents to the broader use of the term as long as the adaptations are conducted with high standards of scientific pertinency and consistency. It is in this spirit that I use the term, faithful to the original idea of a transfer between linguistic levels along a paradigmatic axis, but also as a model for the presence of such structures in other fields.[1]

An important adaptation of deep structure is found in Greimas and Courtés, who add to Chomsky's linguistic analysis a discussion of subjects and predicates within narratives. These elements are seen to exist at a deep level in a general form that awaits its articulation on the surface, in discourse: "Narrativity therefore has gradually appeared as the very organizing principle of all discourse, whether narrative [...] or non-narrative" (Greimas and Courtés, 1982, p. 209). On the surface level of what is spoken among a referent group, the 'predicate' is seen as a complex phenomenon involving an utterance and an enunciation. As a surface structure, it points to the depth semantics that inheres to positive communication:

> These two types of structures are metalinguistic constructions ("deep" and "surface" are two spatial metaphors, relating to the axis of verticality). The one serves to designate the position of departure, the other the point of arrival of a string of transformations. [...] In semiotics the use of this dichotomy is necessarily set in the general theory of the generation of signification. [...] The notion of depth being relative, each domain of the generation of discourse refers back to a "deeper" domain and so on until the deep structure par excellence, which is the elementary structure of signification, is reached.
> (Greimas and Courtés, 1982, pp. 69–70)[2]

Greimas and Courtés note how perilous it can be to negotiate the terrain between linguistics and philosophy, fields whose self-definitions extend between the poles of empirical-technical data (linguistics) and conceptual isotopic metaphors (philosophy). But such a negotiation is precisely the task that Greimas in particular undertakes, as a communication theorist and structural linguist. His lasting impact on the social sciences is due to his having applied a linguistic model to a broad range of disciplines including discourse studies, narratology, literary criticism and educational science.[3] His deep structures establish homologies with the general pedagogical situation, which is created jointly by the particular subject under study, the historical context and the scholar-educator who arranges and responds to the subject.

Jerome S. Bruner advocates the inclusion of the deep structures of narrative and myth in the classroom. He stipulates in his 1965 *Toward a Theory of Instruction* that there are two natural modes of thought: the paradigmatic – logico-scientific thinking that rests on description, explanation and verification – and the narrative, which weaves events together:

> A narrative, or at least a corpus of narratives, may be what philosophy used to be. It may reflect what is believed about the celestial bodies and their relation to man; it may tell how man came into being, how social life was founded, what is believed about death and about life after death; it may codify law and morals [...]. In studying symbolic systems, we want the students to understand myths rather than to learn them.
>
> (Bruner, 1966, p. 89)

Bruner opposes traditional 'theories of stimulus-response conditioning,' as being valuable only for enactive representation. Psychologists who persist in these theories are seen to infantalize subjects. Gestalt theory rather permits the best system for the analysis of the iconic mode, while rational behavior enters the picture when there is internalization of symbolic techniques. With such a theory in mind Bruner proposes a social studies course – 'Man: A Course of Study' – to be organized around four criteria: 'contrast,' "stimulation and use of informed guessing, hypothesis making," "participation – particularly by the use of games that incorporate the formal properties of the phenomena for which the game is an analogue" and "stimulating self-consciousness" (Bruner, 1966, pp. 92–93). To educate to contrast is to train students to recognize what is so obvious as to be overlooked; this relates to questions of cultural differences and thus to conditioning, insularity and ethnocentrism. To teach hypothesis making is also a means to access deep structures insofar as students learn that by forming a theory they are giving a plausible explanation to an as yet unexplained event. Similarly, ludic activity and analogical thinking involve students actively in the learning process. Lastly, by acknowledging the role of the unconscious in learning, students and teachers grow more adept at conceptualizing problems and acquire the necessary research skills to solve them: "The most urgent need of all is to give our pupils the experience of what it is to use a theoretical model, with some sense of what is involved in being aware that one is trying out a theory" (Bruner, 1966, p. 96).

The act of putting theory in the hands of students is a necessary means of processing data and facts and recoding them into generalizable principles and laws. Bruner invites students to generate narratives and other hypothetical explanations of phenomena in order to better understand their humanity and oneness with nature. He uses the term *translation* to refer to the process by which one brings to light the previously unknown parts of one's intellectual itinerary:

> The heart of the educational process consists of providing aids and dialogues for translating experience into more powerful systems of notation and ordering. And it is for this reason that I think a theory of development must be linked both to a theory of knowledge and to a theory of instruction, or be doomed to triviality.
>
> (Bruner, 1966, p. 21)

As with Greimas and Courtés, Bruner's pedagogy mediates horizontally between diverse fields while on the vertical axis of language and expression it advocates a fluid movement between the depths and the surface.

If we may now turn our attention to philology, we will witness another utilizable form of deep structure. As argued by philologist Paul Zumthor, the historical-literary events of the Middle Ages are best perceived in terms of "deep structures that emerge within a circumscribed event [and] become delimited by approximation, in successive and theoretically distinct approaches" (Zumthor, 1986, p. 84). In contrast to those medievalists who fail to negotiate deep structures in their inherent complexity, Zumthor proposes a pluralistic study of texts that denies premature closure to interpretation and allows for multiple hypotheses about the multiple discourses present in the text. Only in such a way, he argues, can one evince the rich internal ambiguities, duplicity and contradictoriness of the medieval text. It is Zumthor's view that the problems that arose with the romantic heritage of medievalism were carried over into the tradition of logical positivism and continued well into the 20th century. Regarding the generation of his professors, Zumthor states, "they attached themselves to contingent criteria, posed as absolutes: unity, organicity and others" (Zumthor, 1986, p. 46). Working with a scientist bias, they objectivized philology and assumed that *facts* were all that existed of relevance to the historical text. These included the assumption that a text possessed an original source, a definitive order and the quality of intransitivity. By restricting their field in this way, the medievalists failed to access its deep structures or to enter into the medieval cosmos and its codes, its historicity and its imaginary, including its duplicities. They "[refused] what was ambiguous, plural, or implied" and "condemned as garbled any opacity in discourse"; as a result of these and similar errors, the scholars manifested the

> prejudice according to which "cultural" history, moving either backward or forward in time, was clarified on the basis of a central epistemic moment, identified with "classicism" (from Descartes to the Encyclopedists) in relation to which any opposition could be defined.
>
> (Zumthor, 1986, 49–50)

Classicism has not helped readers grasp the "deep biological and psychic roots" (Zumthor, 1986, p. 11) of the Middle Ages; instead it has anachronistically applied the criteria of modernity to medieval texts.

Perhaps the most significant emergence of deep structures in the sciences over the last generation has been the deep ecology movement. Here too the precedent of Gestalt theory has provided an important foundation. One of the original expounders of deep ecology, Arne Naess, relates the revolution in global consciousness to the emergence of an ecological self. The deepness of deep ecology stands in contrast to 'shallow' ecology, which opposes environmental degradation for the sake of optimizing the quality of human life and the human standard of living; in contrast, deep ecology concerns the interconnectivity of all life and the need for radical sacrifices by humans if the biosphere is to prosper. Naess studied with the Vienna Circle, and shares many of the assumptions of von Foerster and von Glasersfeld. As a complex thinker he demonstrates a Whiteheadian investment in facts and concretions, and the "stream-and-process character of gestalt experience" (Naess, 2008, p. 194). For too long, the Norwegian philosopher argues, educators have constructed a false dichotomy between the egoistic self and the altruistic self (of morality and self-sacrifice), ignoring the deeper ecological self which works in its own self-interest *and* for the good of the natural community.

A founding premise of deep ecology is that the diversity and complexity of life-forms is a virtue. In writing (with George Sessions) the eight tenets of the 'deep ecology platform,' Naess was careful to not be constrained by the diversity of religious and philosophical orientations of the adherents to deep ecology; in fact, the variety of points of view is deemed a healthy characteristic of the movement, as it wards off the danger of ideology. In keeping with his conviction that one needn't be a disciple of a particular thinker to employ his ideas, Naess finds Kant's explication of the 'inclination' toward the beautiful act to be a valuable tool for promoting deep ecology, given that the person who carries out a beautiful act is following something greater than a sense of moral duty: "The beautiful act is, in Kant's view, a morally complete act because it is benevolent. Benevolent action expands our love to embrace the whole of life. It completes us and perfects us" (Naess, 2008, p. 134).[4] How this idea can be applied in context is seen in Naess's critique of a graduate seminar that has lost its contact with the natural world:

> Even when life-forms are studied at this educational level, the style in which they are taught is from the viewpoint of an observer, not a participant. Field trips are rarely made in silence such that students can hear clearly what trees or tiny animals and plants are telling them. The focus on interaction with fellow students is permitted to go on as if they were alone and not living with a myriad of beings. Nor are students taught to express what they *really* experience and what gestalts they participate in, leaving subject-object relations out. They may obtain their doctorates without ever *sensing* what they are talking about, and if they have gained cognition (not only knowledge) of the third kind (according to Spinoza), they are not stimulated to consider how to *inspire* others, how to *lead* them with few words to acquire the third kind, the understanding love and loving understanding (*intellectualis* amor = *amor* intellectualis).
>
> (Naess, 2008, p. 138)

It is Naess's conviction that we vastly underestimate ourselves and our students. Naess's admiration for the skills of the common man translate into the educational precept, "Learn what engages your feeling." Coextensive with this tenet is an elevation of spontaneity and personal feelings and, conversely, a distrust for the prefabricated modes of mass communication: "What we feel about something belongs to the qualities of the world as we know it. What does not have such qualities is abstract structure" (Naess, 2008, p. 71). In a manner reminiscent of Whitehead's stages of education – which succeed each other as students mature but do not erase each other – Naess discusses the critical importance of 'unlearning.' Optimally, as one replaces an earlier knowledge with a new one, one preserves the positive values associated with the earlier knowledge. The example Naess provides is "the mythopoetical imagination" (Naess, 2002, p. 145), so grand in the mind of the child yet so often diminished in the adult.[5] The above thinkers refer to deep structures as useful schemata that are not entirely knowable but nevertheless essential to the understanding of their fields. The pedagogy that results from their study is not based on such binaristic divisions as conscious/unconscious, subject/object or nature/mind. Rather those polarities are seen to have biological reasons for being, innate sources in the depths of the human organism. As Chomsky has stated,

Speculating on it a bit, I suspect that within a century, looking back towards the present, one will conclude that the truly central component has been the discovery of a deep level. Higher mental processes show, at this level, a fundamental simplicity, perhaps the result of a relatively sudden and recent biological evolution.

(Chomsky in Piattelli Palmarini, 2008, p. 23)

It is due to such realizations that fields like deep ecology and deep rhetoric have emerged, in which the substance and limits of knowledge are explorable in terms of structural descriptions and narratives. As I demonstrate below, these insights can be compared with profit to the epistemological theories of Vico and Dewey.

Knowledge and Metaphysics in Vico and Dewey

In Vico's *New Science*, one found the argument made that human culture evolves in a manner consistent with the expressions of human speech and the 'poetic logic' of humanity. Hayden White has written in this regard of the 'deep structure' of Vico's masterwork, as located in his philosophy of language. It is here one finds "the connection between metaphysics, the science of things in all the forms of their being, and logic, the science of the forms by which they may be signified" (White, 1987, p. 204). Vico's theory proposed a direct relationship between the various phases of figurative language – especially the historic usage of four master tropes: metaphor, metonymy, synecdoche, irony – and human evolution through the phases of civilization. Specifically, Vico's

> tropological analysis of figurative language [allows] for the construction of a model by which both the stages in the evolution of consciousness can be defined and the transitions from one to another of them can be accounted for in terms of 'the modifications of the human mind.'
>
> (White, 1987, p. 209)

In the Vichian view, by heeding metaphysics the teacher is able to immunize the learner from the excesses of materialism. Thus in his 1732 inaugural oration, 'On the Heroic Mind,' Vico advised students and teachers to seek an integrated view of the disciplines:

> All the while that you are under instruction, concentrate solely on collating everything you learn so that the whole may hang together and all be in accord within any one discipline. For this task your guide will be the very nature of the human mind which rejoices in the highest degree in that which forms a unity, comes together, falls into its proper place.
>
> (Vico, 1976, p. 239)

By perceiving the beauty of the human mind, the student is guided by the sublime. Insofar as metaphysics is the discipline that is concerned with wisdom, the eternal and the sublime, it is seen by Vico to be an essential part of the university curriculum:

> Metaphysics will free the intellect from the prison of the senses; logic will free the reasoning power from false opinions; ethics the will from corrupt desires. Rhetoric exists to ensure that the tongue does not betray nor fail the mind, nor the mind in its theme; poetics to calm the uncontrolled turbulence of the imagination; geometry to hold in check innate errors; physics in truth, to rouse you from the blank amazement with which nature and her marvels has transfixed you.
>
> (Vico, 1976, pp. 235–36)

If, as argued in Chapter 6, the awareness of one's ignorance is of critical importance to learning, Vico's metaphysics prioritizes that awareness, given that for him "the appropriate point for metaphysics is first truth, located not in human cognition but in divine understanding," and that "no one [...] has genuine knowledge of true being" (Miner in Vico, 2010, p. x). What human beings can attain with respect to divine understanding is an awareness of their own ignorance.[6]

According to the *verum = factum* principle explored in Chapter 2 (first presented in *On the Most Ancient Wisdom of the Italians* and further elaborated in *New Science*), human beings can only truly know what they themselves have made. This principle serves as the basis of Vico's refutation of both Cartesian metaphysics, which is rooted in the individual self (which humans did not create), and skepticism, according to which human beings can know nothing of the truth. While clearly this is a vast subject, we may say with specific reference to our topic that Vico's metaphysics lies at the heart of what he saw as the ideal curriculum, which elevated the study of language and poetry, history and religion, and served as a basis for self-knowledge and for the study of the other arts and sciences, as well as moral philosophy, metaphysics and theology. In this curriculum – which contrasted with prevailing curricula, which excluded language and poetry, history and religion, as too inexact, and centered instead on dialectics and the mechanistic sciences – there was a prescribed order to the studies. The order corresponded to the developmental stages of the individual and presupposed an interweaving heterarchy of the disciplines. Such an organic and holistic epistemology was a far cry from the Enlightenment encyclopedia. In the order of the studies, metaphysics was to be come after mathematics and physics: "The human mind will be led from the known facts of mathematics to the doubtful in physics to metaphysics, which seeks out those realities which are true, certain, and thoroughly known" (Vico, 1993, p. 137). One discovers the truths of metaphysics as a limit, as the recognition of a good. By giving an approximate form to this limit, humans recognize their ignorance and acquire humility: "For the clarity of metaphysical truth is identical to the clarity of light, which we do not know except through things that are darkened" (Vico, 2010, p. 53).

The fact that metaphysics is ontologically different from other fields of study doesn't mean it is not useful for arriving at a proper contextualization of knowledge. On the contrary, by being situated at the crossroads of what is known – those things humans have made, including history – and not known, including God or the *numen* – it possesses a dual nature: "Divine things [...] are the human mind and God. Metaphysics studies both in order to contribute to science, while theology studies them in order to contribute to religion" (Vico, 1993, p. 133). Since Vico's metaphysics are based on the divine or the one, about which humans can only have *indirect* knowledge, as a reflected beauty, the study of this field requires ingenuity and intuition, faculties which in turn assist one in making ethical decisions when reason fails and perceptions are dimmed.[7] A prime example of this moral faculty is placed in relief in 'On the Heroic Mind,' where Vico stresses the importance to students of aspiring toward the divine and sublime, a goal that is approximated by the speculative and idealizing functions of myth.

Vico marked a new era in the history of pedagogical philosophy, transdisciplinary thinking and the institutional self-study of the university. He attributed great importance to the relation between language, metaphysics and the civil institutions, and held that it is the ethical role of pedagogy to explore this relation through the study of texts.[8] For Vico, "the discipline of a text is how the immediacy from which it originally derived is translated into permanence and transmitted in and by culture" (Said, 2000, p. 92). In this respect Vico is a kindred spirit to John Dewey who, as we see below, updated metaphysics in order to integrate it with the other arts and sciences, grounding it in experience and the knowledge of texts deemed to be inextricable from the tissue of cultural life and the civil institutions.

American pragmatism led to a rejection of both the 'realist' and 'idealist' theories of knowledge; despite important differences between them, Peirce, James and Dewey all held that knowledge was constructed and that this process benefitted from the rigorous use of inference, intuition and instinct. The realist theory of knowledge saw the learner as passive and dependent on external reality for stimulus and direction, while the idealist theory of knowledge saw the learner as an active former of ideas, as enabled by a detachment from the physical sphere. Dewey rejected both theories, arguing that they depend on the 'ubiquity' of knowledge and presuppose a Cartesian split between the object to be known and the knower, the *res estensa* and the *res cogitans*. What he proposed therefore was a third kind of knowledge, reminiscent of Kant's synthetical *a priori* but also of those theorizations we have mentioned by Ricoeur, Piaget, Serres and Naess.

Dewey countered the realists and idealists with a view of knowledge that presupposed a mediation between the individual, the particular situation of difficulty confronted, and the actions taken to resolve it. Without sacrificing its scientific claims, Dewey's constructivist paradigm sought to engage philosophy as a philosophy *of* something, rather than a purely abstract or self-involved discourse. For Dewey, the 'object' of knowledge is no longer an external thing upon which the knower sets his or her sights; it is the inquiry itself. The pedagogical event was a circuit, a dynamic process of exchange and adaptation to reality. To see learning in this way meant to adopt novel approaches to causality and proof; in particular, it meant returning to the Aristotelian concept of final causation as well as taking a fresh look at the nature of predication. Dewey was fond of the medical analogy whereby the physician, who possesses considerable experience and a repository of scientific learning, needs in every case to apply these tools to a new and unique situation, to confront a specific individual and malady, to form a diagnosis and prognosis based on conditions in flux.[9] The analogy of physician to educator provides insight into Dewey's view of predication, which does not depend on a preestablished 'given,' as Cartesian rationalists would assume: "The 'given,' that is to say the existent, is precisely an undetermined and dominant complex quality" (Boisvert, 1988, p. 187). If in the classical theory, the idea of the 'given' understands predication as a simple attribution, in Dewey's theory subjects and predicates interact with one another, forming associations and symbols; thus "the only thing that is unqualifiedly given is the total pervasive quality" (Boisvert, 1988, p. 189).

Metaphysics, as Dewey states, is concerned with 'ultimate traits,' but these are not fixed and atemporal, abstract truths; they evolve, causing metaphysics itself to change. Our knowledge of "ultimate, that is, irreducible traits" is qualitative, since the traits are themselves "specifically diverse existences, interaction, and change" (Dewey, 1960, p. 215). Among those who assumed that such traits were fixed and atemporal in Dewey's day were the positivist practitioners of the quantitative scientific method, a method which, as Dewey clarifies, "exhibits certain irreducible traits *of* the irreducible traits we have mentioned, but it does not replace them" (Dewey, 1960, p. 216). This elucidation allows Dewey to discuss 'potentiality' as it refers to a characteristic of change. The use of this term presupposes the existence of change and a process of becoming (Dewey, 1960, p. 220) that implies not merely diversity but a progressively increasing diversification of a specific thing in a particular direction. Thus potentiality cannot be reduced to "a causal force immanent within a homogeneous something and leading it to change" (Dewey, 1960, p. 221). Dewey seeks to free metaphysics from the "ultimate origins and ultimate ends – that is, from questions of creation and eschatology"; the old metaphysics – mechanical and atemporal – is rejected as time itself is seen to be one of the "ultimate traits of the world" (Dewey, 1960, p. 223).

In Dewey, therefore, as in Vico, the predicates of education are to be found in qualitative knowledge. In Dewey's theory, which steers clear of abstract idealism and positivistic empiricism, the perceptions of the learner are given high value. The nature of the logical 'given' is reassessed, since all that is truly given in the predication of knowledge is the indeterminate in search of a subject-object unity. Dewey argues for the need to address the problem of qualitative objects, not simply in the fields of metaphysics and epistemology, but in the logics of scientific proof and artistic construction. The barrier to understanding that is customarily erected between these two logics – as documented by C. P. Snow's *The Two Cultures* – is in error, being based on a static view of knowledge. In order to eradicate this barrier to understanding, which leads to the "failure to realize the qualitative and artistic nature of formal scientific construction," one must unmask the conventions it is based on and examine the construction and intrinsic meaning of "symbolic or propositional forms" (Dewey, 1960, p. 187). It is precisely these forms that we are considering in this chapter in terms of deep structure and a third, integrative kind of knowledge.

As Vico showed, metaphysics is concerned both with the divine, which is above and beyond the contingencies of history, and the human mind, which exists within an historical framework and is reflective of the need to address the question of ontological change. In this latter capacity, metaphysics stands in a complementary and dialectical relation to the physical sciences. Dewey's naturalistic metaphysics – as perhaps best articulated in the 1925 *Experience and Nature* – similarly rejects the static quality of classical metaphysics (in both its mechanical and spiritualistic manifestations). If that latter metaphysics tended to relegate experience to the status of accidents or contingencies, Dewey posits a metaphysics of the event and of human activity as part of nature by elevating the constitutive value of experience and of history. This metaphysics, like that of Vico, had a practical and useful place within the university curriculum, where it stood to symbolize, at one and the same time, the unity and the heterarchy of knowledge.

Teaching Discovery and Change

The foundations of knowledge today are not the cherished ideas of fifty or a hundred years ago, of quantitative science, positivism and historicism. In the wake of the cybernetic revolution and parallel developments in the other sciences, one has seen the dominant paradigm in scientific thinking shift from the paradigm of 'chance and necessity' (to recall the title of Jacques Monod's classic work *Chance & Necessity: An Essay on the Natural Philosophy of Modern Biology*) to the paradigm of possibilities and constraints, and a complexity-based view of knowledge. If in Monod's view of evolution, life was a most rare and highly improbable event in a world whose "predetermined tendency [is] towards cosmic degradation," in that of Prigogine and Stengers in *Order out of Chaos: Man's New Dialogue with Nature* (1984), life is a relatively frequent phenomenon, as "necessity and regularity are themselves the product of a natural history" (Ceruti and Bocchi, 2002, p. 239).

In terms of scientific methodologies and problem-solving, one might say that classical science, up to and including the 'chance versus necessity' paradigm, considered intuition and subjectivity as being in conflict with the assumption of an Archimedean observation point from which to view objective reality, or the invariant. In the latter 20th century this view was fundamentally altered as the scientific method began to allow for a greater range of possible 'givens' and 'outcomes' than previously. Today that method also welcomes into its purview phenomena that are "*singular*, unrepeatable and contingent (all of which were considered subordinate, residual aspects of the categorial grammar of a fundamental observation point)" (Ceruti, 1994, p. 112). Today's student thus learns to consider all experimental definitions as relative to a particular context.[10]

As just seen in the section 'Knowledge and Metaphysics in Vico and Dewey,' metaphysics has been transformed in the modern era by the process of change that was historically intrinsic to its enduring value. The change was foreseen by Dewey, for whom the intellectual inquiry constituted a circuit belonging no more nor less to the researcher than to the material of the research. A similar insight was to alter the paradigm of classical science, which had assumed a standard of certitude and predictability. After Heisenberg and Gödel, Schrödinger and Prigogine, science recognized uncertainty and unpredictability as part of its working model. As Ceruti has written:

> The science of the end of the 20th century cannot be anything but a science of the general *and* the particular, of the repeatable *and* of the unrepeatable, of invariances *and* of change. [...] The developments of the evolutionary sciences until very recently followed the conception of science indicated by the epistemology elaborated by Pierre Simon de Laplace at the beginning of the 19th century, an epistemology of the science of natural phenomena which was reversible *par excellence* (and therefore not evolutionary), or in other words, classical physics.
>
> (Ceruti, 1994, pp. 112–13)

Heinz von Foerster has written of Ceruti's 'epistemology for a new science' as follows:

> While in the orthodox perception and discussion of this notion, we, the human beings who do the perceiving and the discussion, are eliminated by invoking causation either in its fuzzy form of

"chance" or from its straight form of "necessity," Ceruti re-instates our responsibility into the new architecture of science by founding it not on chance and necessity but on constraints and possibilities.

(von Foerster, in Ceruti, 1994, p. xi)

Similar insights can be gathered today from cognitive science, which speaks of the psyche in terms compatible with cybernetics and the theories of thermodynamics. Varela's theory of autopoiesis is a form of deep structure:

The principle activity of brains [...] is to make continuous self-modifications. The shift requires that we move away from the idea of the world as independent and extrinsic to the idea of a world as inseparable from the structure of these processes of self-modification. This change in stance does not express a mere philosophical preference; it reflects the necessity of understanding cognitive systems not on the basis of their input and output relations but by their operational closure. A system that has operational closure is one in which the results of its processes are those processes themselves.

(Varela, Thompson and Rosch, 1991, p. 137)[11]

The autopoietic view represents the idea of a circuit of self-assessment and self-correction, or positive feedback. The prefix *auto*, implies consciousness and the boundaries of consciousness which change over time, partly as a function of habits and social conditioning and partly as a function of one's use of knowledge and projections and aspirations for the future. The word *poiesis* indicates the central role of making and making with language that lies at the heart of this new epistemology. It is in this sense that the autopoiesis of today's cognitivists assumes its operational closure as a form of deep structure. This contrasts with the earlier holism, as seen, for example, in Gaston Bachelard, who continued to accept the dichotomy between the objectivity of the sciences and the subjectivity of the arts: "Bachelard [...] consummated the rupture [...] between science and the humanities – perceiving on one side a spirit of burning the midnight oil and working and, on the other, a material imagination that sleeps, dreams, and ponders" (Serres and Latour, 1995, p. 31).[12] Michel Serres, who wrote his university thesis with Bachelard, makes the following critique of Bachelard's holism:

The "new scientific spirit" coming into fashion at that time lagged way behind the sciences. Behind mathematics, because, instead of speaking of algebra, topology, and the theory of sets, it referred to non-euclidean geometries, not all that new. Likewise, it lagged behind physics, since it never said a work about information theory nor, later, heard the sound of Hiroshima. It also lagged behind logic, and so on.

(Serres and Latour, 1995, p. 11)

If Bachelard wished to pursue an exclusively rational thought (a category in which he included psychoanalysis) by which to overcome the various prerational obstacles to a purely empirical thought supplied by art, religion and myth, thinkers like Popper, Serres, Latour, Badiou and Bhaskar invited art, religion and myth into the cognitive science agenda.

Bhaskar, a philosopher of science, has stated that the understanding attainable through science depends on the integration of three modes: the mechanical, the actual and the experiential. Bhaskar proposes a synthesis of the problems of pragmatic logic and scientific proof (as seen above in the work of Cassirer, Whitehead and Peirce). In his notational system, one finds a representation of deep structures that confirm that 'experience is in fact significant in science' (Table 7.1):

> Events must occur independently of the experiences in which they are apprehended. Mechanisms, events and experiences thus constitute three overlapping domains of reality, viz. the domains of the *real*, the *actual* and the *empirical*. This is represented in [the] table below.
>
> (Bhaskar, 1978, pp. 56–57)[13]

Bhaskar supports a sociology of science in recognition of the layered nature of scientific process and the independence of natural laws and structures from our perception, knowledge and judgment of them, and thus the need to avoid any Humean and/or positivistic attempts to reduce the process of scientific proof to one of deduction. The 'realistic theory of science' he puts forward is at once a 'transcendental realism' and a reevaluation of theory in the social venue of science as it is made (Bhaskar, 1978, pp. 195, 248).

How the possibilities of scientific discovery are tied to the constraints of physical transcriptions is also the subject of Latour's work on visualization and cognition. By focusing on the 'flattening' of the multifarious data of research into two dimensions, Latour aims at demystifying our understanding of cognitive breakthroughs. He disputes both the 'mentalist' and 'materialist' positions, both of which rely on the juxtaposition of old and new paradigms, the so-called 'grand dichotomies' of mythic/

Table 7.1 Bhaskar's Three Ontological Domains

	Domain of Real	Domain of Actual	Domain of Empirical
Mechanisms	✓		
Events	✓	✓	
Experiences	✓	✓	✓

Bhaskar, 1978, pp. 56–7.

rational, primitive/civilized, before/after. There simply was no sudden emergence of the scientific mind in the 16th century, rather there were numerous unexpected developments in the paradigms of knowledge. One recalls in this context the work of Thomas Kuhn, who demonstrated the dialectical nature of paradigm shift in the sciences and the prominence of humanistic factors in those changes. Kuhn's implicit pedagogy is characterized by an informed gradualism. As he writes,

> When a new candidate for a paradigm is first proposed, it has seldom solved more than a few of the problems that confront it, and most of those solutions are still far from perfect. Until Kepler, the Copernican theory scarcely improved upon the predictions of planetary position made by Ptolemy.
>
> (Kuhn, 1962, p. 156)

What Latour calls the agonistic nature of scientific discovery – the competition among scientists attempting to persuade one another of their discoveries – was presented by Kuhn as well:

> Even in the area of crisis, the balance of argument and counterargument can sometimes be very close indeed. And outside that area the balance will often decisively favor the tradition. Copernicus destroyed a time-honored explanation of terrestrial motion without replacing it; Newton did the same for an older explanation of gravity, Lavoisier for the common properties of metals and so on.
>
> (Kuhn, 1962, p. 157)

Like Kuhn, Latour effectively presents the subject of paradigm shift as incorporating a variety of fields of study. This is critical since the dichotomies usually employed to discuss scientific revolutions provide an effective synopsis of their effects, but not of their causes. The tendency to emphasize changes in mentality or consciousness has meant that too little attention has been paid to the actual physical processes involved, especially in basic techniques of inscription and visualization. Similarly there has been too much emphasis on the economics of change, leading to a materialistic bias that has neglected the study of scientific craftsmanship, specifically the practice of writing and imaging. While scientists often possess contrasting world views and mental orientations, the presence of concrete, novel inscriptions succeeds in attracting their attention to the true breakthroughs. These are reflected in simple schemes that represent the cognitive essence of large amounts of data not previously organized and distilled in such a manner. Such a process of distillation and persuasion is referred to as the "mobilization" of the scientist's findings, in other words the scientist's accomplishments depend on his or her ability to communicate them so as to generate "allies" in what is viewed as a fundamentally "agonistic" process (Latour, 1986, p. 5). The second requirement the scientist encounters is the need for image production to endure in a presentable and 'immutable' form such that its applicability is not diminished in the process of transmission. Recalling the discovery of perspective, Latour calls to mind the 'optical consistency' this brought to human knowledge. In so doing he disputes the pedagogical clichés that tie perspective to the advent of a greater realism:

> Perspective is not interesting because it provides realistic pictures; on the other hand, it is interesting because it creates complete hybrids: nature seen as fiction, and fiction seen as nature, with all the elements made so homogeneous in space that it is now possible to reshuffle them like a pack of cards.
>
> (Latour, 1986, p. 9)[14]

Latour includes in his view of visualization and cognition an appraisal of art history, notably the revolutionary nature of early Dutch painting (as studied by Svetlana Alpers), which amounted to nothing less than a new way of seeing. In the epistemological realm, Latour endorses the "anthropology of geometry and mathematics" as well as the "ethnography of inscription" (1986, pp. 26, 30). These hybrid fields locate the commonality between the arts and sciences and undermine the strict separation of the disciplines that typically involves a dismissal of the more temporal, less predictable discipline by the more abstract and atemporal one. The primacy of the visual and manual activities is exemplified by Galileo's unprecedented ability to assemble on paper, in his annotations, the truths of both geometry and physics. His 'immutable mobiles' are thus another example of the deep structures of knowledge as evinced by his visualization of a fundamental connectedness between fields, "his creation of a geometrical medium in which geometry and physics merge" (Latour, 1986, pp. 7, 24). It is no coincidence that long after the excitement over Galileo's scientific discoveries has faded, we continue to read him because of the precision and elegance of his prose. As one teaches the subject of scientific discovery or paradigm shift, one is teaching about learning itself. The problematic rests in time and how one frames in time the discovery of new hypotheses that promise to alter our assumptions about what is true. Recalling Whitehead's rhythms of education, the learner is always at a critical juncture, progressing, expanding, refining one's knowledge, leaving the old behind. One only has the present as the narrow passage through which memories are examined and redirected toward practical applications for the future. In the present, one is at a threshold of creativity, not unlike the scientific discoverer. For Whitehead, "creativity is the basis of process, and issues into novelty"; it is "the universal principle of reality and causation" (Evans, 1998, pp. 66–67).

As one introduces the topic of scientific discoveries it is useful to survey the range of extant historical possibilities in a theory or visualization and demonstrate how the principals in the debate argued their cases and how a given theory won out (such as Kepler's discovery that the orbits of planets around the sun were elliptical, not circular). Ideally one does this with modesty and circumspection so as not to ideologize the discovery or assume a 'total view.'[15] The introduction of new knowledge invariably changes not only the old knowledge but also the frame and context of the old knowledge. Consider in our own day the theory of exaptation, according to which a trait or feature of an organism is employed for a use other than the one for which it was developed by evolution. On its own, exaptation seems logical enough, but when it is extended into a genetic principle, it has an impact on our assumptions about natural selection itself.[16]

Advancing a Humanistic Pedagogy

> Humanism is essentially the holding of a dislike or contempt for violence. It is in one sense a philosophy of compromise.
> –John Fowles (1988, p. 376)

From Kant forward, the relation of philosophical subjects and predicates, of self-knowledge and knowledge of the world, has presupposed the problem of ethics and judgment. Kant's enduring value for us concerns his pluralistic and dialectical notion of predicates and his expansion of the domain of the knowable to include concepts of action and judgment. Implicit in this expansion is the notion that by accessing the intuitive (visual, poetic, nonverbal) mind, educators can motivate students to modify their behavior. One recalls in this regard the importance Kant gave to values and transcendental reason, and his integration of the practical and theoretical spheres in the heuristics of learning.

In line with the goal of instilling good judgment in students, in this section I explore the challenges of adopting a humanistic pedagogy across the curriculum. I assume that such a pedagogy is intrinsically difficult, given the fact that it opposes those pedagogies focused purely on the word or on quantified catalogues of information that students can consign to memory, and because in the limited time available for instruction there will always be other competing priorities. I assume that such a pedagogy will be dialectical and needs to arrive at compromises between opposing points of view and adopt dialogue and narrative for that purpose.

The virtue of practical wisdom that is our focus here is called phronesis. Phronesis is akin to the ancient Greek skill of *aristos*, or the ability to identify the best strategy for a given situation. In his study of this theme, John Fowles specifies three areas of education: the external, the internal and the synoptic. The goal of optimizing education universally is only met by the synoptic – by the third way – which integrates the external and internal perspectives and avoids the danger of trivialization by quantification, as in the confusion of technology for science.

A prominent educator who has adopted such a third way is Michel Serres. As seen in Chapter 2, Serres' concept of the "third-instructed" in *The Troubadour of Knowledge* is that of an educator able to mediate between the extremes of the humanities and the sciences and their respective pedagogical methods, enabling the student to actively engage with the event of learning as a matter of ethics and judgment. The concept of the "third-instructed" means, among other things, to be "seized" by "the passion of pedagogy" (Serres, 1997, p. 54). Here, as in many of his works, Serres' language grows metaphorical and involves a large number of associations and lateral reasonings; the pedagogical discourse is given a narrative structure in which the philosopher (or 'lover of knowledge') is cast as a sea voyager, swimmer, rugby player or peasant plowing his fields. The intent is to break free from the dualistic discourse that does not tolerate the use of creative modes for the communication of knowledge; "The goal of instruction is the end of instruction, that is to say invention. Invention is the only true intellectual act, the only act of intelligence. The rest? Copying, cheating, reproduction, laziness, convention, battle, sleep. Only discovery awakens" (Serres, 1997, pp. 92–93).[17]

If the 'postmodern condition' or 'affliction' (discussed in Chapter 6) marked a crisis in the neoliberal university, a period of stagnation due to excessive verbalism and the loss of a vivid contract with nature, Serres's pedagogical writings are the perfect antidote. An intellectually robust polymath from Gascony who was for years a French naval officer, Serres possesses an encyclopedic knowledge of the sciences and a conscious disregard for the more intellectualist trappings of academia. Thus in *The Five Senses* (1985), he inserts this parody of the academic 'banquet' or 'colloquium' to which the scholar arrives as a 'statue,' a slave to words alienated from the material world of the senses:

> Arriving at the banquet, the statue interrupts it, neither sitting down, nor drinking, neither smelling nor tasting; it consumes the menu: a mobile dictionary capable of memorizing the list of dishes, recipes and wines, but unable to commemorate a meal.
>
> (Serres, 2008, p. 193)

For Serres, the great discoverers come from the arts as much as the sciences, in what amounts to a continuous cross-pollination between the disciplines: "From Rabelais to Valéry, passing through Molière, Voltaire, or Balzac, ten writers have more or less mastered the science of their time. Science illuminates, fortifies their work, and their work, in turn illuminates and reinforces science" (Serres, 1997, p. 53). These authors – to whom Serres adds the names Leibniz, Goethe, Montaigne and Musil – lived in the fullness of their bodies and passionately taught the necessity of combining the languages of the arts and sciences. Serres affirms the need for deep narrative structures since narrative reflects the movement of history in the macrocosm, like a vast river, just as it reflects the consciousness, intellect and affect of the individual in the microcosm. It is through narrative that empathy can be seen as a form of knowledge. "Learning about misfortune," one can be led to a novel form of "secular prayer" (Serres and Latour, 1995, p. 184), a kind of petitioning.

The modern awareness of a duality of knowledge has led educators to revisit the relationship between the arts and sciences. One of the products of the Keplerian revolution – as symbolized by the cosmological model of the ellipse – was a dual epistemology able to bring attention to both the enlightenment and the occult. This model enables the creation of a third space at the boundaries of the disciplines, a teaching space that Serres found accessible through dialogue, the imagination and the afferent mind.[18] Thus Serres draws out of the notion of Keplerian shift, which involves a bending of time, the idea that time exists in sheets or interruptive folds that can be exploited creatively in narrative. Just as the idea that the planetary system conformed to a perfect circle needed to be supplanted by the model of the ellipse, so did humanity need to alter its solar and rationalist epistemology.

Among the notions that circulated during the 'postmodern' period were that the foundations of knowledge had collapsed or that one was at the end of history.[19] Bateson takes the position that the foundations of knowledge remain intact – the 'eternal verities' – even as the sciences are continuously evolving.[20] The organizational nexus of knowledge changed to allow for a broader understanding of relativity, cognitive science and the interconnected worldview of an integral holism. Within such a view, epistemology has benefited from its comparison to the biological sciences and evolution, which stresses its concreteness and rootedness in natural processes. Postmodernism, in contrast, discouraged this integrative view. After its initial founding in the field of architecture, the movement lapsed into a kind of terminal ambiguity. Briefly stated, as a social construction, postmodernity lacked the certitude of a concrete historical validation.

Cesare Segre compares the era of deconstruction, postmodernity and 'weak thought' to the great interest that arose in non-rational solutions to human problems. The philologist notes that the postmodern and the idea of the 'end of history' are notions based on the past, not the present or future; he suggests that the parallel occurrence in Western culture of an array of esoteric and superstitious practices is no coincidence.[21] Romano Luperini writes similarly of the goals of the postmoderns: "It was necessary to reject foundations and programs, to abhor the great narratives, to return to the origins, to the house of being, to the great foundational myths, to exit from history" (Luperini, 2005, p. 12). The postmodern was the period of a "general anaesthesia, [...] an anaesthesia of the collective life," in particular of the intellectuals. If one sees the postmodern as "an extreme phase of late modernity" (Luperini, 2005,

p. 12), a period of breakdown and stagnation when educators substituted the 'history of identity' thesis for actual history, then today one can begin to recuperate some of the terrain that was lost.

As Edward Said has argued, the focus on values and truth of a properly construed humanism was absent from a number of the disciplinary approaches born out of the post-Vietnam War period's pursuit of social and personal relevance: area studies, feminism, post-colonial studies, post-structuralism and post-modernism. Said makes the point that the purported humanists have abandoned or trivialized humanism's historical focus on universality by adopting anti-foundationalist identity politics and theory-laden postmodernist stances. He suggests that the 'radically multicultural' nature of United States culture demands that one invest such area studies with the same pursuit of universals and the same passion for philology, that one would expect in the traditional curriculum. Said argues that we find ourselves beset with

> antifoundationalism, discourse analysis, automatized and tokenized relativism, and professionalism, among other orthodoxies. [...] The alternatives seem now to be quite impoverishing: either become a technocratic deconstructionist, discourse analyst, new historicist, and so on, or retreat into a nostalgic celebration of some past state of glory associated with what is sentimentally evoked as humanism. What is missing altogether is some intellectual, as opposed to a merely technical, component to humanistic practice that might restore it to a place of relevance in our time.
>
> (Said, 2000, p. 70)

Tony Judt has written as well about the vogue of area studies courses that offer students the chance to study people like themselves, a form of Ricoeur's self as *idem*:

> The shortcoming of all these para-academic programs is not that they concentrate on a given ethnic or geographical minority; it is that they encourage members of that minority to study *themselves* – thereby simultaneously negating the goals of a liberal education and reinforcing the sectarian and ghetto mentalities they purport to undermine.
>
> (Judt, 2010, p. 202)

An alternative to the above scenarios is available: If one invests in the Socratic goal of self-inquiry, the self as *ipse* comes into view. However, as Said notes, when the focus on values and truth and the pursuit of the universal are lacking, the orthodoxies rush in. These are shortcuts to a kind of achievement driven by a consumer-based view of education. Many tertiary institutions have witnessed a falloff in the achievement of legitimate 'learning goals' due to the appeal of streamlined courses that students can complete without engaging in the rigorous and isolated study that is called for.[22] In many cases, educators prepackage their results, simplify instruction and instrumentalize the curriculum. What is lacking from such classes – to return to the Batesonian dyad – are rigor and the imagination. And yet, to engage the imagination and the heuristic power of reflection is not a luxury, but a necessary tool for the enhancement of communication skills and the education of the whole person.

In a 2005 lecture on Academic Freedom, President Lee C. Bollinger of Columbia University stated, "[O]f all the qualities of mind valued in the academic community I would say the most valued is that of having the imaginative range and the mental courage to take in, to explore, the full complexity of the subject" (Bollinger, 2005, n.p.). Bollinger suggests that such complexity can only be perceived and presented by faculty who are able to consider contrasting views judiciously and rigorously. His message on academic freedom is based on confronting difficulty and the variability of phenomena in the academic venue:

> The stress is on seeing the difficulty of things, of being prepared to live closer than we are emotionally inclined to the harsh reality that we live steeped in ignorance and mystery, of being willing to undermine even our common sense for the possibility of seeing something hidden. To be sure, that kind of extreme openness of intellect is exceedingly difficult to master, and, in a profound sense, we never do. Because it runs counter to many of our natural impulses, it requires both daily exercise and a community of people dedicated to keeping it alive....
>
> (Bollinger 2005, n. p.)

The arduous pursuit of the qualities of mind advocated by Bollinger coincides with the notion of a predicate as something as yet undetermined, something to be arrived at by each individual learner in process.

As I have argued in this chapter, that process can be furthered by accessing the deep structures of knowledge. It is clear that when speaking of deep structures one is adopting a metaphor, but the use of that metaphor implies the user's recognition of its efficacious nature, as an index of a knowledge whose exact contours cannot currently be further articulated. As a metaphor, deep structure is an example of what Paul Ricoeur calls 'odd predication':

> The thought process of a metaphor has its initial support in the sentence, that is, in the operation of predication. A metaphor is first and

essentially an "odd" predication that transgresses the semantic and cultural codes of a speaking community.

(Ricoeur, 1995, pp. 160–61)

Coarse tools and approximate techniques can often teach more about a raw material than can the refined ones. The sundial suits the peripatetic.

The existence of deep structures prompts the learner and educator to adopt appropriate tools, including narrative. Narrative is often the aptest way to treat material that is uncertain, contingent or resistant to ordinary means of deduction or analysis. Narrative – with its tropes of interruption, interference and mystery – has the power to explore areas of memory and instinct and is an essential tool in qualitative research and creativity studies. In recognition of the "dearth of narrative methodology in modern education," Mary Elizabeth Moore has advocated for the reintroduction of the "idea that stories can either form world (myth) or transform world (parable)" (Moore, 1988, p. 256). Drawing on Whitehead, Moore stipulates that such "formation and transformation of world would be not only a transformation of human perception, but an actual ordering and reordering of the concrete entities of the world" (Moore, 1988, p. 256).

Variations on these themes were provided from discussions of metaphysics (Vico, Dewey), cognitive science and systems theory (Varela), creativity studies (Bowers), cybernetic epistemology (Ceruti, von Foerster) and complex thought (Morin). All of these educators rely on the exposition of a system of knowledge that is only partially accessible to consciousness, yet which exists within a well-demarcated range of epistemological constraints and possibilities, a relational language legible to one and all, not least because of their recognition of the fundamental role of the emotions, of the affect, in cognitive processes.

Notes

1 For further discussion of the paradigmatic (or associative) axis of language, see Barthes (1988) and Jakobson (1960).
2 The complexity of the predicate is defined by Greimas and Courtés, 1982, p. 242:

> [W]e conceive of the predicate as the relation constitutive of the utterance, *i.e.*, as a function the end terms of which are the actants: by the same token we distinguish two types of elementary utterances (and two types of predicate-relations constitutive of these utterances): utterances of doing and utterances of states.

A related formulation of Greimas's concerns deep structures and narrativity, Ibid., p. 210:

> [We see] in the deep narrative structures the domain which can account for the appearance and development of all (and not merely verbal) signification, which can also assume not only the narrative performances

but also articulate as well the different forms of discursive competence. These semiotic structures, which we continue to call, for lack of a better term, narrative (or better, semio-narrative) structures, are in our view the depository of fundamental signifying forms.

3 See Greimas, 1990, p. 7:

The state of advancement of a science, a criterion difficult to establish, is therefore decisive. The very models that are restrictive for an established science can be arbitrary for a discipline that has a scientific vocation. In both cases the problem of their adequation arises in a different way.

4 The source text is I. Kant, *Versuch einiger Betrachtungen über den* Optimismus ("An attempt at some reflections on optimism"), published in 1759.
5 The mythopoetical imagination is a deep structure – comprising order and disorder – and is often a better tool for defining a literary text than by assigning it to an historical period. See Naess, 2008, p. 194: "The attempts by historiographers to characterize epochs (the Renaissance, Baroque, Enlightenment, Romantic periods) are frowned upon by historians who delight in complexity, not uniformity, in irregularities as much as in regularities."
6 See Miner, in Vico, 2010, p. xi: "Vico's position seems to be that while true being exists and serves as the absolute presupposition of metaphysics, little if anything can be scientifically known or understood about it."
7 See Brennan, 2017, p. 136: "What I do not think has been appreciated about Vico's epistemological redefinition of science is its ethical strain." Brennan notes the same parallel that we are aiming to establish in this chapter between epistemology and the philosophy of education as he compares with insight Vico's intellectual adversary – the scientism of his day – to the quantitivism of our current institutional situation.
8 See Mazzotta, 1999, p. 57:

Because Vico places poetry's "imaginary figments" at the center of the university, we must focus on it in order to grasp what Vico expects of poetry and of the university. [...] The constitutive ambiguities of poetry – its mixing instruction with delight, truth with simulacra, the past with the present – unveil, in turn, the constitutive ambiguities of the idea of the university.

9 This is close to Whitehead's focus on the individual student and situation, as explored by James Williams in "Whitehead's Curse?" (2014).
10 Despite the broadening awareness of this new, more supple scientific paradigm, as Baez and Boyles (2008, pp. 1–33) demonstrate, U. S. governmental funding agencies in the education sector have been moving in the opposite direction, defining education narrowly and positivistically as a science, subject to randomized "clinical" experimentation.
11 See Varela and Bourgine, 1992, p. xii: "As white light seen through a prism, the autonomy of the living is articulated by a number of constitutive capacities such as viability, abduction and adaptability concepts on which research can actually advance."
12 See Bachelard, 1984, pp. 147–48:

There are no simple phenomena; every phenomenon is a fabric of relations. There is no such thing as a simple *nature*, a simple substance; a substance is a web of attributes. And there is no such thing as a simple idea, for as Dupréel has pointed out, no idea can be understood until it has been incorporated into a complex system of thoughts and experiences. Application is complication. Simple ideas are working hypotheses or concepts, which must undergo revision before they can assume their proper epistemological role.

According to the autopoietic view, "simple phenomena," "simple substance[s]" and "simple ideas" not only exist but are basic to the empirical observations upon which cognitivism and the new holism depend.

13 See also Bhaskar, 1978, pp. 56–57:

> The crux of my objection to the doctrine of empirical realism should now be clear. By constituting an ontology based on the category of experience, as expressed in the concept of the empirical world and mediated by the ideas of the actuality of the causal laws and the ubiquity of constant conjunctions, three domains of reality are collapsed into one. This prevents the question of the conditions under which experience is in fact significant in science from being posed; and the ways in which these three levels are brought into harmony or phase with one another from being described.

14 See Latour, 1986, p. 27, regarding common errors in epistemology:

> There are two ways in which the visualization processes we are all interested in may be ignored; one is to grant to the scientific minds what should be granted to the hands, to the eyes and to the signs; the other is to focus exclusively on the signs *qua* signs, without considering the mobilization of which they are but the fine edge.

15 See A. Naess, 2008, p. 155:

> Conceptions of *explicit* total views as found in the history of philosophy are ridden with paradoxes. Either a total view is explicit but fragmentary or it is total but implicit. An analogous conclusion can be reached conceerning the ordinary use of the term *view*. Views are something from somewhere. This somewhere is not part of that something. So we cannot have a total view in this sense, comprising viewed and viewpoint.

16 See Bocchi and Ceruti, 2002, pp. 225–27, on S. J. Gould. See also Lewontin, 1991, p. 82:

> Darwin's alienation of the organism from the environment was an essential first step in a correct description of the way the forces of nature act on each other. The problem is that it was only a *first* step, and we have become frozen there.

17 Serres also writes, 1997, p. 65: "Only philosophy can go deep enough to show that literature goes still deeper than philosophy. [...] Sometimes one can only understand if one liquidates one's knowledge in the loyal narrative of circumstance."

18 Serres employs this notion together with his idea of a non-linear historical time subject to folds, eddies and turbulence; this idea is compatible with his use of term "homeorrhesis" or stability through flowing.

19 Such statements reflect the nominalism of an academy poorly disposed to describe the phenomena of modern science other than by scientism; one sees this in concrete terms in the current rush to STEM classes. See the chapter of E. Touya de Marenne, "Searching for STEM's *telos*," 2016, pp. 69–97, for a persuasive description of the current status in the American academy regarding this issue.

20 See G. Bateson, in Bateson and Bateson, 1987, p. 23: "Today in America it is almost heresy to believe that the roots of thought have any importance."

21 See Segre, 2005, pp. 50–51, "Penso [...] che queste pratiche hanno in comune un modo di rivolgersi alla coscienza che è sostanzialmente astorico, autoreferenziale, e perciò non corregge affatto l'atonia morale" ("I think [...] these practices have in common a way of addressing oneself to the conscience that is substantially ahistorical, self-referential, and for that reason does not correct in the slightest the moral atony").

22 See Arum and Roksa, 2011, pp. 121–44, for a clear presentation of the problem.

Conclusion

Two threads running through this study have been the role of history in defining our pedagogy and the question of language, notably the language of educationalism. If, as Erich Auerbach states, it is the educator's responsibility to convey an historical sensibility to students in a language that endures, that task continues to be undercut by forces in and out of the academy.[1] These forces negatively impact the allocation of resources in a fair and equitable manner that lives up to the spiritual and ethical mission of the university in the Western tradition. They seem to be reshaping the liberal arts curriculum in favor of technology and STEM courses and to the detriment of the humanities. This situation has led to an activist literature that addresses the crisis in sociopolitical and policy terms. That has not been my focus; rather I have sought to examine the predicates of education in a philosophical, humanistic and scientific manner grounded in the contemporary context.

Within this purview there are numerous historical and linguistic protocols to mediate. To begin with there is contemporary history. The 20th century saw horrific and seemingly limitless instances of genocide; it also saw an unprecedented explosion of knowledge. In the globalized information age of the 21st century it is fair to say that educators have an obligation to teach the history of the 20th century in a way that reconciles the extremes of human ingenuity and human destruction. Today's students have grown up in a world irrevocably changed by the acceleration of historical time. While it is simple enough to compile dates and events of great conflicts and discoveries, this does not educate students about the responsibilities of citizenship, the complex networks of human culture or the nature of the good and the true. Then there is the history of the particular discipline at hand, which is connected to a specialized language that the student is challenged to learn and augment over time. This implicates in turn the history of the individual as she traverses the stages of learning. With linguistic protocols running in parallel to the historical ones, teachers must master the language of historical reality, they must be fluent in their disciplinary language but also in the 'language of relations' that stands over and above the disciplinary language; lastly they must speak in the language of values – of ethics and virtues.

Such teachers are not the norm at a time when the dominant paradigm is that of a technologized, performativity-based university tailored to the material demands of the information age. Ironically, that paradigm has failed to exploit the most exciting aspects of the cybernetic revolution: the theory of the observer, recursive function theory, complex systems. At a time when students are asked to process ever more varied sets of information and to convey that information cross-culturally, educational institutions are failing to prepare them in the necessary communication skills, in the organization, articulation and expression of ideas, in discerning what is good and how to be better world citizens.

In Chapter 1 I compared the pedagogical thinking of A. N. Whitehead, Gregory Bateson and Bill Readings. I defined the predicates of education as dynamic, process-derived qualities that depend for their development on a theory of symbolism, seen as an essential tool for communicating the interpenetration of perceptual and cognitive networks in the learner. In contrast to the prevailing rationalistic or analytical languages of the pedagogical sciences, which fail to account for the role of the affective intelligence and the imagination, Whitehead, Bateson and Readings succeed in articulating a philosophy of qualitative education. They consider the question of intellectual self-representation in the academy, the impoverishment of learning that results from the over-specialization and the failure of the quantified curriculum to exhibit its relation to the essential characteristics of intelligent or emotional perception. Whitehead's pedagogy is based on the development of the individual through progressive stages; as students pass from the stage of romance to that of precision then generalization, the mind develops in a rhythm that is biologically appropriate to the organism. As new knowledge is acquired, previous knowledge is removed even as one retains the somatic memory and emotional resonances surrounding it. Bateson's scientific appraisal of the types of learning as progressing through higher recursive stages was shown to be fundamental to his concept of the ecology of mind. Readings, like his two compatriots, privileges the educational event that changes the learner (and is thus non-trivial) and he advocates for a dialogical, Bakhtinian ethos in the academy. He observes that the Humboldtian model for the American academy has been replaced by a market-based and ideological model that he refers to as the University of Excellence, and he articulates positive steps that scholars can take – by constituting peripheral singularities in a culture of dissensus – to counteract this historical change.

In Chapter 2 I turned to Giambattista Vico, who posited for the first time the equivalency of social organization and self-organization. Vico's relational concept of knowledge was invested in the dynamics of becoming. To read Vico today is to be confronted by an archaic and speculative language, rich in references to antiquity and the anthropology of human origins and historical development. The vision of the university he propounds, containing an order of study and a heterarchical organization of the disciplines, represents in many respects the road not taken in the West. Vico conceptualized civilization as the collective project of humanity and therefore as a subject matter that cannot be restricted to a few academic departments. Philology for Vico is the science of the things of man: those things include mythology, the visual arts, the codes of scientific discourse, the legal statutes of jurisprudence and so forth. The Vichian idea that human beings can only know the truth of what they themselves have made is a constructivist idea that I connected to the thought of Cassirer, Piaget and Bateson. Cassirer's pedagogical philosophy is based on his theory of the symbol as a universal and transcendent modality in culture. This unifying theory is pervasive across the disciplines and provides a moral and ethical means for integrating communication about teaching. Cassirer's thought is compatible with Piaget's, which emphasizes the pluralism of experience and the role of dynamic learning in the construction of meaningful order. Piaget's constructivism assumes that an operational bridge exists to link together the hard sciences, the human sciences and the historical disciplines. The chapter's final section connects the constructivist pedagogy to the stoic conception of liberality and intellectual autonomy, returning to Bateson to exemplify that ideal.

Chapter 3 explored the bases for a process theory of learning applicable to the modes of instructional logic employed in today's academy. In contrast to the dualistic pedagogies of the object that juxtapose mind to body, art to science, man to nature, process pedagogy introduces a theory of the observer – of the learning subject – in order to mediate these dichotomies. First, the chapter traces the modern history of process pedagogy beginning with Kant and leading through Cassirer and Whitehead to an array of approaches (context theory, complex thought and edusemiotics) that favor the symbiosis of art and science over the lingering Cartesian separation of 'subjective' mental processes from 'objective' forms of knowledge and social organization. Second, it examines the case of science education, specifically as regards habit formation among students and the need to contextualize and generalize scientific knowledge (as proposed by 'science studies,' a development that offers a qualitative alternative to the myth of scientific objectivity based on purely quantitative research). Third, it explores theories of consilience, comparing the scientistic 'total view' of E. O. Wilson to the more relativistic organic visions of Wendell Berry, Richard Rorty and Stephen Toulmin. Lastly, I examine the educational role played by logical abduction, as first articulated in the modern era by Charles Sanders Peirce, whose pragmatic theories have been extended and applied by a number of scholars.

In Chapter 4 I put the theoretical insights arrived at in Chapter 3 into practice, with specific reference to the model of second language

instruction. Given language's organic relationship to speakers, the learning of a second language implicates by necessity the concepts of *habitus*,
hard wiring of knowledge and affective knowledge.[2] Given this fact, the
model of language instruction provides a paradigm applicable across the
disciplines in syntony with what Cassirer called "the unity of the infinite
variety of languages" (Cassirer in Hamburg, 1964, p. 220). Thus, how
the student learns another language (L2) is comparable to the process
of learning a scientific discipline. A discussion about the use of narrative in the classroom corroborated its effectiveness in eliciting novel and
creative responses from students. If cultivated, such an art can impact
the languages and codes of the individual disciplines, advance the research mission of scholars in those fields and favor the interrelationships
between the disciplines.

Chapter 5 dealt with analogical thinking, faith and the gaps that exist
in knowledge and its representations in the educational enterprise. These
intertwined subjects have a vital function in the construction of intellectual models and formulations of the truth and deserve to be accounted
for in teaching methodologies. In contrast to the binary focus of digital thinking, analogical thinking is variable and modulable. In order to
make the point that analogical thinking assists us in our pursuit of the
truth I enlisted a number of metaphors and analogies – some of them
painful, some of them humorous – that have been used by prominent authors to describe academia. To exemplify the cracks or discontinuities in
consciousness and the inadequacy of the verbalist, logocentric and digital intensification of language, I cited the example of film studies where
too often the feature length film is studied as a kind of literary text on
the screen and not in terms of its perceptual-cognitive novelty. I availed
myself of the theoretical work on that subject by Merleau-Ponty, Gibson
and Varela and on the unique role played by the sense of sight in the
human intelligence. My approach to visual thinking asks students to
examine the basic elements of cinema directly and be skeptical of the
textualization of cinema that turns the viewer into a passive receptacle. (The detour into cinema studies is compatible with discussions else-
where in the book on foreign language instruction, analogical thinking
and dialogics.) I then focus on how the gaps that exist in historical and
literary texts serve as fertile entry points for educators eager to infuse
their classrooms with creativity and imagination. Lastly I consider the
role of discontinuities in the scientific paradigm that arose in the wake
of Heisenberg and Schrödinger, Gödel and Prigogine, when non-linear
models of cause and effect replaced linear ones: "Contemporary evolutionary biology has opened important new frontiers precisely by radically challenging the univocal nature of the 'scientific method'" (Bocchi
and Ceruti, 2002, p. 225).

In Chapter 6 I assessed the ethical questions facing higher educators
as a constitutive – not a supplementary – part of knowledge. I cited

Cassirer on the need for scientists to submit to a 'double judgment,' that is to integrate the morality of their ideas with the quantitative rigor of their research. Since the state or 'system' is primarily interested in its own survival, it tends to ignore the validity of the inward knowledge of the virtues. The recommendation to 'educate the virtues' is built on the distinction between information and knowledge; only the latter, it was shown, can position itself under the sign of the Other: the respect for other disciplines, the respect for Others' rights, the recognition of the Other within oneself, the availability to other cultures and other forms of learning. Profiles of studies by Jonas, Baez and Boyles, and Lewontin reinforced the ethical position taken in the chapter; these exemplary works combine their authors' academic expertise – in philosophy, science studies and genetics – with a conscientious approach to the dangers of technology and the need to replace outdated deterministic and ideologized conceptions of science.

In Chapter 7 I explored the deep structures of knowledge that exist below the surface of our empirical understanding in a variety of fields. I placed into relief the use of such terminology by premier scholars – Chomsky, Greimas, Varela, Serres, Bruner, Zumthor, Naess, M. C. Bateson – in order to treat areas of knowledge that are not predictable or fully analyzable. I focused on the role of humanism in elucidating these structures, whether in deep ecology or psychology, philology or linguistics. Returning to Vico's epistemology and vision of a heterarchy of the disciplines, I compared his metaphysics to that of Dewey, detailing how both thinkers view metaphysics as a science of change coinvolved with history, myth, ethics and the civic and social advance of humanity. I drew a line between the scientistic doctrines that Vico opposed, those that Dewey opposed and the recurrence of similarly reductive doctrines today. Based on this foundation I moved to a discussion of non-behaviorist, non-positivistic theories of science that emerged in the wake of the cybernetic revolution. This emergence was attributed to the maturation and broader understanding of relativity, cognitive science and the interconnected worldview of an integral holism. Within such a view, epistemology has benefited from its comparison to the biological sciences and evolution. The founding of the premises of knowledge on constraints and possibilities was also explicated in terms of a complementarity of objectivism and subjectivism, rooted in the character and nature of natural processes. A related phenomenon is the emergence of contemplative pedagogy.

In 2000 I was awarded a Contemplative Practices Fellowship (CPF) to prepare a graduate seminar on Petrarch. As we studied the author's lyrical poetry in Italian and his Latin prose, students were encouraged to assess the pertinence to the work of Petrarch's practices of contemplation, religious retreat and prayer. They appropriated the texts personally and sought out their deep structures. There was a stimulating sense of cohesion and common purpose, tranquility and respect among the members of the seminar, and much freedom to read 'across' the vast literary production of Petrarch and his later imitators. As Steven Rockefeller, a strong supporter of the CPF program, has written:

> Education in American colleges commonly suffers from a failure to connect information and experience, theory and practice, ideas and solutions to real problems. Much that goes on in the classroom is abstract and unrelated to the living experience of the students. Consequently much of it is not retained beyond the examination period. It is never digested and integrated into a student's real understanding so as to produce growth and wisdom. One remedy to this problem is to find new imaginative ways for students to learn by doing.
>
> (Rockefeller, 1996, p. 8)

One such way that is being explored is the introduction of contemplative practice into the classroom. By respecting silence and inner listening in a communal way, one may introduce meditative practice in a secular way. As Brian Stock has written:

> We have to teach students what contemplative activity is all about. Among other things, they have to be instructed in reading meditative literature, not as they would read modern poems, plays, or novels, but as contemplatives read them, using texts as a means to an end and not considering them, as is the fashion in contemporary literary practice, as ends in themselves.
>
> (Stock, 1996, p. 4)

One of the major purposes of this book has been to restore value to the activity of teaching as a full and equal partner to that of research. Another has been to articulate the central role of the senses and perceptions in constituting and guiding the intelligence, and of a theory of symbolism that draws on the senses. Thus the attention given to cinema, to foreign language instruction (the oral/aural learning experience par excellence), to analogical thinking, the imagination and creativity, and dialogics. So too the periodic attempts throughout the book to detail the systemic problems and obstacles that educators confront in their professions.

As we look to the future of education, one of the clearest guides is Edgar Morin, whose 2001 manual, *Seven Complex Lessons in Education for the Future*, brings together the languages of theorists of various fields to assess the current state of education. Advocating for an open epistemology, understood as a place of uncertainty and dialogics, Morin recommends replacing the current "disjunction-reduction-unidimensionality paradigm" with a "paradigm of distinction-conjunction," so as to introduce into epistemology a "dialogical principle" (Morin, 2001, p. 6). Not coincidentally, Morin cites Vico's *The New Science* in labeling the metasystem he is proposing. Acknowledging his historical distance from the Neapolitan philosopher, Morin adopts the term 'new science' to propose "a multidimensional transformation of what we mean by science, concerning what seems to constitute certain of its intangible imperatives, starting with the inescapability of disciplinary fragmentation and theoretical splitting" (Morin, 2001, p. 30). As with Vico, this direction is "an anti-Cartesian idea, in the sense that Descartes thought that distinction and clarity were the intrinsic characteristics of the truth of an idea" (Morin, 2001, p. 48). In proposing the idea of a complex unity linking analytical-reductionist thinking and global thinking within a 'dialogic,' Morin uncovers in the etymology of the word 'dialogue' the presence of two logics, those of order and disorder. Thus, in the field of organic chemistry, he notes

> the encounter between two types of chemico-physical entities: a stable kind that can reproduce and whose stability can carry a memory that becomes hereditary, such as DNA, and amino acids, which make proteins in multiple forms extremely unstable, which degrade but recreate themselves incessantly from messages that emanate from DNA.
>
> (Morin, 2001, p. 49)

Introducing these macro-concepts of order and disorder to represent the dialogic principle, Morin notes with regret that most academics tend to elevate the one at the cost of the other and thus dissociate the polarity from their epistemological and pedagogical assumptions and practices:

> Order and disorder are two enemies: one abolishes the other, but at the same time, in certain cases, they collaborate and produce organization and complexity. The dialogic principle allows us to maintain duality at the heart of unity. It associates two terms that are at the same time complementary and antagonistic.
>
> (Morin, 2001, p. 49)

In his final chapter, "Ethics for the Human Genre," Morin postulates that "The West also has to integrate virtues of other cultures in order to correct the activism, pragmatism, quantitativism, frenetic consumerism it has unleashed at home and abroad" (Morin, 2001, p. 86). The basis for a human ethics must be "the complex concept of the human genre [...] composed of the individual ↔ society ↔ species triad" (Morin, 2001, p. 87). The reciprocal relation between individual and society is what nourishes and sustains either, especially in the development of an ethics of democracy:

> It is this dialogic of order and disorder that produces all of the living organizations in the universe. [...] We are thus compelled to work with disorder and uncertainty, and in so doing realize that this does not mean letting ourselves be overwhelmed by them; it means, rather, finally coming to terms with them by means of a more dynamic and complex form of learning.
>
> (Morin, 2001, p. 87)

What Morin proposes is for the educator aiming to teach democracy to conceive it as "the continuous regeneration of a complex retroacting loop: citizens produce the democracy that produces citizens" (Morin, 2001, p. 88):

> In the planetary era, the democratic societies of the world must meet the challenge of plurality and ethno-cultural and sociological conflict and diversity, if they are to remain truly democratic. The dangers in the West are that of confusing itself with a "dictatorship of the majority over minorities."
>
> (Morin, 2001, p. 89)

If today we confront a "pathological semantics" (Foerster, 2003, p. 173) in society characterized by the lust for certitude and the obsession with authority, then academia must provide an ethical alternative, a language of reason and mediation.

The challenge for the educator today is analogous to the one faced by Socrates: to evaluate present experience, to uncover doubt, to be a midwife of the truth, to dialogue about what it means to be human. To be a Socratic educator is to *reduce* information, to recover the analogical mode of thinking and the grain of the voice. Novelist J. M. Coetzee has written as follows:

> What I call my philosophy of teaching is in fact a philosophy of learning. It comes out of Plato, modified. Before true learning can occur, I believe, there must be in the student's heart a certain yearning for the truth, a certain fire. The true student burns to know. In the teacher she recognizes, or apprehends, the one who has come closer than herself to the truth. So much does she desire the truth embodied in the teacher that she is prepared to burn her old self up to attain it. For his part, the teacher recognizes and encourages the fire in the student, and responds to it by burning with an intenser light. Thus together the two of them rise to a higher realm. So to speak.
>
> (Coetzee, 2009, p. 163)

How many educators sense this burning? Certainly it is familiar to those process thinkers who persist with an organicist and integrative understanding of humanity's position in nature. If Arne Naess was to praise Whitehead's philosophy over that of more famous philosophers, it was due to his 'maturity' and his understanding of joy.[3] Why this maturity matters, especially in education, is that its opposite opens the door to pessimism, irrationality and despondency.

In closing, I would like to consider this book as an example of what Walter Ong called the interiorization of history, that is an awareness that history is more than an exterior course of events, more than a developing idea in the Hegelian sense. Ong tells us that the cosmos and its history are something alive and ongoing and that in the digital age, time is 'substantial': "Since Einstein, it has been apparent that time is not throwaway waste. Time is constituent of material being, as much as are length, breadth, and thickness" (Ong, 1999, vol. 4, p. 209). One needn't be religious to perceive the spiritual pregnancy of this era in which the realization has grown that history is a process in time that is embodied in the structure of human personality as an interior reality. The faithful meet new uncertainties as they always have, humbly and hopefully, undeterred by the cupidity of individualistic striving yet conscious of the weight of personal responsibility. Within this reality the predicate is "something cried out," it is an "aurally based term" (Ong, 1999, v. 3, p. 103). As such it is a surface manifestation of a deep structure, whether in the languages of the disciplines, the syntax of narratives or the cognitions of the individual.

Notes

1 See E. Auerbach, 1969, p. 6:

> We are [...] threatened with the impoverishment that results from an ahistorical system of education; not only does that threat exist but it also lays claim to dominating us. Whatever we are, we became in history, and only in history can we remain the way we are and develop therefrom: it is the task of philologists, whose province is the world of human history, to demonstrate this so that it penetrates our lives unforgettably.

2 See Snyder, 1990, p. 17:

> Language is learned in the house and in the fields, not at school. Without ever having been taught formal grammar we utter syntactically correct sentences, one after another, for all the waking hours of the years of our life. Without conscious device we constantly reach into the vast wordhoards in the depths of the wild unconscious.

3 See Naess, 2008, p. 125:

> Do the most influential philosophers of our time and culture represent high degrees of maturity and integration? I have in mind not only Heidegger, Sartre, Kierkegaard, and Wittgenstein, but also Marx and Nietzsche. Tentatively, I must answer no. There are lesser-known but perhaps more mature philosophers, like Jaspers and Whitehead.

References

Alighieri, D. (1981). *Literature in the Vernacular* [De vulgari eloquentia] (S. Purcell, Trans. and Introd.). Manchester: Carcanet New Press.

Arum, R. and Roksa, J. (2011). *Academically Adrift: Limited Learning on College Campuses.* Chicago, IL: University of Chicago Press.

Auerbach, E. (1969). Philology and *Weltliteratur* (E. and M. Said, Trans.). *The Centennial Review* 13: 1–17.

Bachelard, G. (1984). *The New Scientific Spirit* (A. Goldhammer, Trans.; Patrick A. Heelan, Foreword). Boston, MA: Beacon Press.

Badiou, A. (2002). *Ethics: An Essay on the Understanding of Evil* (P. Hallward, Trans. and Introd.). London: Verso.

Baez, B. and Boyles, D. (2009). *The Politics of Inquiry: Education Research and the "Culture of Science."* Albany: State University of New York Press.

Barker, Carol M. (2000). *Liberal Arts Education for a Global Society.* New York: Carnegie Corporation.

Barthes, R. (1988). *The Semiotic Challenge* (R. Howard, Trans.). New York: Hill and Wang.

Barthes, R. (1989). *The Rustle of Language* (R. Howard, Trans.). Berkeley: University of California Press.

Bateson, G. (1970). The Message of Reinforcement. In *Language Behavior. A Book of Readings in Communication* (J. Akin, A. Goldberg, G. Myers, & J. Steward, Eds.), pp. 62–72. Paris: Mouton.

Bateson, G. (1972). *Steps to an Ecology of Mind.* New York: Ballantine.

Bateson, G. (1980). *Mind and Nature. A Necessary Unity.* New York: Bantam.

Bateson, G. (1981). Paradigmatic Conservatism. In *Rigor and Imagination. Essays from the Legacy of Gregory Bateson* (C. Wilder-Mott & J. H. Weakland, Eds.), pp. 347–55. New York: Praeger.

Bateson, G. (1991a). God as the Pattern that Connects. *New Perspectives Quarterly* 8, 2: 40–43.

Bateson, G. (1991b). *A Sacred Unity. Further Steps to an Ecology of Mind* (Rodney E. Donaldson, Ed.). New York: Cornelia and Michael Bessie.

Bateson, G. and Bateson, M. C. (1987). *Angels Fear. Towards an Epistemology of the Sacred* New York: Macmillan.

Bateson, G. and Ruesch, J. (1951). *Communication. The Social Matrix of Psychiatry.* New York: W. W. Norton.

Bateson, M. C. (1972). *Our Own Metaphor. A Personal Account of a Conference on the Effects of Conscious Purpose on Human Adaptation.* New York: Knopf.

Bateson, M. C. (1994). *Peripheral Visions. Learning Along the Way*. New York: Harper Collins.

Bearn, G. C. F. (2000). Pointlessness and the University of Beauty. In *Lyotard. Just Education* (P. A. Dhillon & P. Standish, Eds.), pp. 230–68. London: Routledge.

Becker, E. (1973). *The Denial of Death*. New York: Free Press.

Bellah, R. N., et al. (1985). *Habits of the Heart: Individualism and Commitment in American Life*. Berkeley: University of California Press.

Berry, W. (2000). *Life is a Miracle*. Washington, DC: Counterpoint.

Bhaskar, R. (1978). *A Realist Theory of Science*. Sussex: Harvester Press.

Bierce, A. (1958). *The Devil's Dictionary*. New York: Dover.

Bocchi, G. and Ceruti, M. (2002). *The Narrative Universe* (Luca Pellegrini & Alfonso Montuori, Trans.). Cresskill, NJ: Hampton Press.

Boisvert, R. D. (1988). *Dewey's Metaphysics*. New York: Fordham University Press.

Bollinger, L. C. (2005). Benjamin N. Cardozo Lecure on Academic Freedom. http://www.columbia.edu/cu/news/05/03/cardozo_lecture.html.

Bourdieu, P. (1997). *Pascalian Meditations* (R. Nice, Trans.). Stanford, CA: Stanford University Press.

Bowers, C. A. (1993). *Critical Essays on Education, Modernity, and the Recovery of the Ecological Imperative*. New York: Teachers College Press.

Boyer Report. (1995). The National Commission on Educating Undergraduates in the Research University, created in 1995 under the auspices of the Carnegie Foundation for the Advancement of Teaching. http://naples.cc.sunysb.edu/Pres/boyer.nsf.

Brennan, T. (2017). Vico and Modern Scientism. *Italian Culture* 35, 2: 129–42.

Brinton, C. (Ed.) (1959). *The Society of Fellows*. Cambridge, MA: Harvard University Press.

Brumbaugh, R. (1991). Why Whitehead? *Process Studies* 20, 2: 72–77.

Bruner, J. S. (1966). *Toward a Theory of Instruction*. Cambridge, MA: Harvard University Press.

Burke, K. (1969). *A Grammar of Motives*. Berkeley: University of California Press.

Burke, K. (1984). *Attitudes towards History*. Berkeley: University of California Press.

Bybee, M. D. (1991). Abduction and Rhetorical Theory. *Philosophy and Rhetoric*, 24, 4: 281–300.

Calasso, R. (1994). *The Ruin of Kasch* (W. Weaver & S. Sartarelli, Trans.). Cambridge, MA: Harvard University Press.

Calvino, I. (1988). *Six Memos for the Next Millennium*. Cambridge, MA: Harvard University Press.

Campbell, J. (1982). *Grammatical Man. Information, Entropy, Language, and Life*. New York: Simon & Schuster.

Carr, D. (b. 1944–). (1991). *Educating the Virtues. An Essay on the Philosophical Psychology of Moral Development and Education*. London: Routledge.

Carr, D. (b. 1940–). (1999). *The Paradox of Subjectivity. The Self in the Transcendental Tradition*. New York: Oxford University Press.

Casetti, F. (1999). *Theories of Cinema, 1945–1995* (F. Chiostri, E. Gard Bartolini-Salimbeni, & T. Kelso, Trans.). Austin: University of Texas Press.

Cassirer, E. (1953–1957). *The Philosophy of Symbolic Forms* (R. Manheim, Trans.; C. W. Hendel, Pref. and Introd.). 3 vols. vol. 1, *Language*; vol. 2, *Mythic Thought*; vol. 3, *The Phenomenology of Knowledge*. New Haven, CT: Yale University Press.

Cassirer, E. (1957). Science and Ethics: Equal Partnership. *Saturday Review*. New York. March 2, p. 50.

Cassirer, E. (1961). *The Logic of the Humanities* (C. S. Howe, Trans.). New Haven, CT: Yale University Press.

Cassirer, E. (1970). *An Essay on Man*. New York: Bantam.

Cassirer, E. (1996). *The Philosophy of Symbolic Forms. Volume Four: The Metaphysics of Symbolic Forms* (J. M. Krois & D. P. Verene, Ed., J. M. Krois, Trans.). New Haven, CT: Yale University Press.

Ceruti, M. (1994). *Constraints and Possibilities. The Evolution of Knowledge and Knowledge of Evolution* (Alfonso Montuori, Trans.; Heinz von Foerster, Foreword). Lausanne, Switzerland: Gordon & Breach.

Ceruti, M. (2018). *Il tempo della complessità* (Edgar Morin, Pref.). Milan: Raffaello Cortina.

Chomsky, N. (1972). *Language and Mind*. New York: Harcourt Brace Jovanovich.

Chomsky, N. (1998). *On Language*. New York: New Press.

Cocteau, J. (1988). *Diary of an Unknown* (Jesse Browner, Trans.). New York: Paragon House.

Code, L. (2006). *Ecological Thinking: The Politics of Epistemic Location*. Oxford: Oxford University Press.

Coetzee, J. M. (2009). *Summertime*. London: Harvill Secker.

Côté, J. E. and Allahar, A. L. (2011). *Lowering Higher Education: The Rise of Corporate Universities and the Fall of Liberal Education*. Toronto: Toronto University Press.

Crick, F. (1994). *The Astonishing Hypothesis. The Scientific Search for the Soul*. New York: Simon & Schuster.

Cronen, V. E. and Pearce, W. B. (1980). *Communication, Action, and Meaning. The Creation of Social Realities*. New York: Praeger.

Dal Lago, A. (1992). Comunità. Appunti sulla permanenza di un mito. *aut aut* 250: 5–12.

Dal Lago, A. (1998). Sulla non-conoscenza. In *Attraverso Bateson. Ecologia della mente e relazioni sociali* (S. Manghi, Ed.), pp. 153–67. Milan: Raffaello Cortina.

De Tocqueville, A. (1945). *Democracy in America* (H. Reeve, Trans.). 2 vols. New York: Knopf, 1945.

Dewey, J. (1944). *Democracy and Education*. New York: The Free Press.

Dewey, J. (1958). *Experience and Nature*. New York: Dover.

Dewey, J. (1960). *On Experience, Nature and Freedom* (Richard J. Bernstein, Ed. with Introd.). New York: Bobbs-Merrill.

Dewey, J. (1964). *On Education. Selected writings* (Reginald D. Archambault, Ed.). Chicago, IL: University of Chicago Press.

Dewey, J. (1991 [1910]). *How We Think*. Amherst, NY: Prometheus Books.

Dhillon, P. A. (2000). The Sublime Face of Just Education. In *Lyotard. Just Education* (P. A. Dhillon & P. Standish, Eds.), pp. 110–24. London: Routledge.

Ducrot, O. and Todorov, T. (1979). *Encyclopedic Dictionary of the Sciences of Language* (Catherine Porter, Trans.). Baltimore, MD: Johns Hopkins University Press.

Eco, U. (1975). Looking for a Logic of Culture. *The Tell-Tale Sign: A Survey of Semiotics* (Thomas A. Sebeok, Ed.), pp. 9–17. Lisse: Peter de Ridder Press.

Eco, U. (1986). *Travels in Hyper Reality: Essays* (William Weaver, Trans.). San Diego, CA: Harcourt Brace Jovanovich.

Edmundson, M. (1997). On the Uses of a Liberal Education. *Harper's Magazine* 295 (September 1997): 39–47.

Elkins, J. (2001). *Why Art Cannot Be Taught: A Handbook for Art Students.* Urbana: University of Illinois Press.

Evans, M. D. (1998). *Whitehead and Philosophy of Education. The Seamless Coat of Learning.* Amsterdam: Rodopi.

Fann, K. T. (1970). *Peirce's Theory of Abduction.* The Hague: Martinus Nijhoff.

Foerster, H. von (1984). *Observing Systems* (Francisco Varela, Introd.). Seaside, CA: Intersystems Publications.

Foerster, H. von (1995). Ethics and Second-Order Cybernetics. *Stanford Humanities Review* 4, 2. http://www.stanford.edu/group/SHR/42/text/foerster.html.

Foerster, H. von (2003). *Understanding Understanding. Essays on Cybernetics and Cognition.* New York: Springer.

Fornasa, Walter (1998). Maestro perché le cose finiscono in disordine? Epistemologia ecologica e processi educativi. In *Attraverso Bateson. Ecologia della mente e relazioni sociali* (Sergio Manghi, Ed.), pp. 201–12. Milan: Raffaello Cortina.

Fowles, J. (1964). *The Aristos.* Boston, MA: Little, Brown.

Fowles, J. (1998). *Wormholes* (Jan Relf, Ed. and Introd.). New York: Henry Holt.

Gadamer, H.-G. (1975). *Truth and Method.* New York: Continuum.

Gadamer, H.-G. (2001). Education is Self-Education. *Journal of Philosophy of Education* 35, 4: 529–38.

Gardner, H. (1999a). *The Disciplined Mind. What All Students Should Understand.* New York: Simon & Schuster.

Gardner, H. (1999b). *Intelligence Reframed. Multiple Intelligences for the 21st Century.* New York: Basic Books.

Gargani, A. (1985). *Lo stupore e il caso.* Rome: Laterza.

Gibson, J. J. (1966). *The Senses Considered as Perceptual Systems.* New York: Houghton Mifflin.

Gilson, E. (1988). *Linguistics and Philosophy. An Essay on the Philosophical Constants of Language* (John Lyon, Trans.). Notre Dame, IN: University of Notre Dame Press.

Ginsberg, B. (2011). *The Fall of the Faculty the Rise of the All-administrative University and Why It Matters.* Oxford: Oxford University Press.

Glasersfeld, E. von (1995). *Radical Constructivism: A Way of Knowing and Learning.* London: The Falmer Press.

Greimas, A. J. (1990). *Narrative Semiotics and Cognitive Discourses* (Paolo Fabbri & Paul Perron, Foreword; Paul Perron & Frank H. Collins, Trans.). London: Pinter.

Greimas, A. J. and Courtés, J. (1982). *Semiotics and Language. An Analytical Dictionary* (L. Crist, D. Patte, J. Lee, E. McMahon II, G. Phillips, & M. Rengstorf, Trans.). Bloomington: Indiana University Press.

Habermas, J. (1989). *The New Conservatism* (Shierry Weber Nicholsen, Ed., and Trans.; Richard Wolin, Introd.). Cambridge, MA: MIT Press.

Hall, R. A., Jr. (1941). G. B. Vico and Linguistic Theory. *Italica*, 18, 3: 145–54.

Hamburg, C. H. (1964). A Cassirer-Heidegger Seminar. *Philosophy and Phenomenological Research* 25, 2: 208–22.

Hamrick, W. S. (1988). Postliterate Humanity. *Process Studies* 17, 4: 242–43.

Harries-Jones, P. (1995). *A Recursive Vision: Ecological Understanding and Gregory Bateson*. Toronto: University of Toronto Press.

Heims, S. J. (1991). *The Cybernetics Group*. Cambridge, MA: MIT Press, 1991.

Heller, D. E. (2004). The Changing Nature of Financial Aid. *Academe* (July-August), 90, 4: 37.

Herrick, J. (2005). *The History and Theory of Rhetoric. An Introduction*. Boston, MA: Pearson.

Hillman, J. (1990). On Mythical Certitude. *Sphinx*, 3: 224–43.

Humboldt, W. von [1810] (1959). Über die innere und äussere Organisation der höheren Wissenschaftlichen Anstalten. In *Die Idee der deutschen Universität* (E. Anrich, Ed.), pp. 375–86. Darmstadt: Wissenschaftliche Buchgesellschaft.

Illich, I. (1982). *Gender*. New York: Pantheon.

Jakobson, R. (1960). Closing Statement: Linguistics and Poetics. In *Style in Language* (T. A. Sebeok, Ed.), pp. 11–35. Cambridge: MIT Press.

Jay, M. (1993). *Downcast Eyes. The Denigration of Vision in Twentieth-Century French Thought*. Berkeley: University of California Press.

Jonas, H. (1984). *The Imperative of Responsibility. In Search of an Ethics for the Technological Age* (Hans Jonas with David Herr, Trans.). Chicago, IL: University of Chicago Press.

Judt, T. (2010). *The Memory Chalet*. New York: Penguin.

Kant, I. (1951). *The Critique of Judgment* (J. H. Bernard, Trans. and Introd.). New York: Hafner Press.

Kant, I. (2007). *Critique of Pure Reason* (Marcus Weigelt, Trans., Ed. and Introd.). London: Penguin.

Kenner, H. (1995). *Mazes*. Athens: University of Georgia Press.

Kramsch, C. (1993). *Context and Culture in Language Teaching*. Oxford: Oxford University Press.

Krois, J. M. (1987). *Cassirer. Symbolic Forms and History*. New Haven, CT: Yale University Press.

Kuhn, T. S. (1962). *The Structure of Scientific Revolutions*. Chicago, IL: University of Chicago Press.

Latour, B. (1986). Visualization and Cognition: Thinking with Eyes and Hands. In *Knowledge and Society: Studies in the Sociology of Culture Past and Present* (Henrika A. Kuklick & Elizabeth Long, Eds.), vol. 6, pp. 1–40. Greenwich, CT: Jai Press.

Latour, B. (1999). *Pandora's Hope. Essays on the Reality of Science Studies*. Cambridge, MA: Harvard University Press.

Leplin, J. (1997). *A Novel Defense of Scientific Realism*. Oxford. Oxford University Press.

Lewontin, R. C. (1991). *Biology as Ideology. The Doctrine of DNA*. Toronto: House of Anansi.

Lowe, V. (1990). *Alfred North Whitehead. The Man and His Work*. (J. B. Schneewind, Ed.). 2 vols. Baltimore, MD: Johns Hopkins University Press.

Luperini, R. (1998). La classe come comunità ermeneutica. *Allegoria* 28: 104–9.

Luperini, R. (2005). *La fine del postmoderno*. Naples: Guida.

Lyotard, J.-F. (1984). *The Postmodern Condition: A Report on Knowledge* (Geoff Bennington and Brian Massumi, Trans.; Fredric Jameson, Foreword). Minneapolis: University of Minnesota Press.

Lyotard, J.-F. (1988). *Peregrinations. Law, Form, Event*. New York: Columbia University Press.

Lyotard, J.-F. (1993). The Other's Rights. In *On Human Rights* (Stephen Shute & Susan Hurley, Eds.), pp. 135–47. New York: Basic Books.

Lyotard, J.-F. (2000). *The Confession of Augustine* (Richard Beardsworth, Trans.). Stanford, CA: Stanford University Press.

Margulis, L. (1998). *Symbiotic Planet: A New Look at Evolution*. New York: Basic Books.

Margulis, L. and Sagan, D. (2002). *Acquiring Genomes. A Theory of the Origins of Species*. New York: Basic Books.

Mazzotta, G. (1999). *The New Map of the World. The Poetic Philosophy of Giambattista Vico*. Princeton, NJ: Princeton University Press.

Mengaldo, P. V. (1991). *Giudizi di valore*. Turin: Einaudi.

Merleau-Ponty, M. (1964). *Sense and Non-Sense* (H. L. Dreyfus and P. A. Dreyfus, Trans.). Evanston, IL: Northwestern University Press.

Merleau-Ponty, M. (2002). *Phenomenology of Perception* (C. Smith, Trans.). London: Routledge.

Miller, J. H. (1995). The University of Dissensus. *Oxford Literary Review* 17, 1–2: 121–43.

Monod, J. (1972). *Chance & Necessity. An Essay on the Natural Philosophy of Modern Biology* (Austryn Wainhouse, Trans.). New York: Random House.

Moore, M. E. (1988). Narrative Teaching: An Organic Methodology. *Process Studies* 17: 248–61.

Moriarty, S. E. (1996). Abduction: A Theory of Visual Interpretation. *Communication Theory* 6, 2: 167–87.

Morin, E. (2001). *Seven Complex Lessons in Education for the Future*. Paris: UNESCO.

Morin, E. (2005). *The Cinema, or The Imaginary Man* (Lorraine Mortimer, Trans.). Minneapolis: University of Minnesota Press.

Naess, A. (2002). *Life's Philosophy. Reason and Feeling in a Deeper World* (Roland Huntford, Trans.). Athens: University of Georgia Press.

Naess, A. (2008). *Ecology of Wisdom* (Alan Drengson and Bill Devall, Ed.). Berkeley, CA: Counterpoint.

Nardone, G. and Watzlawick, P. (1993). *The Art of Change: Strategic Therapy and Hypnotherapy without Trance*. San Francisco, CA: Jossey-Bass.

Neusner, J. (1995). What Went Wrong on Campus. *Humanitas* 8, 2: 47.

Nussbaum, M. (1997). *Cultivating Humanity. A Classical Defense of Reform in Liberal Education*. Cambridge, MA: Harvard University Press.

Nussbaum, M. (2010). *Not for Profit: Why Democracy Needs the Humanities*. Princeton, NJ: Princeton University Press.

Ong, W. J. (1999). *Faith and Contexts* (T. J. Farrell, Pref.; T. J. Farrell & P. A. Souk, Eds.), vols. 3 and 4 (of 5). Atlanta, GA: Scholars Press.

Palmer, P. (1983). *To Know as We Are Known. Education as a Spiritual Journey*. San Francisco, CA: Harper & Row.

Paulson, W. (2001). *Literary Culture in a World Transformed. A Future for the Humanities*. Ithaca, NY: Cornell University Press

Pearce, W. B. (1989). *Communication and the Human Condition*. Carbondale and Edwardsville: Southern Illinois University Press.

Pearce, W. B. and Cronen, V. E. (1980). *Communication, Action, and Meaning: The Creation of Social Realities*. New York: Praeger.

Peirce, C. S. (1998). *Essential Peirce. Selected Philosophical Writings*, vol. 2 (1893–1913) (Peirce Edition Project, Eds.). Bloomington: Indiana University Press.

Percy, W. (1984). *Lost in the Cosmos. The Last Self-Help Book*. New York: Washington Square Press.

Perley, J. E. (2007). The Spellings Commission Report. *Academe* 93: 134.

Pert, C. (1997). *Molecules of Emotion: Why You Feel the Way You Feel*. New York: Scribner.

Piaget, J. (1970). *Genetic Epistemology* (E. Duckworth, Trans.). New York: Columbia University Press.

Piaget, J. (1972). *Psychology and Epistemology* (P. A. Wells, Trans.). Harmondsworth: Penguin.

Piaget, J. (1977). *The Essential Piaget* (H. E. Gruber & J. J. Vonèche, Eds.). New York: Basic Books.

Piattelli Palmarini, M. (2008). Il cervello non è relativista (Interview with Noam Chomsky). *Corriere della sera*, April 14, 2008, p. 23.

Pirandello, L. (1985). L'eresia catara. *Novelle per un anno* (Mario Costanzo, Ed.; Giovanni Macchia, Introd.). Milan, Mondadori. vol. 1 (of 2), 838–48.

Pollitt, K. (2002). Pierre Bourdieu, 1930–2002. *The Nation*, February 18, 2002: p. 10.

Pound, E. (1970). *Selected Cantos*. New York: New Directions.

Proctor, R. (1998). *Defining the Humanities. How Rediscovering a Tradition can Improve Our Schools. With a Curriculum for Today's Students*. Bloomington: Indiana University Press.

Readings, B. (1991). *Introducing Lyotard*. London: Routledge.

Readings, B. (1995). From Emancipation to Obligation: Sketch for a Heteronomous Politics of Education. In *Education and the Postmodern Condition* (M. Peters, Ed.), pp. 193–207. Westport, CT: Bergin and Garvey.

Readings, B. (1996). *The University in Ruins*. Cambridge: Harvard University Press.

Rescher, N. (1996). *Process Metaphysics*. Albany, NY: SUNY Press.

Rescher, N. (1998). *Complexity. A Philosophical Overview*. New Brunswick, NJ: Transaction.

Ricoeur, P. (1992). *Oneself as Another* (Kathleen Blamey, Trans.). Chicago, IL: University of Chicago Press.

Ricoeur, P. (1995). *Figuring the Sacred: Religion, Narrative, and Imagination* (David Pellauer, Trans.; Mark I. Wallace, Ed.). Minneapolis. MN: Fortress Press.

Rockefeller, S. C. (1996). *Meditation, Social Change, and Undergraduate Education*. Williamsburg, MA: The Center for Contemplative Mind in Society.

Rorty, R. (1998). Against Unity. *The Wilson Quarterly* 22, 1: 28–38.

Rosenzweig, R. M. (1998). *The Political University. Policy, Politics, and Presidential Leadership in the American Research University*. Baltimore, MD: Johns Hopkins University Press.

Said, E. (1994). *Representations of the Intellectual*. New York: Pantheon.

Said, E. (2000). *Reflections on Exile and Other Essays*. Cambridge, MA: Harvard University Press.

Schleifer, R. (2000). *Analogical Thinking. Post-Enlightenment Understanding in Language, Collaboration, and Interpretation*. Ann Arbor: University of Michigan Press.

Scholes, R. (1988). *The Rise and Fall of English: Reconstructing English as a Discipline*. New Haven, CT: Yale University Press.

Scholes, R. (1998). Does English Matter? *Brown Alumni Magazine* 99, 1: 34–39.

Schopenhauer, A. (1974). On Philosophy at the Universities. In *Parerga and Paralipomena* (E. F. J. Payne, Trans.), vol. 1 (of 2), pp. 139–97. Oxford: Clarendon Press.

Schrecker, E. (2010). *The Lost Soul of Higher Education. Corporatization, the Assault on Academic Freedom, and the End of the American University*. New York: New Press.

Segal, L. (1986). *The Dream of Reality. Heinz von Foerster's Constructivism*. New York: W. W. Norton.

Segre, C. (2005). *Tempo di bilanci. La fine del Novecento*. Turin: Einaudi, 2005.

Semetsky, I. (2013). *The Edusemiotics of Images. Essays on the Art–Science of Tarot*. Rotterdam: Sense.

Serres, M. (1995). *The Natural Contract* (Elizabeth MacArthur and William Paulson, Trans.). Ann Arbor: University of Michigan Press.

Serres, M. (1997). *The Troubadour of Knowledge* (Sheila F. Glaser with William Paulson, Trans.). Ann Arbor: University of Michigan Press.

Serres, M. (2008). *The Five Senses. A Philosophy of Mingled Bodies (I)* (Margaret Sankey and Peter Cowley, Trans.). New York: Continuum.

Serres, M. and Latour, B. (1995). *Conversations on Science, Culture, and Time* (Roxanne Lapidus, Trans.). Ann Arbor: University of Michigan Press.

Slaughter, S. and Rhoades, G. (2004). *Academic Capitalism and the New Economy: Markets, State, and Higher Education*. Baltimore, MD: Johns Hopkins University Press.

Snow, C. P. 1959. *The Two Cultures and the Scientific Revolution*. New York: Cambridge University Press.

Snyder, G. (1990). *The Practice of the Wild*. Berkeley, CA: North Point Press.

Soldati, M. (1959). *America, primo amore*. Milan: Mondadori.

Spitzer, L. (1967). *Linguistics and Literary History; Essays in Stylistics*. Princeton, NJ: Princeton University Press.

Steiner, G. (1989). *Real Presences*. Chicago, IL: University of Chicago Press.

Stevens, W. (1951). *The Necessary Angel. Essays on Reality and the Imagination*. New York: Vintage.

Stock, B. (1996). *The Contemplative Life and the Teaching of the Humanities*. Williamsburg, MA: The Center for Contemplative Mind in Society.

Thagard, P. (1988). *Computational Philosophy of Science*. Cambridge, MA, MIT Press.

Thagard, P. (1992). *Conceptual Revolutions*. Princeton, NJ: Princeton University Press.

Thagard, P. and Holyoak, K. J. (1995). *Mental Leaps. Analogy in Creative Thought*. Cambridge, MA: MIT Press.

Toulmin, S. (1996). Concluding Methodological Reflections. Elitism and Democracy among the Sciences. In *Beyond Theory. Changing Organizations through Participation* (Toulmin & B. Gustavsen, Eds.), pp. 203–25. Amsterdam: John Benjamins.

Toulmin, S. (2001). *Return to Reason*. Cambridge, MA: Harvard University Press.

Varela, F. J. (1992). Whence Perceptual Meaning? A Cartography of Current Ideas. In *Understanding Origins. Contemporary Views on the Origin of Life, Mind and Society* (Varela & J. P. Dupuy, Eds.), pp. 235–63. Dordrecht: Kluwer.

Varela, F. J. (1999). *Ethical Know-How. Action, Wisdom, and Cognition*. Stanford, CA: Stanford University Press.

Varela, F. J., Thompson, E., and Rosch, E. (1991). *The Embodied Mind. Cognitive Science and Human Experience*. Cambridge, MA: MIT Press.

Varela, F. J. and Bourgine, P. (1992). Introduction. In *Toward a Practice of Autonomous Systems. Proceedings of the First European Conference on Artificial Life* (F. J. Varela and P. Bourgine, Eds.), pp. xi–xvii. Cambridge, MA: MIT Press.

Verene, Donald P. (2008). Cassirer's Metaphysics. In *The Symbolic Construction of Reality: The Legacy of Ernst Cassirer* (Jeffrey Andrew Barash, Ed.), pp. 93–103. Chicago, IL: University of Chicago Press.

Vico, G. (1968). *The New Science of Giambattista Vico* (T. G. Bergin and M. H. Fisch, Trans.). Ithaca, NY: Cornell University Press.

Vico, G. (1976). On the Heroic Mind. In *Vico and Contemporary Thought* (G. Tagliacozzo, D. Verene, & M. Mooney, Eds.; E. Sewell & A. C. Sirginano, Trans.), pp. 228–45. Atlantic Highlands, NJ: Humanities Press.

Vico, G. (1988). *On the Most Ancient Wisdom of the Italians: Unearthed from the origins of the Latin Language: Including the Disputation with the* Giornale de' letterati d'Italia (L. M. Palmer, Trans., Ed. & Introd.). Ithaca, NY, Cornell University Press.

Vico, G. (1990). *On the Study Methods of Our Time* (Elio Gianturco, Introd., Trans. with Introd.; Donald Phillip Verene, Pref.). Ithaca, NY: Cornell University Press.

Vico, G. (1993). *On Humanistic Education (Six Inaugural Orations, 1699–1707)* (Giorgio A. Pinton and Arthur W. Shippee, Trans.; Donald Phillip Verene, Introd.). Ithaca, NY: Cornell University Press.

Vico, G. (2010). *On the Most Ancient Wisdom of the Italians. Drawn out from the Origins of the Latin Language* (J. Taylor, Trans., R. Miner, Introd.). New Haven, CT: Yale University Press.

Walker, G. and Noda, M. (2000). Remembering the Future: Compiling Knowledge of Another Culture. In *Reflecting on the Past to Shape the Future* (Diane W. Birckbichler, Ed.), pp. 187–212. Lincolnwood, IL: National Textbook Company.

Whewell, W. (1967 [1847]). *The Philosophy of Inductive Sciences* (J. Herivel, Introd.). New York: Johnson Reprint Corporation.

White, H. V. (1987). *The Content of the Form: Narrative Discourse and Historical Representation*. Baltimore, MD: John Hopkins University Press.

Whitehead, A. N. (1925). *Science and the Modern World*. New York: Free Press.

Whitehead, A. N. (1929a). *The Aims of Education and Other Essays*. New York: MacMillan.

Whitehead, A. N. (1929b). *The Function of Reason*. Boston, MA: Beacon Hill.

Whitehead, A. N. (1933). *Adventures of Ideas*. New York: Free Press.

Whitehead, A. N. (1948). *Science and Philosophy*. New York: Philosophical Library.

Whitehead, A. N. (1957). *Process and Reality*. New York: Free Press.

Whitehead, A. N. (1958). *An Introduction to Mathematics*. New York: Oxford University Press.

Whitehead, A. N. (1961a). *Alfred North Whitehead. His Reflections on Man and Nature* (Ruth Nanda Anshen, Selected with Prologue). New York: Harper.

Whitehead, A. N. (1961b). *The Interpretation of Science* (A. H. Johnson, Ed. with Introd.). Indianapolis, IN: Bobbs-Merrill.

Whitehead, A. N. (1968a) *Essays in Science and Philosophy*. New York: Greenwood Press.

Whitehead, A. N. (1968b). *Nature and Life*. New York: Greenwood Press.

Whitehead, A. N. (1971). *Concept of Nature*. Cambridge: Cambridge University Press.

Whitehead, A. N. (1985). *Symbolism. Its Meaning and Effect*. New York: Fordham University Press.

Whitehead, A. N. and Russell, B. (1927). *Principia Mathematica*. 3 vols. New York: Cambridge University Press.

Wiener, N. (1950). *The Human Use of Human Beings*. New York: Doubleday.

Wilden, A. (1979). Changing Frames of Order: Cybernetics and the *Machina Mundi*. In *Communication and Control in Society* (K. Krippendorff, Ed.), pp. 9–29. New York: Gordon and Breach.

Wilden, A. (1987). *The Rules Are No Game. The Strategy of Communication*. London: Routledge & Kegan Paul.

Wilder-Mott, C., and J. H. Weakland (Eds.). (1981). *Rigor and Imagination. Essays from the Legacy of Gregory Bateson*. New York: Praeger.

Williams, J. (2014). Whitehead's Curse? In *The Lure of Whitehead* (N. Gaskill & A. J. Nocek, Eds. and Introd.), pp. 249–66. Minneapolis: University of Minnesota Press.

Williams, R. (1976). *Keywords. A Vocabulary of Culture and Society*. New York: Oxford University Press.

Williams, W. C. (1974). *The Embodiment of Knowledge* (R. Loewinsohn, Ed. and Introd.). New York: New Directions.

Wilson, E. O. (1998). *Consilience. The Unity of Knowledge*. New York: Random House.

Zukovsky, L. (1978). *"A."* Baltimore, MD: Johns Hopkins University Press.

Zumthor, P. (1986). *Speaking of the Middle Ages* (E. Vance, Foreward; S. White, Trans.). Lincoln: University of Nebraska Press.

Index